27.50

D1564480

The Restoration
of Land

Studies in Ecology Volume 6

Studies in Ecology

General editors

D. J. Anderson BSc, PhD
Department of Botany
University of New South Wales
Sydney

P. Greig-Smith MA, ScD
School of Plant Biology
University College of North Wales
Bangor

Frank A. Pitelka PhD
Department of Zoology
University of California, Berkeley

The Restoration of Land

The ecology and reclamation of
derelict and degraded land
By A. D. Bradshaw and
M. J. Chadwick

University of California Press
BERKELEY LOS ANGELES

University of California Press
Berkeley and Los Angeles

Library of Congress
Catalog Card Number 79-64658

ISBN 0-520-03961-0

© Blackwell Scientific Publications 1980

Printed in Great Britain

Contents

Contents

Preface

Recently an awareness has developed that the world's resources are not infinite. In many countries there is now a concern to husband and protect the raw materials on which life depends. Perhaps the most basic resource of all is the land. So laws and regulations are being passed to prevent further destruction of land, and money is being found to restore land which has been destroyed or degraded. Such a transformation in our beliefs and actions was essential, for in the last two decades the rate of exploitation and destruction of land has increased to alarming proportions.

It is tempting in all this, and sometimes satisfying, to take up an extremist position. Some people suggest man is capable, through technological advances, of taking care of all the problems presented by the demands of continued economic growth. Others prophesy imminent disaster and urge the rapid evolution to a post-industrial society. The wilderness solution however is as illusory as is a return to 'normal' rapid economic growth conditions. The future must lie in some kind of middle way in which resources are carefully utilized, husbanded and recycled. And the most important resource to be treated in this way is the land.

But land is not a simple commodity that can be stored and replaced, destroyed and remade, or even recycled in exactly the same way as manufactured goods. It is a complex biological system built up over long periods of time. If we are to restore it we must understand how it functions biologically, physically and chemically. If we do not understand it we may not restore it properly or we may only be able to restore it at great expense, in the same way that someone without proper engineering knowledge cannot effectively repair a piece of machinery.

So our objective in this book is to show how theory must be combined with practice to achieve successful land restoration. Because the people involved in reclamation are most often engineers, planners and landscape architects, we have written it with them in mind, although for biologists and soil scientists the book will show the scope that exists for the practical application of their knowledge. A few years ago it would not have been possible to write a book of this sort because too little scientific work had been carried out on the restoration of land, and solutions to restoration problems were *ad hoc*, or not available, or expensive. Today the situation is very different, owing to

Pasture, Sonoma County,
California by Ansel Adams.

Shall we not learn from life its laws, dynamics, balances?
Learn to base our needs not on death, destruction, waste, but
on renewal.
In wisdom and in gentleness learn to walk again with Eden's
angels?
Learn at last to shape a civilisation in harmony with the earth.
ANSEL ADAMS and NANCY NEWHALL
This is the American Earth, 1960

the work of scientists in universities, industry and government. There are now few land restoration problems for which there is no satisfactory or potential solution. It is now clear that we need not think of land as a resource which can only be used for a single purpose, but something which can be used for one purpose and then subsequently for another: land is now a resource that can be recycled.

The problems involved in land restoration have no national boundaries so a world-wide view point is essential. But two people in one small country have their limitations, despite the dereliction in their back yards. We have had advice from many different people and organisations. They have been very generous in their help. We have also had the benefit of each being surrounded at York and Liverpool by a group of enthusiastic research students and assistants who have done much to provide the clear scientific understanding of many of the problems of land restoration. A quick look through the book will indicate just how much we are indebted to them, as well as to others, for facts and explanations. Their contributions are acknowledged in the text. What will not be clear however is their enthusiasm and tenacity in making land restoration, for them and for us, an absorbing and fascinating subject, requiring as much intellectual effort as any more theoretical parts of biology.

In singling out anyone we fall into the trap of reducing our indebtedness to others. But we must acknowledge our debt to the late Professor R. Alun Roberts of the Department of Agricultural Botany of the University College of North Wales where he first demonstrated to us, as young lecturer and student, that land is a resource to be used, improved and restored.

We have both had the opportunity to visit different parts of the world to see restoration in progress in very different situations to our own. One of us (A.D.B.) spent six weeks in Australia at the invitation of the Australian Mining Industry Council, and two separate visits to the multiracial University of Rhodesia, and visits to West Virginia, Utah and Belgium. The other (M.J.C.) has benefited from visits to the Ruhr, Silesia in Poland, Pennsylvania, West Virginia, Georgia and Florida and also had the opportunity to see reclamation work in the Ukrainian Soviet Socialist Republic when leading a British Government Delegation to the Soviet Union. On these visits we met and made friends with many people. Their ideas and work play an important part in this book.

At home we have the good fortune to work in collaboration with central and local government, industry, and research institutions. In particular we have been associated in joint ventures with the Department of the Environment, the Welsh Office, Cheshire, Derbyshire, Durham, Gwent, Mid-Glamorgan, Northumberland, South Yorkshire and West Yorkshire County Councils as well as the Greater

Manchester and Lancashire Joint Reclamation team. We have also collaborated with the National Coal Board, Imperial Chemical Industries, Laporte Industries, English China Clays and the Institute of Terrestrial Ecology. All these have not only provided us with problems, ideas and facilities, but by reminding us of the problems of reality, stopped us from being too academic.

Then we must acknowledge those who have wrestled with our writings and given us the benefit of their criticising, particularly Michael Johnson, Jan Kowal and R. E. White. But we would not wish to imply their responsibility for what is here: that is ours. To translate the material to paper we have relied on Sandra Collins, Eunice Owens and Janet Wilson for the typing, Ann Vaughan-Williams for the drawings, Tony Tollitt and Dick Hunter for the photographs, and Robert Campbell for the publishing. We could not have kinder and more efficient help.

Our wives and families have been haunted with this book, or the glimmerings or it, for several years. Then in the final stages they have had to put up with a great deal. Without their incessant support and editorial assistance, even when it seemed that book was taking precedence over them, the book could never have been completed.

A.D.B.   M.J.C.

Department of Botany   *Derelict Land Reclamation*
University of Liverpool   *Research Unit*
                              Department of Biology
                              University of York

January 1979

1 The Problem

1.1 ABOUT THIS BOOK

Land is one of our most real assets and one of our major natural resources. For primitive man land provided most of the food he ate, the food for his domestic animals and the animals he hunted, the products he used for shelter and for clothing; even water could be obtained from the earth by digging wells. Land was a valuable life-supporting resource to be tended carefully and preserved.

As our demands have become greater and our numbers have increased, land has become exploited for many other materials. Energy resources of peat and coal are required to supplement dwindling reserves from forests. Metalliferous and non-metalliferous ores have been discovered and are being used for many purposes. Rocks, sand, gravel and clay are being extracted for building and for constructional work. Land is being used to store water to supplement that available from wells, rivers, and natural lakes. Gradually land has become needed for the waste products of increasing industrial activities and our more sophisticated style of living. The way different industries have disturbed land by surface mining in one developed country is given in Table 1.1. It is difficult to see how we could live in comfort without the product of most of these activities.

Table 1.1. Many industries cause land dereliction: the extent of land disturbed by surface mining in the USA up to 1965 due to particular industries

Coal	531,360 hectares
Sand & Gravel	336,960
Stone	103,680
Gold	77,760
Phosphate	77,760
Iron	64,800
Clay	38,880
Other (mainly copper)	64,800
Total	1,296,000

Land which was once biologically productive has been degraded or totally destroyed, and left in a state that it cannot be used even for leisure or recreation activities. Added to this are increasing population pressures and a threatening world-wide shortage of food. Land is not a resource which automatically renews itself like rainfall or sunlight. So we are now having to consider the way we are

1

using this critical natural resource; the profligate days are over. We have to be prepared to restore exploited land to a condition approaching its original biological potential for both food production and amenity. The problem of land restoration has arrived.

The problem is one of world-wide dimensions. It is seen most clearly within highly developed, industrialised nations. However, the economy of these nations has often required the exploitation of resources in less developed and more remote areas, sometimes merely the degradation of land by agricultural use. Restoration problems therefore exist throughout the world. This book will deal with a variety of problems on a global scale but of necessity will emphasise the problem areas, the more heavily industrialised regions, where there has been massive degradation.

The problems of land restoration are intimately associated with problems that have arisen from the degradation of other natural resources, particularly air and water. Materials move from one resource to another, from land to water, into the air and back again to the land so that no resource is isolated from another. But still, because we are terrestrial animals, the problems of land degradation seem particularly pressing. This book is devoted to the degradation of land in the knowledge that the degradation of air and water are intimately interconnected with it.

Land that has suffered from man's industrial activities may be described as *spoiled* or *degraded*, *disturbed* or *devastated*, *derelict* or *damaged*. Some of these terms are used interchangeably, others have well defined and distinct meanings. For example, the term 'derelict land' may be used in the legal sense to refer to 'land which has been relinquished or abandoned by its owner'. However, governmental use in Britain has given it a wider meaning: 'land so damaged by industrial or other development that it is incapable of beneficial use without treatment', but this definition only applies if the land is disused and abandoned. Much land that is damaged by industrial and other development is still in active use. And thus the term 'disturbed land' has been introduced to cover conditions where the land is damaged and degraded, or unsightly, and needs to be treated in some way to bring it back along the upward spiral to increased biological productivity.

Sometimes attempts at the renewal of the degraded resource are given different names. *Reclamation* is often used where some new use of the land will be involved; *rehabilitation* is sometimes confined to improvements of a visual nature. *Restoration* may be used only where land is to be returned to its former use and *renewal* or *redemption* may be used in a form that enables flexibility in planning its re-use. The term *revegetation* is generally confined to situations where the original vegetation has been destroyed and its reappearance in some form is to be encouraged. In this book *restoration* is used as a blanket term to describe all those activities which seek to upgrade damaged land or to re-create land that has been destroyed and to bring it back into beneficial use, in a form in which the biological potential is restored.

The task of understanding how to restore derelict land is not an easy one, because it involves understanding soils and plants and how they interact with each other. It also involves understanding how land is degraded and disturbed and which factors are of critical importance. It must find out how to overcome them. It is essentially a task for the biologist and agricultural scientist, even although the engineer must be involved in the physical problems. But it is also a problem for the landscape architect, and the land agent and accountant for the underlying financial and legal problems.

1.2   THE EXTENT

We have degraded our land resource in a variety of ways and to very different degrees. We have moved complete mountains and destroyed appreciable amounts of whole islands: but we have also degraded the land almost imperceptibly, by acid rainfall that results from smelting operations and the burning of fuel. Productive areas have become covered by mining waste or the waste of chemical industries; land has disappeared below the water table due to mining subsidence.

The area may not seem very great in terms of the total available to us. For example, land disturbed by mining in the United States of America is probably less than 0·2 per cent of the U S land surface. In Great Britain in 1971, dere-

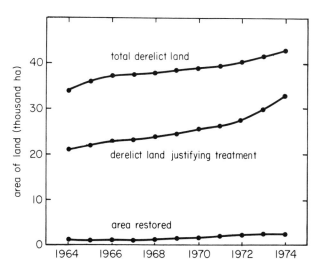

Figure 1.1. Changes over ten years in the amount of derelict land in England: reclamation is keeping up with the production of derelict land but the backlog remains.

The Extent

lict land was estimated in the order of 55 000 ha, 0·4 per cent of the land surface. But these are areas of a scarce resource, often located in the regions of the densest population, and where a large number of people suffer from its degradation. In Britain, and elsewhere, the need to restore this land is now widely accepted and is given a measure of priority by Governments and other bodies.

Figure 1.1 gives some indication of the changes that have occurred in the extent of dereliction in England over 10 years to 1974. Wales has about 20 per cent and Scotland 15 per cent of that in England. It has been estimated that at present the rate of production of derelict land in Britain is between 1200 and 1600 ha per annum. In some years, in Britain, rates of reclamation have exceeded the rate at which derelict land is being produced, but rather infrequently. In England, over 2000 ha were restored in 1972 and details of the progress of derelict land reclamation, in recent years, are given in Table 1.2. The extent of land rendered derelict in the USA by mining and the progress in reclamation are shown in Table 1.3.

Table 1.2. We have yet to make a substantial contribution to restoring derelict land: local progress in derelict land reclamation in England

Region	April 1974 Derelict land	April 1974 Justifying restoration	April 1974– March 1975 Restored	April 1975– March 1976 Restored
North	9411	7757	498	700 hectares
Yorkshire– Humberside	5451	4635	256	313
North West	8015	7212	131	330
East Midlands	5171	4660	95	343
West Midlands	4667	4235	136	528
South West	6415	1762	56	39
East Anglia	1783	1280	26	61
South East	2360	1527	125	146
Total	43273	33068	1323	2460

1.3   A PROBLEM OF SOIL

The most important part of the land resource is the biologically active surface layers—the soil. This provides the rooting medium for plants and is the source of almost all the nutrients they require. As vegetation develops to maturity over periods, often many hundreds of years, the soil structure and fertility build up. Organic matter from the plant roots and surface debris is incorporated into the soil along with animal remains and a complex, stable and fertile soil system, with a well developed structure, is built up over the centuries. It is this active system that is so easily destroyed or degraded when industrial processes produce derelict land (Figure 1.2).

Chapter 1: The Problem

Table 1.3. In ten years half a million extra hectares: the extent of land disturbed by surface- or strip-mining in the USA up to 1965 and 1974

		Total	Land requiring reclamation
New	1965	60,517	37,531
England	1974	66,742	44,005
Middle	1965	490,743	282,356
Atlantic	1974	636,442	308,085
South	1965	131,930	81,385
Atlantic	1974	166,857	88,096
East North	1965	137,936	68,898
Central	1974	206,361	95,588
East South	1965	88,394	67,675
Central	1974	119,239	96,752
West North	1965	153,135	107,527
Central	1974	218,522	144,105
West South	1965	99,895	77,840
Central	1974	138,755	109,104
Mountain	1965	85,202	51,533
	1974	139,872	96,203
Pacific	1965	82,295	51,054
	1974	91,728	43,408
Total	1965	1,290,047	825,799
	1974	1,784,517	1,025,344

Often the top soil is removed from the site and disposed of as the underlying strata are bared to obtain access to materials at depth. This is true of operations for gaining brick clay, where land is stripped for peat, sand and gravel, and where quarries are opened up to obtain stone, slate and shale. Where more modern mining procedures are adopted much of the soil may be stored. This is particularly true where opencast or strip-mining is carried out to gain coal, ironstone or other metalliferous ores. But the top soil may well become buried under huge piles of waste, such as when deep-mined waste has been tipped in colliery spoil heaps, where smelter slags and wastes have been dumped, where waste from chemical factories has been disposed of, and also where pulverised fuel ash from power stations is spread out in great quantities.

Figure 1.2 Where mining for bauxite began: these mines at Les Baux in the Alpilles in Southern France result in the total destruction of the native 'garigue' vegetation.

Figure 1.3. Opencast mining for coal in England—a massive environmental disturbance: yet the land can be completely restored afterwards (see Chapter 9).

Where open-pit mining occurs, as in the china clay industry and mining for non-ferrous metals, there are not only big holes in the ground, subject to flooding, but also even larger waste disposal areas. Wastes are often dumped in steep-sided spoil heaps: the steep slopes are unstable and subject to erosion. Handling and tipping very often result in compaction and loss of soil structure: some materials may be very fine and be left loose and porous. There may be poor drainage or drought. Surface conditions lead to extremes of surface temperature, wind erosion and sand blasting effects. All of these provide an inhospitable physical environment for plant growth.

Added to these effects will be various chemical factors, usually characteristic of the spoil material, that inhibit plant growth. There may be lack of nutrients or particular toxicity problems. Fresh waste material usually lacks the soil microorganisms and animals that are responsible for producing characteristics of soil that render it a fertile medium for plant growth.

These problems must be overcome if the land is to be upgraded from its derelict state and is once again to support healthy plant growth and mature and stable plant and animal communities. When this process begins the substrates will begin to take on again some of the features of a fertile soil. Plants will grow more successfully and in turn give rise to residues which will improve the physical and

Chapter 1: The Problem

chemical characteristics of the substrate. The beginning of this successful renewal of the degraded resource is the aim of derelict land reclamation and the reason why it presents such a fascinating set of ecological problems.

1.4   THE EFFECTS ON SURROUNDINGS

The interrelated nature of industrial dereliction problems have been stressed already. Derelict land problems are not merely concerned with the restricted acreage of the derelict land itself. The presence of derelict land in a region can have considerable effects over a very wide area. From a visual point of view spoil heaps can dominate an entire landscape.

Material that blows from the heaps may give rise to obvious dust in the air. But it can also lead to fine particulate matter in the atmosphere that is a burden of unwanted polluting material. This has been shown to occur in the Swansea Valley long after industrial processing and waste production has ceased, and considerable aerial burdens of heavy metals can still be detected. Where waste material is burnt (as with domestic refuse) or catches fire spontaneously (which used to occur with coal waste tipped in a manner which allowed air within the waste piles) then noxious gases may be added to the atmosphere.

Old mine workings can produce large quantities of acid drainage water containing toxic substances in solution which pollute streams, rivers and lakes. Heavy rain can give rise to flash floods which cause severe erosion of waste heaps and severe contamination of water courses. The results of heavy metal mining in Wales, America and Australia in the last century still have their effects on aquatic organisms of streams that pass through the area, and there are many areas that are still degraded as a result of mining in the early part of this century.

The problems can combine to give a whole series of degraded landscapes and environments. The effect that

Figure 1.4. Old colliery spoil heaps such as these used to ignite easily and become very unpleasant since they emitted large amounts of sulphur dioxide; the fires were difficult to put out.

The Effects on Surroundings

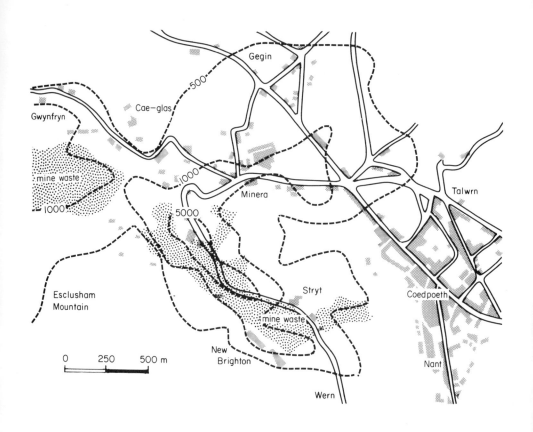

Chapter 1: The Problem

these have on man can lead to an unfortunate positive feedback: deterioration of the environment engenders a less responsible attitude for the environment in which the community lives, in the form of litter, vandalism and lack of planning. Hence a rapid downward spiral of deterioration takes place. It can involve the land values, housing and job opportunities of a whole region. The economic deterioration can be so great that there is complete collapse of whole communities. This situation has been vividly described in the coal mining areas of the Appalachians. The ultimate challenge of derelict land problems and land restoration is to counteract all these tendencies and to bring about a complete environmental renewal.

FURTHER READING

Anon. 1967. *Surface Mining and Our Environment*. Washington: US Dept. of Interior.
Barr J. 1969. *Derelict Britain*. Harmondsworth: Penguin Books.
Caudill H.M. 1976. *The Watches of the Night*. New York: Atlantic–Little, Brown.
Coghill I. 1971. *Australia's Mineral Wealth*. Melbourne: Sorrett Publishing.
Down C.G. & Stocks J. 1977. *Environmental Impact of Mining*. London: Applied Science Publishers.
Fairbrother N. 1970. *New Lives, New Landscapes*. London: Architectural Press.
Simmons I.G. 1974. *The Ecology of Natural Resources*. London: Edward Arnold.
Wallwork K.L. 1974. *Derelict Land*. Newton Abbott: David and Charles.

Figure 1.5. The distribution of lead (ppm) in the soils of agricultural land around Minera lead/zinc mine in North Wales: long after the mine has closed heavy metals remain and could be a serious problem.

'I will lay waste the mountains and hills, and dry up all their herbage; I will turn the rivers into islands, and dry up the pools.'
Isaiah 42: 15.

Figure 1.6. The end of a coal mining era: a region caught in a downward spiral of degradation of land and of economic opportunities.

2　The Possibilities

2.1 ## 2.1　RESTORATION PHILOSOPHIES

One American reclamation expert's maxim was, 'If you can't put it back like it was before you got it out, then don't do it!'. As a statement of aims for land restoration, in situations where land is increasingly being lost to productive uses, the American's philosophy has much to recommend it. It embodies the sentiments that land is a valuable and scarce resource that should be husbanded with care. However, in modern, industrial societies it can be a counsel of perfection leading only to despair and frustration. This does not mean that wasteful use of land or lax and irresponsible attitudes to land reclamation can be condoned. But it must be realised that advanced societies make many essential demands upon land, which are generally for the public good, and the eventual restoration of degraded land must be planned for in relation to prevailing ecological constraints.

There are examples of land that has suffered the upheaval of mining, and has been restored to its former use in the same or in an improved condition. Much of the very successful work carried out by the Opencast Executive of the National Coal Board in the United Kingdom has been directed towards the complete restoration of land to its former use, usually agriculture: the land has often been improved as a result. Other mining activities have been followed by restoration to some form of biological productivity which represents a change in the land-use from its original condition. Agricultural land which has been disturbed through mining and tipping operations can often be returned to productive forestry or vice versa. Where this is not appropriate, it can be restored for recreational purposes (playing fields, running tracks, boating and yachting lakes), to provide amenity areas and public open space, to allow areas to develop for conservation of wild species which can be used for education, or to provide areas for housing, industrial purposes, public services and commerce.

Whatever final land-use is adopted following restoration, it is imperative that it should fit in to the needs of the surrounding area and be compatible with other forms of land-use that occur nearby. It is not sensible to establish grazing areas for sheep close to high density housing

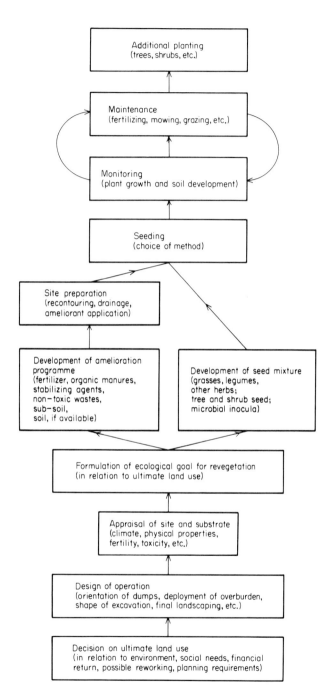

Figure 2.1. The steps involved in the development of a successful restoration scheme: at each step careful observations and experiments must be made to ensure that the operations are planned correctly.

Additional planting
(trees, shrubs, etc.)

Maintenance
(fertilizing, mowing, grazing, etc.)

Monitoring
(plant growth and soil development)

Seeding
(choice of method)

Site preparation
(recontouring, drainage,
ameliorant application)

Development of amelioration
programme
(fertilizer, organic manures,
stabilizing agents,
non-toxic wastes,
sub-soil,
soil, if available)

Development of seed mixture
(grasses, legumes,
other herbs;
tree and shrub seed;
microbial inocula)

Formulation of ecological goal for revegetation
(in relation to ultimate land use)

Appraisal of site and substrate
(climate, physical properties,
fertility, toxicity, etc.)

Design of operation
(orientation of dumps, deployment of overburden,
shape of excavation, final landscaping, etc.)

Decision on ultimate land use
(in relation to environment, social needs, financial
return, possible reworking, planning requirements)

Restoration Philosophies

where domestic pets are a severe threat to farm livestock. Similarly, it is not appropriate to establish nature reserves in areas where the need is for recreation and there will be heavy public pressure. The planning of the eventual land-use must take account of overall plans for the area. This must include, as far as possible, the proper ecological integration of the reclaimed area into the surrounding landscape. This desirable feature often is not achieved and a superficial cosmetic treatment passes for land restoration.

Planning of operations at the site level is also of critical importance if the land restoration scheme is to be ecologically based. It is not too early to plan the restoration scheme before the first dumping of the waste material. The disposal of waste should take account of the orientation and shape of the tips to be formed and the way in which different waste materials are deployed on the site. This will require a knowledge of the chemical and physical properties of the waste material: to some extent this knowledge will place constraints on the formulation of ecological goals for the restored areas. The procedures and considerations that are necessary in the design of a successful revegetation scheme must be properly ordered (Figure 2.1).

If site operations and revegetation procedures are planned in the way suggested there will be minimum delay between the use of the land for mining or waste disposal and its restoration to some other use. Too often the time that elapses between the beginning of the use of the site for mining or waste disposal and its eventual restoration to some other use is a period of many years, so the whole of an area remains unsightly and unproductive. This has led to the evolution of a special philosophy of progressive reclamation which is seen in its most advanced form in the Ruhr in the Federal Republic of Germany.

In the disposal of colliery waste from deep-mined coal operations in the Ruhr, the spoil is tipped in several layers. Each succeeding and higher layer has a basal area that is less than the layer below. Eventually the whole waste heap appears in the form of a step pyramid, each level connected to the one below, and eventually to base level, by a spiral

Figure 2.2. Progressive reclamation of colliery spoil heaps in the Ruhr: a lower layer with trees well established, a layer more recently planted, and the roadway giving access to further tipping.

Chapter 2: The Possibilities

Figure 2.3. Progressive restoration of sand and gravel workings with areas left untouched so that the final landscape is attractive and allows a wide variety of uses: (1) extraction continuing while restoration by tree planting begins (2) fully restored nature and recreation area within a current working

roadway. When tipping ceases on the first layer and commences on the second layer the sides of the first-tipped material are prepared for planting, usually with trees, so that some form of restoration begins and is carried out while tipping is still in progress on the level above. The area of land is being used for two purposes: tipping of waste material and restoration to forestry. The process may be repeated giving four, five or six layers of tipping (Figure 2.2). This process dispenses with the necessity to leave the area of land, that has been tipped upon, for a period of time before restoration commences.

This philosophy is not only appropriate for the restoration of areas upon which waste materials are tipped. It can also be the basis of the utilisation and restoration of sand and gravel areas. Of a total area that can be worked for sand and gravel, in the Federal Republic of Germany only part usually will be designated for extraction. Small parts of the area will be left to form the nucleus of the productive land and associated water. Extraction begins and almost immediately the interleaving areas that are preserved become the basis of walkways and areas that will allow use of the water areas for fishing, bathing and sailing. But while the area is being used for these purposes extraction continues in another part of the area (Figure 2.3). A progressive system is once again being put into operation.

Restoration Philosophies

2.2 END USES OF RESTORED LAND

In the early years of reclamation in England at least half of all land that was restored was eventually used for housing and associated purposes (Table 2.1). In some urban areas residential uses were as high as two-thirds of the reclaimed land. Almost another third to one-half was used for industrial purposes or to provide open space and recreation facilities. Little restored land was returned to agriculture. There is some indication however, that the proportion being restored to agriculture is increasing.

Table 2.1. Reclaimed derelict land meets many requirements: the uses of restored land (percentage area) in England

Use	Urban Areas England 1946–70	Potteries 1952	Black Country 1952	Lancashire 1954–72
Residential and associated urban uses	52·0	55·7	66·8	9·9
Industrial use	23·0	16·6	20·7	11·7
Open space and recreation	20·0	18·1	12·5	29·7
Agriculture	5·0	9·6	0	38·0
Tree planting	0	0	0	10·7

From a land manager's point of view one of the most exciting challenges of derelict land is that there is often no restriction on the after-use of the restored land. The slate is wiped clean, as it were, and there is an opportunity for imaginative land-use re-thinking to take place (Table 2.2). There is no need to view the after-use in traditional ways. For example, it has been recently suggested that fuel might be obtained on a significant scale from short rotation crops (including shrubs and trees). If this occurred in countries where land is in short supply, quite obviously it would not be sensible to divert prime agricultural or forestry land to this purpose. Thus restored derelict land becomes a candidate for energy plantation use.

Table 2.2. Restoration of derelict land presents opportunities: the variety of land-uses possible

Production	Amenity	Other uses
Arable agriculture	Country parks	Industry
Grassland agriculture	Nature reserves	Reservoirs
Forestry	Educational areas	Housing
Energy plantations	Camp sites	Playgrounds
Glasshouse crops	Golf courses	Commercial development
Small scale horticulture	Urban parks	Public authority building

2.3　NATURE CONSERVATION AND WILDERNESS

There is an alternative strategy appropriate to many areas—nature conservation. Many people will be surprised to know that of the 3000 sites recognised officially as sites of special scientific interest in England and Wales, 75 are quarries and other mineral workings. Since old quarries or similar spaces are empty, the soil and plants have been removed and all that remains is bare ground and rock, this provides a refuge for plants that cannot stand the competition of the more vigorous plants that grow on good soil. There are many of these plants—such as the bee orchid *Ophrys apifera* and the gentian *Gentianella amarella*—uncommon plants of great beauty and interest.

So unreclaimed areas can be a refuge for rarities. But because they are left alone they can also become wilderness places where the various stages of development of ordinary plant communities can be seen, the open grassy vegetation which will lead to mature grassland, the scrub that will lead to woodland (Figure 2.4). In many highly developed countries most of the 'undeveloped' land is for agriculture or forestry: there are few areas where nature is left untouched to develop as it will into scrub and rough woodland.

A wilderness of plants will automatically become a wilderness for animals which will be attracted by the protec-

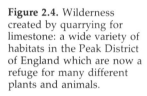

Figure 2.4. Wilderness created by quarrying for limestone: a wide variety of habitats in the Peak District of England which are now a refuge for many different plants and animals.

tion and food provided by the plants and the unusual habitat. On strip-mined areas in the Tennessee River drainage basin, the Tennessee Valley Authority has planted areas specifically to encourage wild life with considerable success. The Central Forest Park being created in Stoke on Trent on old colliery tips and marl holes is aimed at bringing wild life into an urban area. It may be worthwhile bringing in special plants such as rushes and water plants for ducks and wildfowl as at Sevenoaks, Kent (Chapter 10).

Individual species can also be introduced for their own sake. Not so long ago we would have been horrified at doing this sort of thing, but the pressure on the native flora of our country, and of others as heavily developed, is enormous. Every year sees habitats destroyed and the distribution of species becoming more restricted. We shall have to contemplate using derelict land positively as nature reserves and informal wilderness areas.

In the middle of East Anglia there is a series of shallow lakes and rivers, the Norfolk Broads. They are a complex of plant communities, open water, reedswamp, marsh, and fen woodland (Figure 2.5). In each there is an assemblage of unique plants and animals. The special qualities of the Broads have long been recognised. Over the past 50 years they have all been acquired as nature reserves, so that now the area is the greatest concentration of nature reserves in a single type of environment anywhere in Britain.

Figure 2.5. An area of outstanding beauty and a haven for wild life which was once part of a vast series of peat cuttings: the Norfolk Broads in East Anglia (see Figure 2.6).

Chapter 2: The Possibilities

No area could seem more natural and further removed from derelict land. However, in 1960 a meticulous report showed that the Broads are nothing more than a series of peat diggings, the derelict land of a mediaeval open-cast fuel industry. The major evidence is based on the shape of the Broads themselves; they have vertical sides and curious baulks (Figure 2.6). But there is also forgotten historical evidence of peat cutting activity extending over four centuries until about A.D. 1500. There has been plenty of time for that derelict land to heal. But it should be a lesson to our rather tidy twentieth-century minds that wildernesses may be important and that nature conservation is a very possible endpoint for some derelict land (Table 2.3).

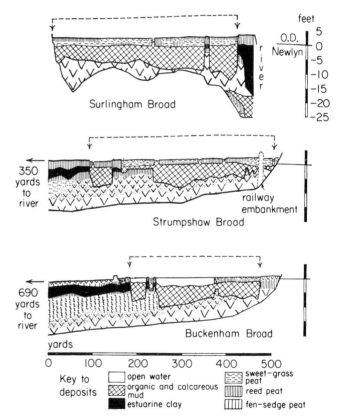

Figure 2.6. Sections through the peat and silt deposits of the Norfolk Broads show that the original deposits are interrupted by steep-sided basins separated by vertical baulks: these basins, the present-day broads, are the remains of a mediaeval peat industry.

2.4   COST OF LAND RESTORATION

The total costs of the restoration of derelict land, particularly in urban areas, may be very high. The costs will include the site acquisition, earth moving, drainage works, fencing, surface treatment and landscaping, fertilisers, seeds and plant material. To this has to be added for many sites the cost of specialist engineering works that are necessary for sealing shafts and other features of the pre-

Table 2.3. Wildlife follows waste: examples of derelict sites in England which are now nature reserves or are officially recognised as sites of scientific importance

Disused quarries		
Miller's Dale, Derbyshire	CNT/SSSI	Carboniferous limestone quarry with rich grassland flora and scrub.
Bishop Middleham Quarry, Durham	CNT/SSSI	Magnesium limestone quarry with many uncommon species.
Clint's Quarry, Egremont, Cumbria	SSSI	Carboniferous limestone quarry with rich grassland flora and orchids.
Barnack Hills and Holes, Northamptonshire	NNR	Mediaeval Jurassic limestone quarries with very rich grassland flora containing rarities.
Disused pits		
Grays, Thurrock, Essex	SSSI	Old chalk pit with complex of calcareous vegetation.
Cherry Hinton Pits, Cambridge	CNT/SSSI	Chalk pits of very different ages showing stages of recolonisation.
Roswell Pits, Ely, Cambridgeshire	CNT/SSSI	Clay pits of different ages with rich flora and fauna, marsh and open water.
Sevenoaks Gravel Pit, Kent	WAGBI/SSSI	Gravel pit developed to give rich bird populations.
Felmersham Pit, Bedfordshire	CNT/SSSI	Gravel pit rich in birds, plants and insects.
Disused mines and chemical wastes		
Sandbach Flashes, Cheshire	SSSI	Old brine beds with birds and unusual salt-tolerant plants.
Plumley Reserve, Cheshire	CNT/SSSI	Old lime wastes from Solvay process with many uncommon birds and plants.
Alvacote Pools, Staffordshire	CNT/SSSI	Colliery subsidence lakes now a regional wildfowl refuge.
High Plains and Garrigill, Alston, Cumbria	SSSI	Old lead mines with large populations of unusual metal tolerant plants.

Fairburn Ings, Ferrybridge, Yorks	RSPB	Colliery subsidence lake important for wintering birds.

Peat cuttings

Barton Broad, Norfolk	NNR	Mediaeval peat cuttings with complete complex of open water, fen and woodland.
Moorthwaite Moss, Cumbria	SSSI	Peat cuttings with excellent growth of bog-moss (*Sphagnum*) etc.
Shapwick Heath, Somerset	SSSI	Complex of nutrient-rich and poor vegetation in recent peat cuttings.

NNR National Nature Reserve
CNT County Naturalist Trust Nature Reserve
SSSI Site of Special Scientific Interest
RSPB Royal Society for Protection of Birds Reserve
WAGBI Wildfowlers Association of Great Britain Reserve

vious use of the site. Once restoration has been completed there will still be charges that must be made against the operation, loan charges on the capital raised to purchase the site and to carry out the reclamation work and also charges for site maintenance and supervision.

In the United Kingdom it is difficult to present figures that give a realistic impression of cost in up-to-date terms. However, in terms of cost in the mid-1970's these could be anything up to £20 000 per ha. Only a small proportion of this cost is due to work which might be termed biological reclamation. Although this activity represents a high risk feature of the total operation it constitutes only a small part of the total cost (Table 2.4).

Table 2.4. The cost of treatment is only a small proportion of the total: costs for various features of land restoration for recreational use in an English County Borough (1970–5) (total cost £15,230/ha.)

Operation	Percentage
Land acquisition	24·1
Preparatory engineering	24·3
Treatment and landscaping	35·3
Salaries and overheads	2·5
Loan charges	11·9
Site maintenance	1·9

In the mid-1960's a number of options were presented for reclaiming derelict land to industrial use in the Swansea Valley. On a 39 ha site industrial development was to take

Cost of Land Restoration

place on about 4 ha. Surfaced roads and the provision of services to the industrial site were included within the reclamation costs. If the whole site were reclaimed the estimated cost was to be £7786 per ha: but if only the 4 ha needed for the industrial development were reclaimed in such a way as to allow overall restoration of the remaining part of the site at some future date the cost would have been £26 960 per ha.

In England average costs of reclamation were put at £1600 per ha pre-1966; £3200, 1968–9; double this in 1976, with costs varying from region to region (Table 2.5). It is

Table 2.5. The full costs vary: average costs of derelict land restoration for schemes approved in 1976 and 1977 in five English Regions

Region	Cost (£) per ha.	
	1976	1977
West Midlands	4885	8707
North-west	6806	12765
Yorkshire & Humberside	6970	5915
East Midlands	7906	5715
Northern	9937	9556

interesting to compare these costs with those given for only the simplest reclamation procedures for opencast sites by the Maryland coal industry in the USA (Table 2.6).

It may appear that any of the costs quoted are excessive and well above what might be regarded as the normal value of the land. Certainly the aim in all reclamation must be to keep costs as low as possible, commensurate with achieving a proper result. What must be borne in mind in viewing these figures is, however, that quite often the purchase of land for purposes similar to those of the restored land would be in excess of these restoration costs. This can be translated into the simple and often forgotten concept that the land may be able to be sold after restoration at a price that covers the whole cost of initial acquisition and restoration. In some areas, such as gravel workings, the costs of restoration may be small and the subsequent real estate values so high that a substantial profit is possible.

Table 2.6. The costs of very simple procedures may not be excessive: estimated reclamation costs following strip-mining in Maryland, USA

Year	Cost ($) per ha.
1967	1075
1968	1137
1969	1186
1970	1248

2.5   BENEFITS OF LAND RESTORATION

It is obvious that if land is restored to biological productivity or to a condition where it can once again be utilised for a range of purposes valuable to a community this will re-

Chapter 2: The Possibilities

present a direct improvement of the area on which the restoration has been carried out. But in addition the surrounding areas will also benefit. The improvement of a site to a condition which integrates well into the surrounding landscape and removes intrusive landscape characteristics, upgrades the environment of a region far beyond the confines of the site that is restored. Visual improvement of the area can begin to upgrade a whole range of environmental characteristics: the built environment is kept in better repair, road surfaces and verges become worth maintaining, planning consents are more rigorously considered, there is less vandalism and the general appearance is respected. To this can be added specific improvements of environmental conditions; reduction of dust burden in the air, reduction or elimination of gaseous additions to the atmosphere due to tip burning, reduction of particulate matter and noxious chemicals deposited in streams and water courses, and elimination of illegal tipping.

The transformation that occurs in an area where planned and sensitive land restoration is practised enables whole communities and areas to begin to upgrade social and economic conditions. One improvement will follow another and amenities and facilities are improved. It is difficult to provide a cost-benefit analysis of this situation although it is not difficult to find examples of where this has occurred.

Figure 2.7. Land restoration can lead to improved social amenities: a large hotel now occupies part of a reclaimed colliery spoil heap in West Yorkshire.

2.6   PLANNING REQUIREMENTS AND FINANCIAL SUPPORT

In Britain Local Authorities were given the power to acquire derelict land in order to bring it back into use by the *Town and Country Planning Act 1944*. These powers were little used and repealed by the *Town and Country Planning Act 1947*. Two years later a considerable advance was achieved through Section 89 of the *National Parks and Access to the Countryside Act 1949* (as amended by Section 6 of the *Local Authorities (Land) Act 1963*). This allows County and District Councils to carry out works to enable derelict, neglected or unsightly land to be treated, not only to bring it back into use but also to improve its appearance. Under certain conditions compulsory purchase may be authorised.

Other legislation gives Local Authorities powers not specifically granted for derelict land which, nonetheless, may be exercised in relation to it. For example, Section 112(1) of the *Town and Country Planning Act 1971* allows acquisition of land by Local Authorities for development for housing or public open space. Thus derelict land may be acquired and restored before subsequently being put to these uses.

The Mines and Quarries (Tips) Act 1969 places responsibility on Local Authorities for ensuring that disused tips are not a danger to the public due to instability. Land restoration may feature as part of the necessary remedial work (and be eligible for an Exchequer contribution to the total cost).

As previously emphasised, costs of land restoration may be high and legislation exists which makes available grants to Local Authorities for both the acquisition and reclamation of derelict land. Section 9 of the *Local Government Act 1966* makes a 50 per cent grant available anywhere. Section 8 of the *Local Employment Act 1972* allows a grant of 100 per cent of approved costs in respect of land in the special development, development, intermediate and derelict land clearance areas. Section 97(1)(c) of the *National Parks and Access to the Countryside Act 1949* allows grants of 75 per cent of approved costs for land reclamation in national parks and areas of outstanding beauty unless these also are covered by the categories stipulated by the *Local Employment Act 1972*, when they also would qualify for the 100 per cent grant.

Grants may be available for tree planting from the Countryside Commission for amenity planting, or from the Forestry Commissions for areas of 1 ha or over to establish utilisable crops of timber. Grants from the Sports Council towards the costs of restoring land for sport and recreation are also a possibility.

The Mineral Workings Act 1951 provided for the establishment of a fund for financing the restoration of land made derelict by open-cast ironstone working, and in an area covered by this Act the Local Authority may carry out restoration work either on the mined land or land adjoining it.

Since 1 April 1974 there has been a significant advance in land restoration possibilities in relation to deep-mined colliery spoil. Previously land in use for tipping on 1 July 1948 was not subject to any provision being made for restoration

Figure 2.8. Successful restoration can eventually give back to farming highly productive land: land restored 20 years ago at Bickershaw in Lancashire.

Figure 2.9. Imagination in refuse disposal: In the 1930s Liverpool was faced with the problem of the disposal of its refuse: a wall built into the River Mersey formed an ideal dumping site, which is now an attractive riverside park—Otterspool Promenade.

or after-treatment of the tips by the National Coal Board. Any restoration work on such tips had to be undertaken by Local Authorities. However, since this date, as a result of an amendment to the *Town and Country Planning General Development Order 1973*, a County Planning Authority may require the National Coal Board to submit a scheme, aimed at ensuring that waste material is tipped in such a way as to facilitate subsequent landscaping and restoration to improve visual amenity. The initiative here lies squarely on the shoulders of the planning authority and unfortunately places no *a priori* obligation on the National Coal Board.

Disposal practices and techniques are the key to successful land restoration and it is unfortunate that major producers of solid waste are not required as a matter of course to submit disposal schemes. However, the *Control of Pollution Act 1974* provides for a systematic approach to the collection and disposal of certain kinds of waste (household, industrial and commercial, but not wastes from mines or quarries or agricultural waste). This Act has meant that surveys of waste disposal methods and sites will eventually have to be undertaken by Local Authorities leading to the formulation of comprehensive formal disposal plans, followed, it is to be hoped, by imaginative land restoration schemes. The potential for imaginative schemes is considerable (Figure 2.9).

An interesting study, performed by the Local Government Operational Research Unit, looked in detail at various integrated waste disposal strategies. Wastes were classified into *hazardous*, *biodegradable* and *inert*. For each waste, volumes were calculated, pre-treatments (if any) determined, potential disposal sites identified and environmental criteria established (in relation to public health, water

pollution and amenity standards). A computer model was used to find the minimum cost allocation of wastes to potential disposal sites. This approach was an imaginative one which appreciated that by considering waste disposal and derelict land together Local Authorities could augment both their available tipping areas and the supply of useful land. The study remains a blueprint for the integration of waste disposal and land restoration.

In the USSR exploitation of minerals is now generally governed by a 'hectare for hectare' philosophy. Thus permission to mine is only generally granted if a guarantee is given that an equal area of mined land will be completely restored.

Until 1977 individual states in the USA exercised primary jurisdiction over the restoration of mined lands. Generally, State legislation authorised a State agency to issue permits to mine on receipt of scientific data on the mine site, mining and reclamation plans, and a bond or other security to cover the restoration plan.

Surface and mineral rights are owned separately, and diversified ownership among private individuals, the federal government and the State governments exist. Until 1976, it had been the policy of the federal government to allow the individual states to act for it where federally owned coal was being mined, but the Federal Surface Mining Control and Reclamation Act was passed in 1977 and changed this.

The Federal Surface Mining Act created overall regulations for coal mine reclamation and established minimum reclamation performance standards. The standards include restoration to the approximate original contour, segregation and replacement of topsoil, establishment of vegetation comparable to pre-mining conditions and protection from adverse hydrological effects. Operators must take responsibility for successful revegetation for five years after seeding; in areas where annual precipitation is less than 66 cm (most of the western United States) this is increased to 10 years.

Thus, from 1977 reclamation is initially the responsibility of the Office of Surface Mining within the US Department of the Interior but individual states may be allowed to take this over if they develop State programmes that comply with the procedures in the Surface Mining Act and enforce performance standards at least as stringent as the federal ones. They may adopt more stringent standards if they wish to but if they do not develop State programmes, they have no regulatory authority over coal mine reclamation.

The Surface Mining Act places a levy per ton on all coal produced in the United States. This fund will be used to finance the restoration of areas that were not reclaimed in the past and other projects to alleviate off-site impacts of the unreclaimed areas.

Chapter 2: The Possibilities

The Federal Surface Mining Act applies only to coal mining, and state laws still authorise the regulation of reclamation activities on other types of mines.

Probably the most closely co-ordinated system of mining, waste disposal and restoration is to be found in the Ruhr Region in the Federal Republic of Germany. In 1920 a law established an association to deal with 'all matters relevant to the encouragement of settlement activity' or regional planning, as we would now say, in the Ruhr. This was the *Siedlungsverband Ruhrkohlenbezirk* which became promoted to the status of a regional planning organisation by the Regional Planning Act of 1962 (Figure 2.10). The SVR is responsible for an area development plan which includes refuse disposal planning and land utilisation policy. Open space and amenity areas must be secured, often by the renewal of derelict areas. It determines the location of tips, decides whether there is a need for the combining of waste materials, approves landscaping plans and suggests planting schemes and procedures. The result is integrated planning control for land restoration.

The SVR consults local authorities and then prepares an integrated land utilisation scheme. This allows for the expansion of green belts, establishment of recreation areas, preserves landscapes of particular value, promotes forestry and integrates waste disposal with the recultivation of derelict land and industrial and mining waste rehabilita-

Figure 2.10. An example of a well-integrated system for democratic planning control: the structure of the Ruhr Planning Authority.

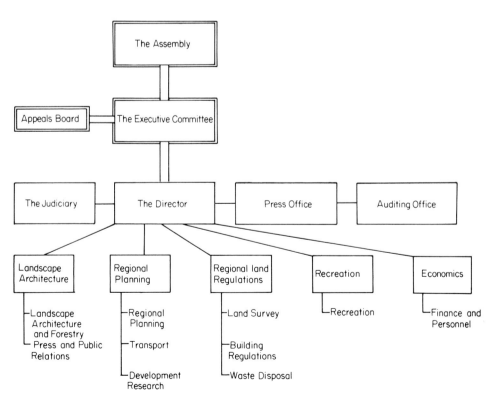

Planning Requirements and Financial Support

tion. Basic research is initiated by the Authority and this enables the SVR to give sound advice to all companies disposing of waste material when formulating the conditions of tipping. This is part of the SVR achievement in planning: it not only sets conditions, it promotes research and gives advice on how the conditions can be met. In doing this it co-ordinates activities in two *Land*, 18 cities, 6 rural districts and parts of three others, in a way that is complementary.

FURTHER READING

Bradshaw A.D. 1977. Conservation problems in the future. *Proc. Roy. Soc. Lond.* B **197**, 77–96.

Cairns J., Dickson K.L. & Herricks E.E. (eds.). 1977. *Recovery and Restoration of Damaged Ecosystems*. Charlottesville: Univ. Press of Virginia.

Darmer G. 1972. *Landschaft und Tagebau*, Hannover: Patzer.

Department of the Environment. 1975. *Aggregates—The Way Ahead*. London: Her Majesty's Stationery Office.

Department of the Environment. 1975. *Planning Control over Mineral Workings*. London: Her Majesty's Stationery Office.

Hilton K.J. (ed.). 1967. *The Lower Swansea Valley Project*. London: Longman.

Holdgate M.W. & Woodman M.J. (eds.). 1978. *The Breakdown and Restoration of Ecosystems*. New York: Plenum Press.

Imes A.C. & Wali M.K. 1977. An ecological-legal assessment of mined land reclamation laws. *North Dakota Law Review* **53**, 359–99.

Oppenberg F. & Kardas A. 1974. *Der Naturpark Hohe Mark*. Duisberg: Mercator.

Oxenham J.R. 1966. *Reclaiming Derelict Land*. London: Faber and Faber.

Senior D. (ed.) 1964. *Derelict Land—a study of industrial dereliction and how it may be redeemed*. London: Civic Trust.

'And it was commanded them that they should not hurt the grass of the earth neither any green thing, neither any tree.'
Revelation 9: 4.

3   Plants and Soil

Only plants amongst living organisms are able to manufacture their own sources of energy from simple, inorganic molecules. Animals, fungi and bacteria rely on a ready-made supply of organic material which they break down to obtain energy, but plants contain a green pigment, chlorophyll, which enables them to build up complex carbohydrates from carbon dioxide in the air and water from the soil, utilising light energy from the sun. This process is called photosynthesis.

Carbohydrates are the starting point for the formation of many other substances found in plants: fats, proteins, enzymes, vitamins, all of which contain other elements which are obtained by the plant from the soil, in solution. If all the essential elements are available to the plant, the energy initially obtained from the sun can be utilised to build up the plant body and it will grow—increase in weight.

3.1   PLANT REQUIREMENTS

All the elements essential for plant growth, except carbon and oxygen, are obtained by terrestrial plants from the soil. These mineral nutrients enter the plant through the roots. The plant root has an outer layer of cells, some of which are elongated into root hairs. Water and nutrients are absorbed

Table 3.1. The nutrient requirements of plants: the composition of a culture solution (Long Ashton) suitable for the satisfactory growth of plants

macronutrients		g/l	mM
potassium nitrate	KNO_3	0·404	4
calcium nitrate (anhydrous)	$Ca(NO_3)_2$	0·656	4
magnesium sulphate	$MgSO_4.7H_2O$	0·368	1·5
sodium dihydrogen phosphate	$NaH_2PO_4.2H_2O$	0·208	1·33
micronutrients			
iron citrate	Fe citrate.$5H_2O$	0·036	0·1
manganese sulphate	$MnSO_4.4H_2O$	0·0022	0·01
zinc sulphate	$ZnSO_4.7H_2O$	0·00029	0·001
copper sulphate	$CuSO_4.5H_2O$	0·0025	0·001
boric acid	H_3BO_3	0·0031	0·05
sodium molybdate	$Na_2MoO_4.2H_2O$	0·00012	0·0005
sodium chloride	$NaCl$	0·0058	0·1
cobalt sulphate	$CoSO_4.7H_2O$	0·000056	0·0002

by this outer layer of cells, but the rates at which this occurs from the soil solution can be very different. The nutrients, in the form of electrically charged components, ions, may enter more rapidly than water.

Relatively few inorganic nutrient elements are required by plants (Table 3.1). Some, the macronutrients, are necessary in large amounts: nitrogen, phosphorus, sulphur, calcium, magnesium and potassium; others are termed micronutrients as they are required only in trace amounts: iron, manganese, boron, copper, zinc and molybdenum. Others (sodium, chlorine, cobalt, vanadium and a few more) may be essential for particular species. The typical levels found in plants are shown in Figure 3.1.

Lack of any of these elements causes the plant to grow poorly and show deficiency symptoms. Since nutrients have very different functions, lack of them gives rise to distinct effects, which can be sufficiently characteristic to show which element is in short supply. This is discussed

Figure 3.1. Typical concentrations of mineral nutrient elements in plants, and concentrations in solution sufficient for satisfactory growth in sand culture.

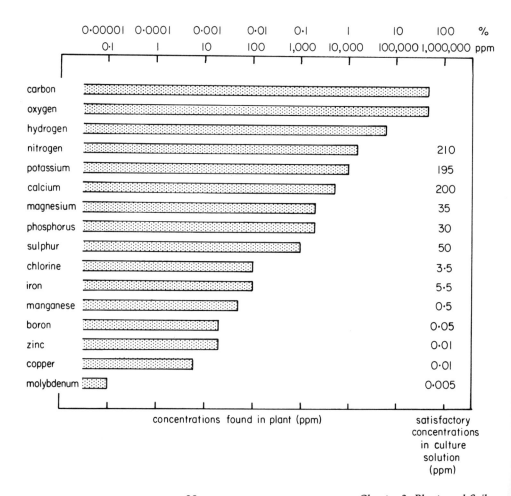

	satisfactory concentrations in culture solution (ppm)
carbon	
oxygen	
hydrogen	
nitrogen	210
potassium	195
calcium	200
magnesium	35
phosphorus	30
sulphur	50
chlorine	3·5
iron	5·5
manganese	0·5
boron	0·05
zinc	0·01
copper	0·01
molybdenum	0·005

concentrations found in plant (ppm)

further in Chapter 7. The concentrations of elements which are sufficient for satisfactory growth are extremely low, but there must be a continuous supply, otherwise the continued demands of the plant will soon exhaust what is available. In culture experiments this is achieved by a continuous flow of solution or by replacing it frequently. In most soils there are stores of nutrients which are slowly released into the soil solution as ions. As the ions are absorbed more are supplied by diffusion or flow to the root or by the root growing into a less depleted zone.

Although all plants require the essential elements, the amounts required by different species are not the same. In general crop plants require more of each nutrient than wild plants, and plants that grow quickly require more than plants that grow slowly, because rapid growth demands more nutrients. Species can have very different nutrient requirements which relate to the natural habitats in which they normally grow (Figure 3.2). Ryegrass (*Lolium perenne*)

Figure 3.2. Species can have very different mineral nutrient requirements: the responses of different grasses to nitrogen and phosphorus in sand culture.

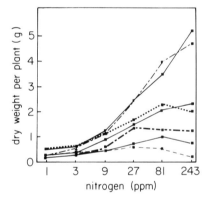
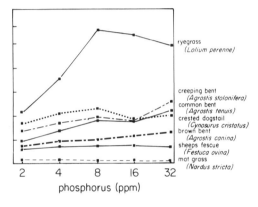

and creeping bent (*Agrostis stolonifera*) are found growing naturally in fertile places such as rich meadows and not on very poor soils: brown bent (*Agrostis canina*) and mat grass (*Nardus stricta*) can occur on very poor soils. This sort of variation in what different species need is important when we come to consider what sort of species to plant on derelict land. It will not be much use planting ryegrass on waste materials that contain little nitrogen or phosphorus without adding extra nutrients, otherwise it will soon die (Figure 3.3).

Although all species take up the whole range of mineral nutrients from the soil a few species are able to obtain the nitrogen they need from the air by means of a special relationship with bacteria. Leguminous plants such as clovers, lupins, vetches and gorse form root nodules which contain the bacterium, *Rhizobium*. This is able to form nitrogenous compounds, with the aid of carbohydrates from their host plant. The nitrogenous compounds are passed on to the plant. If the legume is growing with another plant, such as a grass, this benefits too, since the nitrogen-

Figure 3.3. Rye grass dying on a colliery spoil at Bullcroft Colliery site in Yorkshire: the soil conditions despite reclamation are too extreme for this species—another more tolerant species (left) was more successful.

Plant Requirements

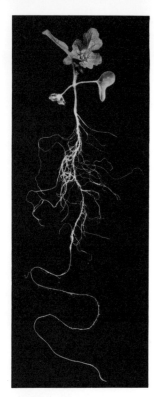

Figure 3.4. The roots of a mustard plant: root systems of plants are diffuse and delicate, adapted to absorbing water and nutrients from a large volume of soil.

ous compounds pass from the legume to the grass. Some other plants which are not legumes have similar relationships with other nitrogen fixing organisms; the common alder, *Alnus glutinosa*, has nodules containing a nitrogen fixing actinomycete, *Frankia alni*, and the snowbrush, *Ceanothus velutinus*, has a similar microorganism.

Plants consist of about 90 per cent water and lose 1 to 10 times their water content every day to the air by evaporation from their leaves. A constant supply of water is therefore essential for growth. The water enters the plant through the root mainly by passive physical processes which ultimately depend on the negative pressures developed in the cells inside the plant by the loss of water to the atmosphere from the leaves.

Water and nutrients are diffused throughout the soil: so the root system of a plant is also very diffuse: a single rye plant (*Secale cereale*) can have 623 km (387 miles) of roots. The plant is anchored into the ground by the main roots and the rest of the roots are exceedingly thin and delicate to give a large surface area (Figure 3.4).

But even so roots cost the plant something to produce. If for any reason a plant is prevented from growing properly then the growth of the roots will suffer as much as the growth of the shoots. This has important consequences since without a well-developed root system the plant will have its nutrient and water supply severely limited.

Besides the substances that a plant needs from the soil there are a number of substances in soil which can be harmful if the concentration rises above very low levels. The most common are aluminium and manganese. An elevated concentration of aluminium causes damage to the roots themselves while high manganese in the tops of the plants causes them to go yellow and stunted. High levels of heavy metals such as copper, zinc and lead are toxic to plants: they are not usually common but they may occur in derelict land soils. They can have severe effects: 0·5 parts per million (ppm) of copper or 10 ppm lead or zinc in solution can stop root growth completely.

Sodium is not an element that plants normally need nor is it toxic at ordinary levels. But it can accumulate in soils, particularly in arid climates, and may be involved in industrial processes and pose a problem for derelict land restoration. If it reaches concentrations of about 1 per cent, which is about half the concentration in sea water, it can cause a general reduction of plant growth: beyond a concentration of 2 per cent very few plants can grow. Magnesium can become toxic in the same way, even though it is required by plants at low concentrations.

Finally, most plants flourish best in conditions which are not too acid or too alkaline. Acidity and alkalinity are due to the concentration of hydrogen ions in the soil solution. When the hydrogen ion concentration in solution is high, the soil is too acid: when it is very low the soil is too

Chapter 3: Plants and Soil

alkaline. Plants can tolerate wide ranges of hydrogen ion concentration and the main effect of hydrogen ion concentration on plants is an indirect one which will be discussed later.

3.2   SOIL TEXTURE AND STRUCTURE

A natural soil is derived from mineral matter originating from igneous rocks. The rocks have broken down over long periods of time and the particles have often been moved from one place to another and been reformed into new, sedimentary rocks before they are finally altered again to form a soil. The inorganic soil particles are the resistant fragments which remain after this long process of breakdown and weathering. Some will be inert material like quartz but others physically and chemically active, like clay minerals. The soil will also contain other decomposition products such as oxides, carbonates and phosphates, and the half-decayed remains of plants, animals and microorganisms. And there will be the soil water, which will contain soluble salts derived from the other materials.

The soil particles are usually a heterogeneous mixture ranging from gravel, particles more than 2 mm in diameter, to clay, particles less than 0·002 mm in diameter. The range of particles is given in Table 3.2. Quartz particles are inert and form an unreactive matrix of the soil. Feldspars and other primary minerals slowly release nutrients by weathering and eventually form secondary minerals, such as clay minerals, with important physico-chemical properties concerned with ion exchange. Decayed organic matter may

Table 3.2. Soil is made up of particles which vary considerably in size: the different soil particles and their properties

United States system	inter-national system	approximate number of particles per gram	approximate surface area, cm² per gram	visibility of individual particles	physical character	mineralogical composition
very coarse sand / coarse sand / medium sand	coarse sand	5.4×10^2	21	visible to naked eye	loose and single-grained; not sticky or plastic	mainly quartz with some rock fragments
fine sand / very fine sand	fine sand	5.4×10^5	210	visible to naked eye	loose and single-grained; not sticky or plastic	mainly quartz and feldspar with some ferromagnesians
silt	silt	5.4×10^8	2,100	visible under microscope	smooth and floury; only slightly cohesive	mainly quartz and feldspar with some ferromagnesians, mica, and clay minerals
clay	clay	7.2×10^{11}	23,000	invisible under microscope except in upper range; many particles resolved by electron microscope	sticky and plastic when moist; hard and cohesive when dry	mainly clay minerals with some quartz

diameter of particles, mm: 2·0, 1·0, 0·5, 0·25, 0·1, 0·05, 0·002, 0·000

31

exceed the clay minerals in ion exchange properties. Oxides, carbonates and phosphates can be important in cementing particles together but have also far-reaching buffering effects in the soil.

Since particles have these different physical and chemical properties, soils having different mixes of particles can vary considerably in their overall properties. A soil made of sand and gravel is very free draining and retains little plant nutrients: a soil made of clay particles may drain badly and become almost totally impervious to water if compressed, but retains nutrients well because of its ion exchange properties.

The other important physical component of soil is the dead organic matter left by plants, animals and micro-organisms. Much of this is half decayed, fibrous and water retentive. As decay proceeds it becomes a structureless but complex brown material—humus. This has important physical properties and helps to bind soil particles into aggregates.

But the soil also contains many small organisms. Fungal filaments ramify through the soil, bacteria form small colonies and secrete gummy substances around themselves, and there is a wide variety of minute soil animals, such as protozoa, mites and springtails, which are constantly affecting the soil on a small scale, particularly in aiding the breakdown of organic material.

Earthworms burrow through soil, eating organic matter and large quantities of soil particles, leaving behind as many as six million burrows to an acre or $1500/m^2$. They excrete the soil particles together with some organic matter in finely divided form, much of it onto the surface of the soil, sufficient to add a new layer of soil about 18 cm thick in 30 years.

The total soil is therefore a complex biological system (Figure 3.5). On the one hand there are the factors which are tending to cement soil particles together such as products of microorganisms and uncombined oxides and salts. On the other hand there are the factors tending to aerate and break up the soil, such as earthworms and other animals, plant roots and also physical agents, frost, water and temperature.

As a result soils normally have a characteristic structure. The soil particles are aggregated into crumbs with spaces between, which can be filled with air, other gases or water, from which roots obtain water and nutrients. Without this crumb structure a soil composed of fine particles can have a very high bulk density and become almost impervious to root growth, water and oxygen; a soil composed of coarse particles is usually structureless and unstable.

Figure 3.5. Soil has a remarkable complexity: the structure of a normal soil magnified 200 times by a scanning electron microscope showing mineral particles, organic matter and microorganisms.

3.3 NUTRIENT SUPPLY

An ideal soil acts as a store of nutrients, releasing them slowly. Only minute fractions of the nutrients in a soil are in a form readily available to plants. The way nutrients are stored and released differs for the various nutrients.

Nitrogen is in many ways the most important single nutrient that a plant obtains from the soil (Figure 3.1) and is nearly always in short supply. It is an important component of proteins and therefore of all protoplasm. It is usually assimilated by plants in the form of nitrate NO_3^-. All nitrates are extremely soluble and since the nitrate ion is a negatively charged anion, it is not readily held by soil materials which have few positively charged sites to combine with anions. As a result nitrates are readily leached from soils, washed out by percolating rain water.

Nitrogen is not a normal component of the primaeval rocks from which soils are derived. It exists mainly as gaseous nitrogen in the air and only gets into the soil by the activities of nitrogen-fixing microorganisms which are able to reduce it to NH_4^+. The most important of these, the bacterium *Rhizobium*, is symbiotically associated with the roots of leguminous plants. There are other nitrogen-fixing bacteria and blue-green algae which live free in the soil.

The amount of nitrogen fixed by the rhizobia associated with white clover in pastures is about 100–200 kg/ha/yr, but it can be up to 500 kg/ha/yr. Under alder thickets on Alaskan glacial moraines the rate of nitrogen accumulation is about 60 kg/ha/yr. In other areas symbiotic nitrogen-fixing bacteria can be very few and only very small quantities of nitrogen are fixed by free living microorganisms, usually not more than 5 kg/ha/yr, but sometimes up to 30 kg/ha/yr. A further small supply of nitrogen, about 5–10 kg/ha/yr comes dissolved in rain: in industrial areas this can be as much as 30 kg/ha/yr (Table 3.3).

Table 3.3. There is a small supply of nutrients from the atmosphere: mean annual nutrient input from rain at three colliery spoil sites in industrial northern England (in kg/ha)

| site | Na | K | Ca | Mg | P | N | | | | rainfall (cm) |
						NH$_4$	NO$_3$	organic	total	
Mitchell	10·32	2·04	11·07	2·48	0·22	4·58	2·98	0·90	8·46	52·96
Maltby	10·37	5·80	17·36	5·39	0·35	4·11	3·03	1·44	8·58	63·88
Bullcroft	16·00	2·95	23·03	4·88	0·28	4·63	3·43	1·52	9·58	63·38

The nitrogen in soils begins its existence mainly in an organic form. When this gets broken down the nitrogen is eventually released in the form of nitrate which will get absorbed by plants and returned to the soil in an organic form, if it is not lost by leaching. Organic matter is therefore the important store normally holding about 5000 kg/ha of nitrogen.

The organic matter decays slowly under the influence of decomposer microorganisms. The nitrogen is excreted as a by-product in the form of ammonia, NH_3, or the ammonium ion NH_4^+. The rate of breakdown is affected by temperature, aeration, and moisture.

The ammonium can be oxidised to nitrate. But some of the ammonium, being positively charged, is held by the soil and only released slowly. The nitrate not immediately used by plants or microorganisms is rapidly leached away and lost although some is converted back to other forms of nitrogen and held in the deeper layers of the soil, available there for deeper-rooting plants.

Phosphorus is an essential part of the enzyme systems of plants and is very important in the actively growing parts. It is taken up from the soil as the $H_2PO_4^-$ or HPO_4^{-2} phosphate ion. It is released into soils by the decay of phosphorus-rich minerals such as apatite and fluorapatite. Many soils are derived from materials containing little phosphorus, such as the Millstone Grit in northern England, and are very deficient. In tropical soils the phosphorus has usually been removed by leaching.

But the most important characteristic of phosphorus is that it is chemically reactive as phosphate and will combine with many components of the soil, such as iron and aluminium in acid soils and calcium in alkaline soils, form-

Chapter 3: Plants and Soil

ing complex insoluble components. As a result very little of the phosphorus is in a readily available state. Phosphorus added to soils becomes locked up in the same way. However the phosphorus-containing compounds may not be completely insoluble and release phosphorus slowly.

Most of the phosphorus taken up by plants will return to the soil in an organic form: in some soils over half the total phosphorus can be in organic matter. This phosphorus is released when the organic matter decays, rather like nitrogen.

The way in which phosphorus is complexed has one other consequence. Soluble available phosphorus does not move far from its source. Most plant roots appear to take up the phosphorus originating less than one, or at the most, two millimetres from the roots. Plants only take up the phosphorus where their roots are, and a poor root system for any reason means a limited source of phosphorus. So trouble due to one cause can lead to troubles with something else.

Many plants have a special, mycorrhizal, relationship with a fungus, which grows either outside the root or actually within the root tissues. The presence of mycorrhiza can considerably increase the supply of phosphorus eventually available to the plant. The phosphorus at first accumulates in the mycorrhizal sheath around the root and then is gradually transferred to the higher plant itself. The process may require energy from the plant. Mycorrhizal associations are widespread and important. Without inoculation pine trees planted in the West African savannas, for instance, will not grow at all.

Sulphur is as essential to plants as phosphorus (Figure 3.1). It is used by plants as the sulphate anion SO_4^{--}. Most rocks contain some sulphur, usually as sulphide, so that it is rarely in short supply, but there are areas of the world, for example the Coast Range of California and the West African savannas, where a sulphur shortage occurs probably due to frequent fires. In industrial areas there is a considerable supply of sulphur from the air, as sulphuric acid and sulphur dioxide produced by burning coal and oil.

In some soils, particularly those formed from clays and shales, sulphur levels can be very high, in the form of iron pyrites, FeS_2, but normally sulphur is in the form of sulphate, or in organic matter. Sulphur compounds are rather insoluble so there is only a little loss from soils by leaching except in some tropical soils.

Cations. The rest of the major nutrients required by plants are in the form of positively charged ions (cations). Rocks, and the soils derived from them, differ markedly in the amount of cations they contain. Basic rocks such as limestones and volcanic tuffs contain large quantities, acidic rocks such as sandstones and volcanic rhyolites little (see Chapter 10).

But the supply of cations is not so much dependent on

Nutrient Supply

what is stored, as on how much of the store is available. The soil contains clay minerals of three main types: the kaolinite group formed of units of one layer of aluminium oxide joined to one of silicon oxide, and the group formed of units of two layers of silicon oxide and one of aluminium oxide. This group contains non-expanding types, micaceous clays, and the expanding montmorillonite type. The units of kaolinite are held by hydrogen bonds, the units of the other group by various cations. Micaceous clays and montmorillonite are therefore richer in cations than kaolinite and their lattice acts as a store (Figure 3.6). But all types have surface negative charges which retain cations in a readily exchangeable form.

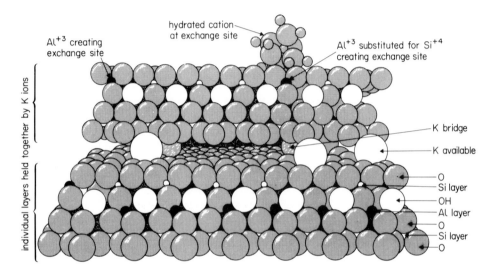

Figure 3.6. A model of the clay illite showing
(i) aluminium (Al^{+3}) substituted for silicon (SI^{+4}) creating negatively charged exchange sites on the surfaces of the illite units
(ii) a hydrated cation adsorbed onto an exchange site
(iii) bridges between the illite units formed by potassium (K)
(iv) available potassium exposed at the edge of a unit.

Cations are also stored within undecomposed organic matter which came from previous plants. Since organic matter has negative charges it also acts as an exchangeable store. Cations, like other elements, are used by plants in a water soluble state. The concentration in solution is replenished by the exchangeable material on the clay and organic matter fractions.

Potassium is the most common nutrient cation in plants (Figure 3.1), being involved in many biological processes. Its origin in soils is from the many potassium-rich minerals such as orthoclase, biotite and muscovite. It may be between the crystal units of the clay minerals of the micaceous type such as illite or superficially on the surface of all clay types and more readily available. Other soil minerals and the organic matter hold lesser amounts.

Soils containing clays retain potassium easily. But in those soils where there is little clay or organic matter, potassium is lost readily, particularly in areas of high rainfall. In hot, wet climates the clays themselves are destroyed, giving soil very deficient in potassium.

Calcium is an essential plant nutrient for both cell function and structure. But it is also important because it is a very dominating cation in many soils, determining pH which in turn controls other factors. It has an important effect on the structural arrangement of clay particles, causing them to flocculate.

Calcium is a common element occurring in minerals such as feldspars, hornblende and dolomite, or in the simple form of calcium carbonate. There are, however, many areas where there is neither free calcium nor much calcium combined in any form: the only calcium may be in organic matter.

Calcium can also be stored, like potassium, in an exchangeable form. But it is not stored within the clay lattice itself. So most of the calcium is readily available and may be leached fairly readily from the soils; in a moist temperate climate the amount is at least 150 kg/ha/yr. So in areas of high rainfall there may be a serious deficiency of calcium solely due to leaching.

Magnesium is a constituent of chlorophyll so is essential to plants, but is not needed in very large amounts. It originates from many minerals and is usually in the soil in the form of silicates. It occurs abundantly in the clay minerals from which it can be released. It is not usually in short supply and is usually readily available. It is most likely to be deficient in sandy soils and highly leached tropical soils.

Sodium. There is no clear evidence that sodium is an essential nutrient, although a few species grow better when it is present. Sodium is very mobile and in conditions where there is strong evaporation and a water supply from below, it can accumulate in soil to toxic levels. Normally it is not present in large amounts, being too readily leached.

Trace elements (micronutrients). All the preceding elements are required in relatively large amounts by plants. The other group of elements are required only in very small amounts (Figure 3.1). But they are still very important, and if a plant does not obtain sufficient of any one of them its growth will be adversely affected.

In normal soils there are usually sufficient micronutrients since such small quantities are required, but particular rocks such as sandstone can be deficient in them and give rise to soils which are deficient for one or more elements; excessive leaching can also have the same effect. Since plants accumulate micronutrients, the organic matter is always an important source of micronutrients.

3.4 NUTRIENT CYCLING AND ORGANIC MATTER

The supply of nutrients to plants from the soil is not a one-way affair. If it were, the world would have run out of nutrients long ago. When plants die their remains fall to the ground and decompose: their roots decompose in situ. The organic matter produced becomes an important source of plant nutrients, and as a result the nutrients used by plants pass from plant to soil to plant in an endless cycle (Figure 3.7). In this way there is considerable conservation of nutrients, and when they are returned to the soil they are in a form which will make them readily available to a new set of plants.

This cycling through organic matter is an important feature of all soils. In some situations, especially in the wet tropics, the organic matter breaks down very quickly and

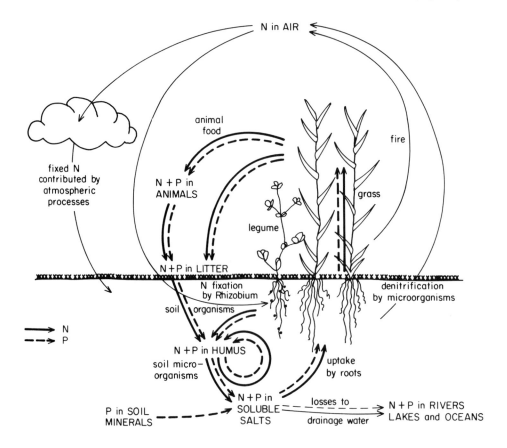

typical values for a fertile grassland in a temperate climate

	stores (kg/ha)			transfers (kg/ha/yr)	
	N	P		N	P
PLANTS	300	50	atmospheric	10	0·5
ANIMALS	20	6	fixation	50	0
LITTER	200	30	litter and roots	70	10
SOIL ORGANISMS	100	30	animals	30	5
HUMUS	5000	1000	mineralisation	100	15
AVAILABLE	30	50	leaching	5	0·2
MINERALS	0	5000	denitrification	5	0
			fire	0–100	0
			plant uptake	100	15

the nutrients are quickly taken up again by plants: a higher proportion of the nutrients are stored in the living plants. In temperate regions there is usually a much greater store of organic matter, but the cycle is still very active.

In all situations losses from the cycle occur particularly by leaching. These will be made up by the release of further nutrients from the soil minerals and by some nutrients brought in the rain (Table 3.3). If the rate of loss is more than the rate of replacement then the cycle will slowly become exhausted. This is obvious in high-rainfall areas where calcium becomes deficient.

Nitrogen supply to plants is enormously dependent on cycling, since it is not contained in soil minerals. Nearly all the nitrogen that a plant obtains from the soil is derived from previous plants. Losses from the cycle of nitrogen are made up by the various microorganisms which fix nitrogen from the air. In Figure 3.7 the system is accumulating nitrogen because fixation is greater than the losses. But nitrogen fixation demands a great deal of energy and is not always as high as this. Under conditions wher fixation does not occur the nitrogen cycle sooner or later slows down and very little plant growth is possible.

Organic matter is the key to cycling and this is the reason why we hold it in such respect. Before the advent of chemical fertilisers almost the only way of ensuring that nutrient levels were maintained was to see that all organic matter was returned to the soil.

But there is another attribute of organic matter which is important. The breakdown of organic matter by microorganisms releases the nutrients in a soluble form at rates suited to uptake by plant roots. Organic matter represents an accumulation of nutrients which have been released from parent minerals only slowly and over a long period. Nutrients which were scarcely available have been converted into a form where they are readily available and can be rapidly cycled.

A primitive soil left by the retreat of a glacier, or deposited on a shore line by the sea, begins by having no organic matter. Although it may contain a large quantity of nutrients these may not be in a form which is readily available, and the nitrogen which must be fixed by microorganisms will have had no time to accumulate. So soils without organic matter are likely to be much less fertile than the same material which has had time to develop into a proper soil. This is an important principle which obviously applies to derelict land. But it does not mean that plants cannot exist without organic matter. It can readily be replaced by nutrients supplied artificially, but it is not easy to supply them in the slow progressive manner achieved by organic matter.

Nutrient Cycling and Organic Matter

Water culture experiments show that plants can tolerate wide ranges of acidity or alkalinity. But in soils there are marked effects, mainly due to secondary causes.

Acidity or alkalinity depends on the concentration of hydrogen ions, H^+, in the soil solution. Soils which are acidic tend to have a pH below 5, and those which are alkaline a pH above 8. Soil becomes acid because of a deficiency of bases such as calcium: alkaline soils have an excess of calcium or sodium.

Hydrogen ions are not only present in the soil solution, but also stored on charged sites, attached to soil particles like other ions. This exchangeable hydrogen ion fraction is important since it controls the degree to which the soil will tend to revert to its original acidity if this is changed by the addition of alkaline materials.

The secondary effects of pH in soils are complex. On the one hand it can cause nutrients to become unavailable: on the other hand it can cause elements which are micro-nutrients and other elements which are not nutrients to become available to plants in toxic amounts (Figure 3.8). It affects organic matter decay and nutrient release, and also nutrient retention because the cation exchange capacity of clays is reduced as acidity increases.

Figure 3.8. The pH of a soil affects many of its biological and chemical characteristics: there are many consequent repercussions on plant growth.

In alkaline soils where the pH is more than about 8, the major problem is that the micronutrients iron, manganese and boron become difficult for the plant to absorb. Phosphate becomes unavailable because it changes into insoluble compounds which plants cannot use.

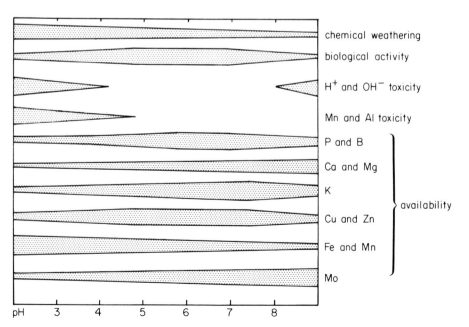

chemical weathering

biological activity

H^+ and OH^- toxicity

Mn and Al toxicity

P and B

Ca and Mg

K

Cu and Zn

Fe and Mn

Mo

availability

pH   3   4   5   6   7   8

Chapter 3: Plants and Soil

In acid soils, quite apart from a deficiency of calcium, there is a serious excess of aluminium and manganese. These two elements are present in nearly all soils but usually in a form unavailable to plants. But when the pH drops below 4–5, they become more soluble and can have direct toxic effects (Figure 3.9). The aluminium also has an indirect effect. Together with iron, it combines with phosphate forming insoluble compounds in which the phosphate is not available to plants. In very acid soils microbial activity is reduced. As a result, release of nitrogen and other nutrients can be very low so that there is a considerable nutrient deficiency.

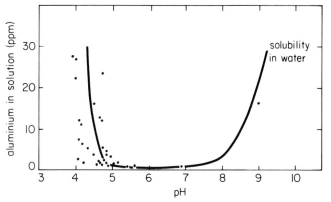

Figure 3.9. High levels of aluminium at low pH exclude many plants from acid soils: a graph showing the effect of pH on the solubility of aluminium in water and the concentrations of aluminium found in soil solutions.

Plants differ in their ability to tolerate this complexity of problems (Figure 3.10). Natural vegetation on acid soils has a characteristic set of species, often called calcifuges, which can tolerate both the toxicity and nutrient shortage. They grow slowly, and also have more efficient powers of uptake. Calcicoles, species characteristic of soils in the alkaline range, have a different but analogous set of capabilities. There are only a few species which can tolerate the complete range of pH found in nature.

Figure 3.10. Species can differ considerably in their preferences for soils of particular pH: the occurrence of ten grass species on different soils in the Sheffield region of England.

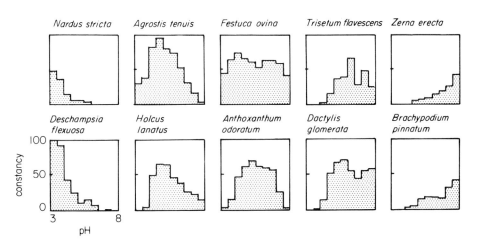

Soil Acidity

3.6 SOIL PROFILES

If a soil is examined by excavating a pit it will nearly always be found to consist of layers which are the outcome of the processes that have been discussed in this chapter. There is usually a layer in which the soil is enriched by organic matter, either decayed or still more or less unchanged. At the same time, under the influence of rainfall, most soils possess layers from which there has been loss of nutrients and other materials by leaching, and lower layers which have received the products of this leaching. It is possible to recognise sequences of layers or horizons that give a soil distinct features, known as the soil profile.

In most temperate-region soils there is a horizon near the surface which is subject to loss of material (ions and soil particles), a horizon which receives the material from above, and a horizon of the almost unchanged parent material from which the soil has developed. These horizons may be sub-divided but are termed, in the usual system of classification, sequentially the A, B and C horizons. Although the A horizon may have lost certain nutrients it is also usually the zone in which organic matter and much of the biological activity of the soil will be found. There may be a distinct layer of organic matter on the actual surface, known as the O or A_o horizon. These two horizons correspond, very approximately, to the general term 'top soil'. The B (and C) horizons correspond to 'sub soil', but, of course, the terms are frequently used much less specifically than this. We normally expect the top soil to be the most fertile part of the soil, but under certain conditions the lower layers may be equally or more fertile.

3.7 WATER SUPPLY

Water is a crucial material for plant growth: most of the hydrogen and oxygen in Figure 3.1 comes from water. But plants are immensely prodigal of water, continuously losing it from their leaves by evaporation. The cells in their leaves are adapted to take up carbon dioxide from the atmosphere, and as a result cannot help losing water from the same cells. Most plants use at least 250 kg of water for each 1 kg of dry matter they produce, in drier regions as much as 800 kg.

Ground covered with plants loses water in much the same way that an open water surface loses water, depending on the temperature of the water surface, the dryness of the air, and the speed of the wind which removes the damp air from the water surface. The temperature of the water surface itself will depend on the input of radiation from the sky.

The amount of water lost from a soil through plants can

Figure 3.11. In different regions of the world there can be very different balances between monthly rainfall and water used by crops (evapotranspiration): deficits are made good by water stored in the soil: where the deficit is large plants must be drought-tolerant to survive unless irrigation is provided.

be set against the input of water from rain throughout the year. Rainfall in Britain is fairly uniformly spread over the whole year, but during the summer, because of the high rates of water loss, there is a net deficit in some regions. In other regions of the world the deficits can be much more pronounced (Figure 3.11). Over shorter periods it must be realised that transpiration by plants is a continuous process whereas water input by rain never is.

The importance of the soil in providing a store of water therefore becomes obvious. The amount available to plants will depend on the amount held per unit volume of soil and the depth of soil into which roots penetrate. The amount of water that a soil can hold depends considerably on its texture. Sandy soils may be able to hold only one quarter as much as a soil made of peat or silty loam. The water which

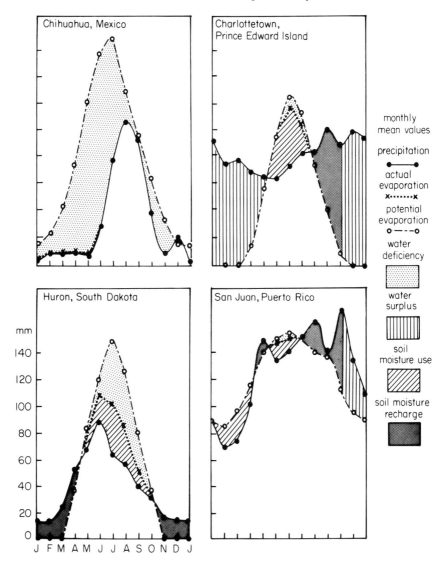

is valuable to plants is not the total in the soil, but the available water capacity which is the difference between the amount of water that can be held by the soil against gravity (the field capacity) and the amount held by the soil when plants begin to wilt. Since these two points are rather difficult to measure they are now usually defined indirectly by the water potential (ψ)—the force required to extract water from the soil. Field capacity is usually taken as ψ = –0·33 bars and wilting point ψ = –15 bars. These values are largely constant from soil to soil but correspond to different ranges of percentage moisture (Table 3.4).

Table 3.4. Soils differ considerably in their retention of water: the available water capacity in different soils

soil type	field capacity (% water)	permanent wilting point (% water)	available water capacity (cm) (assuming rooting depth of 30 cm)
sand	6·7	1·8	1·98
sandy loam	19·8	7·9	4·75
fine sandy loam	25·6	9·5	6·40
silty loam	35·3	12·7	7·05
clay loam	30·1	16·3	4·15
clay	39·4	22·1	4·83
peat	156·8	70·6	9·05

Organic matter plays a part in improving the water-holding capacity of soils, particularly light sandy ones. If the organic matter content of a sandy soil is increased by presence of 25 per cent peat, its available water capacity should be doubled (Table 3.4). In fact smaller quantities of organic matter than this can have the same effect, because of the effect organic matter has on overall soil structure.

Most herbaceous plants root down to a depth of 60 cm and more vigorous species can root down to twice this depth. Trees may well root down to a depth of 3 m. This provides all plants with a reasonably large store of water to draw on in seasons when rainfall is less than evaporation. It is also possible in the deeper layers of the soil that the water store is recharged from underground sources.

If for any reason a plant cannot develop a good root system, perhaps because of toxicity or nutrient deficiency, then it will only have a very small store of water to draw on in the surface layer of the soil. The plant can die of drought even where there is an adequate supply of water in deeper layers of the soil. On coal waste heaps, for instance, lack of nutrients leads to great reduction of root systems (Figure 3.12).

Species differ in their use of water and their ability to tolerate dry periods. Species in arid regions may have physiological mechanisms leading to more economical use of water. Some may be adapted to store water by being succulent. Others evade surface drought by very deep roots or by going into a period of dormancy. So there are few regions where plants are completely absent because of drought.

Chapter 3: Plants and Soil

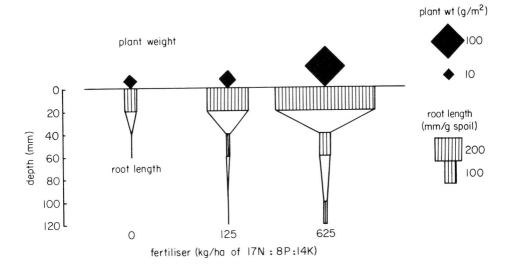

Figure 3.12. The root growth of plants is as much affected by lack of plant nutrients as is shoot growth: in this experiment ryegrass plants on colliery spoil provided with insufficient nutrients have such poor roots that they could die of drought.

FURTHER READING

Black C.A. 1968. *Soil-plant Relationships* (2nd edition). New York: John Wiley and Sons.

Cooke G.W. 1967. *The Control of Soil Fertility*. London: Crosby Lockwood.

Foth H.D. 1978. *Fundamentals of Soil Science* (6th edition). New York: John Wiley and Sons.

Hewitt E.J. & Smith T.A. 1975. *Plant Mineral Nutrition*. London: English Universities Press.

Richards B.N. 1974. *Introduction to the Soil Ecosystem*. London: Longman.

Rodin L.E. & Bazilevich N.I. 1967. *Production and Mineral Cycling in Terrestrial Vegetation*. Edinburgh: Oliver and Boyd.

Russell E.W. 1974. *Soil Conditions and Plant Growth* (12th edition). London: Longman.

*'To see the world in a grain of sand
And a heaven in a wild flower
Hold infinity in the palm of your hand
And eternity in an hour'*
WILLIAM BLAKE
Auguries of Innocence *Circa* 1800.

4 Natural Soils and Their Improvement

Man has always been exploiting and reclaiming land. The whole development of agriculture has depended upon a zealous replacement of the natural sparse vegetation by agricultural crops. The early agriculturalist was however the victim of his environment. He could only remove the original vegetation and accept the soil as he found it. As a result the very early cultivators, from Neolithic to early Iron Age, who were limited in what they could cultivate by their primitive implements, had to accept extremely poor soils, usually on either extremely acid or extremely calcareous rocks, and the poor crops that resulted. It was only when technology improved with the coming of the Anglo-Saxons, who had developed a mould-board plough, that the rich loam soils could be cultivated. At this stage the poorer soils were deserted and have remained uncultivated ever since.

Recently, however, the agriculturist in Britain has been able with modern techniques to go back to these soils and reclaim them, so that now some of them yield as well as the naturally more fertile soils. In other countries which early settlers found areas impossible to cultivate which are now in full-scale agriculture because we now have a proper understanding of what was wrong with the soils and how they can be corrected.

Since agricultural land reclamation and improvement has led the way in showing how derelict land can be restored, we must look at some selected examples.

4.1 A RANGE OF NORMAL SOILS

We need a yardstick by which soils can be judged, which gives us some idea of the sort of soil textures and nutrient compositions which are associated with satisfactory growth. Table 4.1 gives a range of examples of British soils on which the growth of agricultural crops is satisfactory, although under modern agriculture, further fertilisers and lime may be given. Common experience has established levels of nutrients which are considered satisfactory for growth of common species and these are given in the same table for guidance, although Figure 3.2 shows that species differ in their requirements.

Contrasted with these are soils which are not so satisfactory for plant growth. These are in areas which have never been cultivated or which were originally cultivated by primitive man but subsequently went out of cultivation. They are often deficient only in one or two respects and therefore can be brought back into productive cultivation by modern methods. For each soil the particular characteristics which are likely to be a cause of trouble are marked.

The same considerations can be given to soils on a world scale, although the effects of climate may be sometimes over-riding. As a yardstick to all the soils the glacial moraine soil from the Antarctic is included. It is a raw and undeveloped material, low in organic matter and available nutrients, particularly nitrogen. But is the sort of raw material from which many productive soils of the world have been derived.

Until recently the land classifications used in most parts of the world paid particular attention to the total of nutrient and physical characteristics of the soils of the regions being classified. Now with the advent of modern methods of improvement, much more emphasis is put on those characteristics, such as fundamental physical and drainage properties, which cannot be overcome by modern farming techniques. The resulting assessments, termed 'land-use capability classifications', are rapidly replacing the earlier classifications. Land improvement and reclamation are concepts well understood by the farming community.

4.2.   CHALK DOWNLAND— MACRONUTRIENT DEFICIENCY

The chalk downs are a very characteristic part of Britain. Extensively settled in Neolithic times, they were deserted at the end of the Iron Age, and have remained uncultivated until recent times except for a period in the middle of the nineteenth century.

Chalk is almost pure calcium carbonate. As a result the soils that are formed from it, known as rendzinas, are thin, extremely deficient and dominated by the presence of calcium carbonate (Table 4.1). As a consequence the natural vegetation is very distinctive and characteristic. When the original woodland has been cleared a poor, although very attractive, grassland develops, dominated by a number of slow-growing plants such as sheep's fescue (*Festuca ovina*), quaking grass (*Briza media*), salad burnet (*Poterium sanguisorba*), glaucous sedge (*Carex flacca*) and wild thyme (*Thymus praecox*). The productivity of such areas is extremely poor, less than 300 kg/ha of dry matter per annum.

A superficial examination of chalk down grassland suggests that the limiting factor is shortage of water. In a dry period in the summer the surface soil is dusty and the plants look parched. The native plants, such as the salad burnet, have deep roots capable of obtaining water from deep down. But closer analysis shows that the chalk rock has considerable power of water retention and that there is no greater shortage of water in chalk soil than in other soils. The over-riding problem is shortage of major plant nutrients, especially phosphorus and potassium, assisted by an excess of calcium, which together also depress the accumulation of nitrogen since legumes will not flourish under these conditions.

Reclamation of these areas for agriculture has been very simple. The old grassland has been ploughed, usually quite deeply to about 20 cm. A period of time may then be allowed for the old turf to decompose, during which a crop such as rape is grown, heavily fertilised with 500 kg/ha of standard concentrated complete fertiliser. Then after this crop, or immediately after the initial ploughing, a normal cereal crop can be grown, providing it is given a heavy fertiliser dressing as was done for the rape. Yields can be the same as on more ordinary soils (3–4 tonnes/ha).

After two or three barley crops the land may be put back to grass, but this time using highly productive species such as ryegrass (*Lolium perenne*), timothy (*Phleum pratense*),

Table 4.1. A basis for comparison: physical and chemical characteristics of some British and world soils

| % | particle fraction | | | loss on ignition | p |
	sand %	silt %	clay %	%	
British soils—productive					
Silty loam (Lincs)	40	35	25	3	6
Sandy loam (Cheshire)	65	20	15	2·5	5
Clay loam (Cambs)	30	40	30	2·5	6
Alluvial meadow (Yorks)	35	40	25	7	5
—unproductive					
Chalk grassland (Berks)	42	28	30	7	8
Upland pasture (Dyfed)	50	35	15	8	5
Nardus fell (Cumbria)	55	15	30	12	4
Sandy heath (Norfolk)	75	15	10	6	4
World wide soils—productive					
Prairie silt loam (US)	[20]	[65]	[15]	4	6
Steppe chernozem (USSR)	20	55	25	7	7
—unproductive					
Rain forest podsol (Borneo)	[20]	[10]	[70]	12	
Savanna latosol (W.Africa)	[60]	[30]	[10]	4	
Moraine (Signy, Antarctica)	30	10	60	1	
levels for normal plant growth	low high				

Values underlined are those likely to the cause of low productivity in common species
Values in brackets are estimates from other similar sites
Analytical methods are those given in Allen (1974)

meadow fescue (*Festuca pratense*) and cocksfoot (*Dactylis glomerata*), together with white clover (*Trifolium repens*). But this grass will need 50 kg/ha of P, 100 kg/ha of K, and at least 50 kg/ha of N on establishment, which is a heavy dressing, and more in subsequent years. With this treatment grass yields of 5000 kg/ha can be expected.

As a result the chalk lands are now some of the most productive areas of Britain (Figure 4.1). Because the soils are light in texture and free-draining they are easy to cultivate, so there is now little old downland left except on the inaccessible steeper slopes which cannot be cultivated.

Figure 4.1. Poor native grassland on chalk can be replaced by excellent arable and grass crops if major plant nutrients are provided: oats on newly ploughed chalk grassland in Sussex.

4.3   AUSTRALIAN DESERTS— MICRONUTRIENT DEFICIENCY

When the settlers moved into South Australia, they found an area of desert colonised by mallee, a shrub community of eucalypts such as *Eucalyptus incrassata* and broom brush (*Melaleuca uncinata*) in the region south of Adelaide.

Attempts to cultivate it failed despite the fact there was adequate rainfall (over 350 mm) and in adjoining areas farming was perfectly possible on excellent grassland, and the area became known as the Ninety Mile Desert. It

on hange acity 100 g	\multicolumn{7}{c	}{available plant nutrients (ppm)}	mineralisable N ppm	total N %
	K	Ca	Mg	Fe	P	NH$_4$–N	NO$_3$–N		
	350	2000	300	10	30	15	10	300	0·2
	100	700	80	40	10	10	5	140	0·1
	300	2500	600	60	15	20	5	[150]	0·2
	250	3000	350	5	25	20	3	100	0·4
	120	>20000	600	2	14	<1	20	60	0·3
	100	250	100	50	3	25	10	120	0·2
	80	160	50	220	2	30	1	20	0·2
	60	250	40	60	3	8	2	[50]	0·2
	250	2000	500	100	50	[5]	[10]	[150]	0·25
	400	3000	300	30	30	[5]	[10]	[100]	0·2
	200	150	100	50	6	30	5	[50]	0·1
	100	800	250	250	1	[4]	[2]	[10]	0·07
	40	600	80	50	5	1	<1	[5]	0·02
	100	500	50	5	5	2	2	50	0·1
	300	2000	300	200	20	20	20	200	1·0

Figure 4.2. Good grass growth in southern Australia depends on the use of very small quantities of zinc and copper: reclaimed grassland and original scrub in the Coonalpyn Downs, S. Australia.

remained uncultivated until the 1950s when it was discovered that levels of major plant nutrients in the soil were quite adequate, and could anyway be supplemented by fertilisers, but the crucial factor was an acute micronutrient deficiency, of zinc and copper.

A mere 7 kg/ha of zinc sulphate and 7 kg/ha of copper sulphate served to transform the area into a highly productive area of grazing capable of supporting four sheep to the hectare instead of one sheep to 10 hectares it used to carry. As a final seal on the transformation, the area is now called the Coonalpyn Downs (Figure 4.2).

For Eastern Australia, particularly the Southern Tablelands near Canberra, the picture is the same. The same poverty despite 500 mm rainfall is due to a lack of phosphorus and molybdenum. Phosphorus has always been known to be necessary for clover growth, but addition did not seem to have the effects in these areas that it should have done. Clover was helped however by alkaline materials such as wood ash and lime, which were thought to counter the acidity of the soils. But in 1942 it was found that the acidity is not important and molybdenum is the key, just 50 gm of molybdenum per hectare (1 oz/acre). When added with phosphate this is sufficient to get excellent growth of subterranean clover (*Trifolium subterraneum*) and therefore highly productive pasture land.

4.4 HILL GRAZINGS OF WALES—ACIDITY

An archeological map of Wales shows extensive Iron Age settlements of hill and slopes at about 300 m altitude. Today some signs of their old enclosures and fields can still be seen, because between that period and the present day the land has been deserted except for sheep. Hard rocks deficient in nutrients and a high rainfall combine to give a nutrient-poor acidic soil, so acid that organic matter breakdown is prevented and 10 cm of peaty organic matter remains on the soil surface. Such soils are known as peaty podzols (Table 4.1).

The vegetation under sheep grazing consists of a grassland dominated by bent grass (*Agrostis tenuis*) and sheep's fescue (*Festuca ovina*) and sometimes heather (*Calluna vulgaris*). There are a few herbs particularly tormentil (*Potentilla erecta*) and heath bedstraw (*Galium saxatile*). There is no white clover (*Trifolium repens*). The acidity and lack of nutrients means that growth is very reduced; 500 kg/ha of dry matter per annum is usual. In terms of sheep production this means only about 2 sheep can be allowed to graze each hectare during the summer months.

When farming was at its peak during the last century, attempts were made to improve these grazings, mainly by the use of farmyard manure. But the real step forward in transforming these areas has depended upon understanding the critical factors controlling production. The dominant problem is acidity which prevents organic matter breakdown, and causes excessive amounts of aluminium and manganese to be free in the soil. The first need is therefore for heavy dressings of lime, as much as 50 tonnes/ha repeated every few years. But these soils are also short of phosphorus so that at least 50 kg/ha of P must be added, traditionally in the form of basic slag at 1200 kg/ha.

But it is not sensible to add these lime and fertiliser dressings to the original vegetation because the turf does not contain species capable of responding to the fertiliser. The original grassland is ploughed: in this way the organic matter becomes buried in the soil with the lime and fertiliser. Then a seeds mixture is sown on top with a small amount of complete fertiliser, perhaps 300 kg/ha. The seeds mixture, which can be complex, has two important components, ryegrass (*Lolium perenne*), and white clover (*Trifolium repens*) to provide the crucial source of nitrogen. It is uneconomic to provide the nitrogen in the form of fertiliser every year particularly because it quickly leached away. The lime and phosphate are not so quickly leached: but even so they must be re-applied every few years or the grassland degenerates.

The resulting grassland can yield 5000 kg/ha of dry matter/yr and the number of sheep that can be carried will have increased five- or ten-fold (Figure 4.3). The soil develops a completely different character as the organic matter breaks down by increased microbial activity and becomes incorporated in the soil by the activities of earthworms and small soil animals, which although they have no place in the original podzol soon spread and multiply under the new conditions. Ultimately the soil takes on the appearance and structure of a brown earth.

Figure 4.3. The poor heather lands of Wales can be converted to productive pastures if they are ploughed, limed, fertilised, and sown with productive grasses: land recently reclaimed from heather on the Llandegla Moors, Clwyd.

4.5 BRECKLAND HEATHS—NUTRIENT DEFICIENCY AND ACIDITY

In the east of England there is an area of about 700 km² of dry sandy soils, not long ago covered with a poor heath vegetation, derelict fields and scattered trees. It is the haunt of the rabbit, the stone curlew (*Burhinus oedicnemus*) and the ringed plover (*Charadrius hiaticula*), and of various rare plants, which take advantage of the poor open vegetation. Its history goes back to the Neolithic period, for it was one of the first areas in Britain to be settled and cultivated by primitive man, because of its easily cultivated soils and thin forest cover. Areas were cultivated until the soils were exhausted and were then left to recuperate—a type of shifting cultivation still widely practised in the tropics.

Such a system has continued intermittently to the present century. There were large fields called 'brakes' which were each cultivated for a few years and then left to recover their fertility naturally before being cultivated again (Figure 4.4). It is this system which gave rise to the name 'Breckland'. The soils were so poor that continuous cultivation was not possible; sometimes wind erosion of the worn-out brakes led to disastrous sandstorms and even dune formation, described by Evelyn in 1677 as 'like the Deserts of Libya'. The problem was a combination of poor sandy texture, extremes of acidity and alkalinity determined by the varying presence of chalk in the sand, considerable lack of organic matter and plant nutrients, and

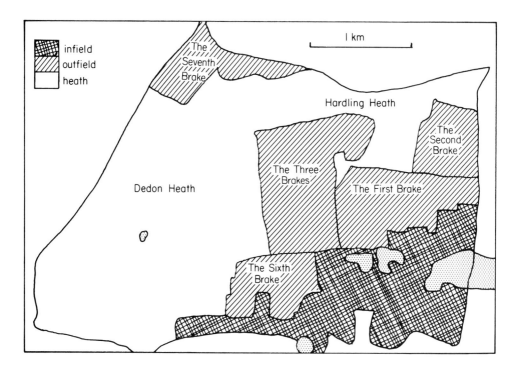

Figure 4.4. In the Breckland, the heath was temporarily enclosed and cultivated for a few years until it was exhausted: a map of the field system in West Wretham, Norfolk in 1741.

surface drought enhanced by the dryness of the climate, the driest in Britain.

Yet now the area is covered with a productive agriculture initiated in the 1930s and developed to cover most of the area during World War II. This has been achieved by a combination of approaches. It was found that it was first necessary to replace the missing major plant nutrients. This is easy with fertilisers, and involves added nitrogen, phosphorus and potassium. In acid areas where there is chalk close below the surface it was brought up by deep ploughing, otherwise heavy dressings of lime were given. Then secondly, grass leys were established involving particularly a grass, cocksfoot (*Dactylis glomerata*), and a vigorous legume, lucerne (*Medicago sativa*), which are deep-rooting and drought-tolerant. These are grazed, and so the soil benefits not only from the organic matter produced directly by the plants but also from the animal droppings.

These leys are left for a few years and then ploughed in and replaced by cereals and root crops. These are continued for several years, well-fertilised until the soil has deteriorated particularly in respect of organic matter, when a ley is re-established.

This system with modifications has enabled a vigorous agriculture to be pursued throughout the area. In many ways it is an up-to-date version of the old brake system, but with input of nutrients and use of sown legumes to provide nitrogen. It has been so successful that there is now very little of the original vegetation left and conservationists are extremely concerned about the rare and unusual flora, which has affinities with the flora of the steppes.

At the same time large areas of the very acid, deep sands have been used for forestry. The Forestry Commission has established one of its largest forests, Thetford Chase, in the area. Except for the relics of shelter belts planted in the last century, the area was treeless. The forest is therefore completely new, established by hand-planting of stock raised in nurseries, mostly of Scots pine (*Pinus sylvestris*). This species is tolerant of drought, soils low in nutrients, and frosts. They need little special attention, although a small quantity of fertiliser (usually rock phosphate) is given in the early stages.

It is now a flourishing area of agriculture and forestry, and new industry at the main town Thetford. Evelyn would indeed be surprised to see the area today.

4.6   ARID LANDS—DROUGHT

In a warm, dry climate a single crop grown properly can use at least 50 cm of water, although wild plants can use less. If this is not available crops either fail or are considerably reduced. The rainfall of arid regions is notoriously variable, so even if there is an apparently adequate mean annual rainfall this can be so unreliable as to make cropping hazardous or impossible.

At the same time the soils that form have developed under extreme conditions. Lack of moisture means that temperatures will rise quickly during the day and this will be followed by rapid cooling at night. This sets up considerable stresses in rock which shatter into angular particles. The weathering of the rock is mainly physical, and little chemical alteration occurs due to the lack of moisture. There are soils in desert regions that are little more than rock particles and lack the organic matter or clay minerals which give so much stability to more normal soils.

Arid regions are frequently subject to strong winds which carry the smaller rock particles and have a sand-blasting effect on rocks and larger particles. Often the wind removes the smaller particles leaving behind sand with a very uniform particle size. The lack of organic matter and smaller-sized particles has a considerable effect on the moisture-holding capacity of the soil (see Table 3.4). Paradoxically in desert regions with clay soils the small amount of water added to the soil as rainfall may be virtually unavailable because of the retention properties of the clay.

Another characteristic of desert soils is that reserves of some plant nutrients may be very low. The source of nitrogen, the organic matter from which it is slowly released, is virtually absent because of high temperatures. In addition, the generally high pH values that prevail mean that any nitrogen added to the soil will be converted to nitrate nitrogen and, at times of cloudbursts quickly lost by leaching from the porous soil material. High pH values also ensure that other nutrients, for example phosphorus, are quickly fixed in forms unavailable to plants. Thus desert soils can be extremely difficult substrates on which to establish a vegetation cover of any sort.

But the addition of water to these areas, particularly clay-dominated areas, by irrigation can totally transform them. If the water supply is controlled it can be added economically in quantities to suit the requirements of the developing crop. The prediction of irrigation need has been brought to a high level of sophistication. Many different methods of application have been developed, by flooding in large areas, by ditches, by sprinklers (which can be enormous covering 60 hectares), or by sub-irrigation. With a controlled supply of water the physical inadequacies of the original soil can be largely overcome. The nutrient deficiencies can be overcome by fertilisers and leguminous crops. As a result some of the most productive areas of the world are now in regions such as the Imperial Valley in California where rainfall is negligible (Figure 4.5).

Figure 4.5. Agriculture entirely dependent on irrigation in the Imperial Valley, California: the rainfall is only 125 mm (5 in) and before irrigation it was an area of desert.

4.7   SALINE AND ALKALINE SOILS—TOXICITY

In humid areas, where precipitation exceeds evaporation over the whole year, and where soils are free-draining, it is unusual for free salts to accumulate within the soil. Rainfall, generally being free of most elements except in very low concentrations, percolates through the soil layers and salts, produced by weathering, dissolve in the water and are carried, in a very dilute form in drainage water, into

55   *Saline and Alkaline Soils—Toxicity*

streams and rivers. The soil holds many ions against leaching through its exchange capacity and these may be preferentially absorbed at different depths in the soil, but there is no accumulation of soluble salts.

In contrast, in areas of low precipitation, there is insufficient rainfall to leach out the salts produced during weathering and they accumulate near the surface of the soil or, if rainfall is slightly higher, at some level beneath the surface. Very often the accumulation occurs well within the rooting zone of plants. In some arid and semi-arid regions the accumulation may be accentuated in low-lying areas by soluble salts carried by drainage water from surrounding areas.

Where the water table is near the surface salinity can become severe, especially if evaporation rates are high. Many examples exist throughout arid regions, including Tunisia, Iraq, the United States and Rajasthan. Saline basins found in the Sinai desert in Egypt and the Salt Desert near the Shithatha Oasis in Iraq show surface encrustations of salt in low-lying areas during all but the infrequent rainy periods. The vegetation is dominated by salt-tolerant species whose close relatives are usually found in coastal salt marshes.

A high soluble salt content is also found in soils that originate in coastal areas, deltas and estuaries. Here the source of salts is the sea which periodically inundates such areas, or a mixture of sea and river water.

Other soils accumulate high levels of salts due to the use of water, containing a heavy load of soluble salts for irrigation, in insufficient quantities to leach away the soluble salts accumulated when the water evaporates. Overhead irrigation is often used to give less volume of water than would be used by other irrigation methods, and salts accumulate. Surface irrigation, in which furrows and ridges are used, often gives rise to localised conditions of increased salinity.

Soils with a high soluble salt content can be classified on the basis of the degree of the soluble salt content and in relation to the dominant ion. *Saline* soils have a high soluble salt content but lower domination by sodium than *alkali* (sodic) soils in which the exchangeable sodium percentage is more than 15.

Plant species differ very much in their ability to tolerate a high soluble salt content in the rooting medium. As the soluble salt content rises, fewer and fewer plant species are able to grow satisfactorily (Figure 4.6). Examples of sensitive species are white clover (*Trifolium repens*) and meadow foxtail (*Alopecurus pratensis*); tolerant species are bermuda grass (*Cynodon dactylon*) and rhodes grass (*Chloris gayana*).

Salinity may be combated simply by supplying sufficient water, from time to time, to ensure that the accumulated salts are leached away. Where surface irrigation is practised this must be carried out frequently enough to prevent the build-up of saline conditions. At the same time an effective drainage must be provided or else the leached salts will merely accumulate lower down in the soil profile and as the water builds up so will the salinity of the soil. The ground water table has to be kept at least 3 m below the surface. Excess of sodium in alkali soils can be overcome by applications of calcium sulphate (see Chapter 12).

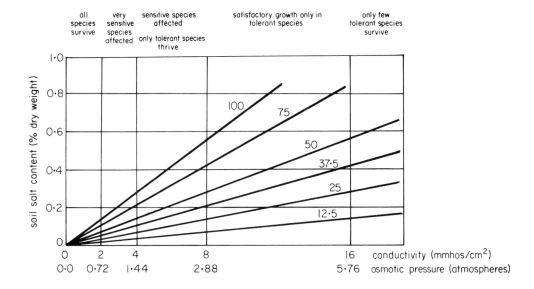

Figure 4.6. Moisture, salinity, and growth of different species: the diagonal lines represent the values for different amounts of soil moisture: the drier the soil the more severe the effects of a particular salt content.

In the Gezira, in the Sudan, irrigation has been carried on only since 1912; in Iraq since the third millennium B.C. Salinisation is a problem in parts of Iraq but is not in the Sudan. The reason for the difference is not dependent on the time scale, or on the salt concentration of the original soil or the irrigation water; it is to be found in the relative permeability of the two soils. In Iraq the soils are permeable but are not always well-drained, so that the water table rises in some areas under heavy rates of irrigation, bringing salts to the surface. In the Sudan the heavy clay soil is impermeable and there are good ditches to collect the water that moves away laterally. As a result the water table is not influenced to the same extent by the irrigation rate, so the water table does not rise bringing with it salts from the saline subsoil.

Judging the correct application rates is a tricky business. There must be enough water to give excess over that required by the crop in order that leaching may occur but not so much that the water table rises by dangerous proportions. But in many parts of the world salinity is successfully combated and intensive agriculture maintained.

Saline and Alkaline Soils—Toxicity

FURTHER READING

Normal soils

Klingebiel A.A. & Montgomery P.H. 1961. *Land Capability Classification*. US Dept. Agric. Soil Conserv. Serv. Agric. Handbook No. 210. Washington: US Dept. Agriculture.

Mackney D. 1974. Land use capability classification in the United Kingdom. In: *Land Capability Classification*. Min. Agric. Fish Food. Tech. Bull. 30, 4–11. London: HMSO.

Ministry of Agriculture, Fisheries & Food. 1966. *Agricultural land classification*. Agricultural land service, Techn. Report 11. London: Ministry of Agriculture, Fisheries & Food.

Chalk downs

Jesse R.H.B. 1960. *A Survey of the Agriculture of Sussex*. London: Royal Agricultural Society of England.

Australian deserts

Anderson A.J. & Underwood E.J. 1959. Trace element deserts. *Scient. Am.* **200**, 95–105.

Moore R.M. (ed.) 1975. *Australian Grasslands*. Canberra: Australian National University Press.

East Anglian heaths

Darby H.C. (ed.) 1938. *The Cambridge Region*. London: Cambridge Univ. Press.

Martelli G. 1952. *Elveden Enterprise*. London: Faber.

Welsh uplands

Jones L.I. 1967. *Studies on Hill Land in Wales*. Welsh Plant Breeding Station, Tech. Bull. 2. Aberystwyth: Welsh Plant Breeding Station.

Milton W.E.J. 1940. The effect of manuring, grazing and cutting on the yield, botanical and chemical composition of natural hill pastures. I. Yield and botanical composition. *J. Ecol.* **28**, 326–56.

Arid and saline areas

Arnon I. 1972. *Crop Production in Dry Regions*. London: Leonard Hill.

Cloudsley-Thompson J.L. & Chadwick M.J. 1964. *Life in Deserts*. London: Foulis.

Kelley W.P. 1951. *Alkali Soils*. New York: Reinhold.

Kovda V.A., Berg C. Van den & Hagan R.M. 1973. *Irrigation, Drainage and Salinity*. FAO/UNESCO London: Hutchinson.

Richards L.A. (ed.). 1954. *Diagnosis and Improvement of Saline and Alkali Soils*. Washington: US Dept. of Agriculture.

'By the deficiency or absence of one necessary constituent, all the others being present, the soil is rendered barren for all those crops to the life of which that one constituent is indispensable.'

LIEBIG.

Chemistry in its Application to Agriculture and Physiology, 1840.

5   Derelict Land Problems

The improvement of derelict land looks as though it might be very difficult. The complete lack of vegetation on many sites suggests problems much worse than those we have been considering in Chapter 4. In some ways this is true because derelict land soils are nearly all derived from mining or earth-moving and so are therefore raw undeveloped materials, either subsoil or rock. They have never had time to evolve a proper soil structure.

But although this may produce problems, it is also a cause for hope. There may really be little wrong with the materials of an area of derelict land which time will not solve. The natural processes of soil building should gradually be able to build up a soil of satisfactory structure and nutrient content. A satisfactory vegetation cover can develop naturally on some sites quite rapidly.

But it is hardly ever practical to wait for nature to take its course; and certain sorts of derelict land have particular problems which time and nature will not heal. There are not many things that can be wrong with derelict land materials since plants have simple requirements. If we can understand what they are and how they can be overcome then we shall be able to develop a logical and efficient approach to the problems of land restoration.

Subsequently we shall examine the problems of individual materials and their solutions in more detail. But as a background to this chapter, and as a key to the whole approach, the particular things wrong with different materials are given in Table 5.1.

5.1   TEXTURE AND STRUCTURE

Few derelict land materials have a texture or structure approaching normal soils. In many cases they are made of a single material, such as clay or hard rock, ground to a specific maximum particle size (Table 5.2). They will initially have no organic matter and no microbial activity to aggregate the material into a satisfactory crumb structure. The outcome of this is variable, for there are many natural highly productive soils, such as silty loams derived from marine silts, and arid zone soils, which have anomalous texture and structure, but which can make excellent farmland. But at the extremes there may be real problems.

Table 5.1. The great variety of materials and their properties: the characteristics of wastes and degraded land of different origins likely to cause revegetation problems

materials	texture & structure	stability	water supply	surface temperature
			physical environment	
colliery spoil	OOO	OOO/o	O/o	o/●●●
strip mining	OOO/o	OOO/o	OO/o	o/●●●
fly ash	OO/o	O	O	O
oil shale	OO	OOO/o	OO	o/●●
iron ore mining	OOO/o	OO/o	O/o	O
bauxite mining	O	O	O	O
heavy metal wastes	OOO	OOO/o	OO/o	O
gold wastes	OOO	OOO	O	O
china clay wastes	OOO	OO	OO	O
acid rocks	OOO	o	OO	O
calcareous rocks	OOO	o	OO	O
sand & gravel	O/o	o	O	O
coastal sands	OO/o	OOO/o	O/o	O
land from sea	OO	o	O	O
urban wastes	OOO/o	o	O	O
roadsides	OOO/o	OOO	OO/o	O/o

deficiency			adequate	excess		
severe	moderate	slight		slight	moderate	sev
OOO	OO	O	o	●	●●	

relative to the establishment of a soil/plant ecosystem appropriate to the material: variations in severity are due to variation in materials and situati

Table 5.2. Materials can have very different textures: the particle size composition of different materials

	sand >0·02 mm	silt 0·02–0·002 mm	clay <0·002 mm
colliery spoil			
Yorkshire	64	27	9
overburden			
Indiana	55	27	18
W.Virginia	20	59	21
fly ash			
Yorkshire	38	59	3
iron ore overburden			
Northants	39	6	55
heavy metal tailings			
Derbyshire (old)	32	35	33
(new)	53	31	16
gold sandwaste			
Johannesburg	90	9	1
china clay waste			
Cornwall	97	2	1
good loam soil	60	20	20

Heavy clays such as those produced by iron stone working in Northamptonshire can be incredibly obstinate materials, varying in the season from a consistency of butter to a consistency of concrete. The coarse rock materials produced when the country rock surrounding a metalliferous vein is excavated, or thrown out as waste from the slate industry, are the opposite extreme—so open

		chemical environment		
cro rients	micro nutrients	pH	toxic materials	salinity
·O	o	OOO/o	o	o/●●
O/o	o	OOO/o	o	o/●●
O	o	●/●●●	●●	o
O	o	OO/o	o	o/●
O	o	o	o	o
O	o	o	o	o
O	o	OOO/ ●	●/●●●	o/●●●
O	o	OOO	o	o
O	o	O	o	o
O	o	O	o	o
O	o	●	o	o
O/o	o	O/o	o	o
O	o	o	o	o/●
O	o	o/●	o	●●●
O	o	o	o/●●	o
O	o	O/o	o	o/●●

and porous that it is difficult for anything to grow in them. Often such materials may in other respects be satisfactory material for plant growth, and contain considerable stores of plant nutrients.

Materials of a more normal constitution can also have an unsatisfactory structure as a result of the use of heavy earth-moving machinery. Colliery spoil has reasonable physical properties but because of lack of organic matter can become consolidated to a rock-like consistency by the passage of wheeled machinery (Figure 5.1). These can exert pressures of 5 kg/cm² and double the bulk density of the spoil by their passage: crawler tractors exert less than 0·7 kg/cm². Although the action of frost etc. can loosen the surface layers of consolidated material it takes some years and the material underneath is not changed, and its solidity remains a barrier to proper root growth and the infiltration of water unless vegetation is established (Table 5.3).

Figure 5.1. Heavy earth-moving machinery causes considerable compaction and loss of soil structure: this grader exerts a pressure of 5 kg/cm² when fully loaded.

Table 5.3. Spoil materials suffer badly from compression because of their poor structure: the bulk densities and infiltration rates of colliery spoils subjected to compression, compared with a normal soil

		bulk density (g/cm³)	infiltration rate (cm/min)		
				compressed	
spoil			uncom-pressed	0·5	5 kg/cm²
Robin Hood	unvegetated	1·44	0·32	0·12	0·02
	vegetated	1·19	1·11	0·10	0·05
Crigglestone	unvegetated	1·69	0·10	0·02	0·01
	vegetated	1·46	0·40	0·13	0·05
Water Haigh	unvegetated	1·48	0·31	0·26	0·05
	vegetated	1·50	0·67	0·25	0·05
Water Haigh	pasture	0·89	11·11	5·88	0·29

Texture and Structure

5.2   STABILITY

A large proportion of the waste materials produced by the present-day mining industry lies between the two extremes of fineness and coarseness. In the extraction of metal ores the mined material may be ground finely with particle sizes below 0·2 mm. After the metal ores have been removed the tailings have to be dumped. Since it has such a fine particle size it should have reasonable physical characteristics, able to permit plant growth and retain adequate amounts of water.

But such materials have been formed from hard unweathered rocks and so may not contain much of the finest clay fraction (Table 5.2). There is also no organic matter or microbial activity. As a result they may be very unstable, easily blown by the wind when they are dry and eroded by heavy rain when they are wet (Figure 5.2).

Other materials, not produced by grinding, may have the same properties, for example the sand heaps produced by the china clay industry. But even materials which have a fairly normal range of particle sizes including a clay fraction, such as colliery spoil (Table 5.2), are readily eroded particularly by heavy rain.

Much of the instability of these materials is because they have no vegetation cover and not because of their struc-

Figure 5.2. Derelict land materials may erode very easily: these metalliferous tailings at Parc Mine, Gwynedd, Wales have lost 10 000 tonnes of waste containing 1 per cent lead and zinc into an important salmon river.

ture. Instability in the absence of vegetation cover can occur even on good soils, as the farmers of the Middle West found to their cost in the mid-1930s. When vegetation cover over a good soil was killed by severe aerial pollution in areas surrounding the lower Swansea valley 50 cm of top soil was washed away in 20 years. The same erosion can be seen in vast areas around the nickel smelters at Sudbury, Ontario.

Part of the instability is due to topography, since erosion will be greatest on steep slopes. A lot of the materials making up derelict land have been dumped by conveyor or dragline and are in steep-sided heaps at the natural angle of rest, about 30°, which makes them vulnerable to severe erosion. But again if vegetation cover could once be established the effect of steepness of slopes would be removed since there are plenty of slopes covered with natural vegetation steeper than this. The value of a proper vegetation cover in stabilising steep banks can be seen in Figure 5.3.

Figure 5.3. If vegetation is not properly maintained it loses its stabilising effects: in this tailings dam wall in Cornwall the central section has received no fertiliser aftercare, the rest has been properly treated.

5.3   WATER SUPPLY

Any material, like rock waste, whose particles are solid and above 10 mm diameter can hold very little water because the spaces between the particles are too large to hold water by capillarity. Materials whose particle size is below 10 mm will hold more water, but good water storage is not provided until the particle size is below 0·2 mm.

But the effectiveness of the water storage is relative to the distribution of rain through the year. A heap of 0·2 mm material in the south-west of England in a region where the rainfall is distributed throughout the year and there is high humidity will not suffer from drought, whereas the same material in a climate with a six-month dry season will suffer considerable drought.

The surface of a heap will tend to be rather different from lower down. In a material of rather poor water-holding capacity such as fine sand a considerable amount of water will be stored in the body of the heap (Figure 5.4). But the surface layers may dry out completely during a dry spell. The same can occur even on a colliery shale which has a better water-holding capacity.

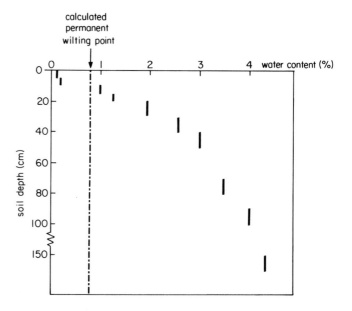

Figure 5.4. Waste materials often contain too little moisture for plant growth at the surface but usually adequate below: the water content of sand waste in Cornwall after 8 weeks' drought.

So there may be a problem of surface drought to be overcome. But if a plant can only get established and develop adequate roots it will be able to tap the water lower down without difficulty. This is true not only in temperate regions but also in arid areas: a pile of fine tailings in an arid region may be able to store more water than normal soils and permit good plant growth after the initial establishment problems have been overcome.

In a heap made mostly of coarse material there will always be a percentage of fine material. After a short period the fine material will have been washed down into the lower parts of the heap. Then, although the upper layers of the heap may be extremely open and porous, there may be sufficient accumulation of fine material lower down to give adequate water storage. Again, plants established with deep roots will be proof against drought.

5.4 SURFACE TEMPERATURE

When the sun shines on normal vegetation the heat absorbed by the plants is lost in two ways. Firstly it is lost by convection as air moves over the leaves: plants growing in desert conditions tend to have finely divided leaves to assist this process. Secondly, it is lost by the evaporation of water from the leaves. These processes keep leaves within a few degrees of the temperature of the surrounding air.

Derelict land which has no vegetation cover can behave very differently. In the first place it may be dark in colour which will result in a much greater amount of heat being absorbed. Secondly, convection is much more difficult since there is only one continuous surface over which the air can move. Thirdly, after the initial water is lost there is no evaporative cooling.

As a result the temperature of the soil surface can rise considerably. Temperatures of 60°C have been recorded on colliery waste in the USA. Plants growing sparsely under these conditions will tend to lose water so rapidly that they cannot maintain their water content and die. But they may also be directly damaged by the heat. The temperature is highest at the soil surface, and so the plant is killed at this point and collapses: this is known as heat girdling. It is unlikely to occur in cool temperate climates.

5.5 NUTRIENT SUPPLY

It is very rare indeed to find derelict land in which there is not a nutrient shortage (Table 5.4). The soil will be most deficient in nitrogen; nearly all nitrogen in soil originates from the atmosphere, so materials from below ground are rarely likely to contain any. An adequate supply of nitrogen is crucial for plant growth, so this factor is probably the most critical in preventing the establishment of vegetation on derelict land, at least until natural nitrogen-fixing processes become established. But many other nutrients, which are derived from soil minerals may also be deficient, particularly phosphorus since this is an important nutrient which is usually scarce or locked up in unweathered minerals. In some materials, particularly those with a high silica content, potassium may be very deficient, although in others it may be plentiful. Some micronutrients may also be lacking.

In a properly developed soil there is not only a long-term store of nutrients, but also a labile pool related to the ion exchange capacity of the material. In a newly formed material, this labile pool will not exist because there will have been no opportunity for nutrients to move into the labile pool from elsewhere in the material. As a result it will be necessary to charge this pool, as well as supply the immediate needs of the plants. What this will entail depends on the constitution of the soil, but heavy additions of more than one nutrient may be necessary (Figure 5.5).

The material may not possess any means by which this labile pool can be formed, particularly if there is no organic matter and no other particles with charged sites on their surface to give an adequate ion exchange capacity, such as in the pure silica sand left by the china clay industry. In this

Table 5.4. Materials can have very different chemical compositions: chemical characteristics of different wastes and degraded areas

	N	P	K	Ca
colliery spoil	OOO	OOO	O	OOO/o
strip mining	OO	OOO	O	OOO/o
fly ash	OOO	O	O	O
oil shale	OOO	O	O	OO
iron ore mining	OOO	OOO	O	O/
bauxite (strip mining)	OO	OO	O	O
(red mud)	OOO	OOO	O	OO/o
heavy metal wastes	OOO	OOO	O	OOO/
gold wastes	OOO	OO	O	OOO/o
china clay wastes	OOO	OOO	O	O
acid rocks	OOO	OOO	O	OO
calcareous rocks	OOO	OOO	O	
sand and gravel	OO/o	O/o	O/o	O/o
coastal sands	OO	O	O	O
land from sea	O	O	O	O/
urban wastes	O	O	O	O
road sides	OO	OO	O	O/

deficiency			adequate	excess		
severe	moderate	slight		slight	moderate	seve
OOO	OO	O	o	●	●●	●

relative to the establishment of a soil/plant ecosystem appropriate to th material

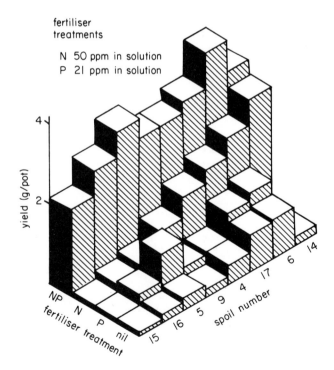

fertiliser treatments

N 50 ppm in solution
P 21 ppm in solution

yield (g/pot)

4

2

NP
N
P
nil
fertiliser treatment

15
16
5
9
4
17
6
14
spoil number

Figure 5.5. The commonest factor limiting growth on derelict land materials is a lack of major plant nutrients: when, as here on different strip-mine spoils the deficient nutrients are provided, growth can be excellent.

	pH	ion exchange capacity	Na	heavy metals	other toxins
●●	OOO/o	OO	/●	O	O
●●	OOO/o	O	/●	O	O
o		●/●●●	O	o/●●	boron
●●	OO/o	O	o/●●	O	O
●	O		O	O	O
	O		O	O	O
		●●●	O	●●●	aluminate
●●	OOO/●	OO	O	●/●●●	O
	OOO	OOO	O	O	O
	O	OOO	O	O	O
	OO	OO	O	O	O
		●	O	O	O
	O/o	O	O	O	O
	O	O	O	O	O
	o/●	O	●●●	O	O
	O	O	O	o/●	various
	O/o	O	o/●●	O	O

case there is no way in which soluble nutrients such as nitrogen and potassium, which are added to the material, can be held. As a result any soluble nutrients which are not immediately taken up by the plants will get leached away into lower layers out of reach of the plants (Figure 5.6). It will be necessary to add nutrients in small amounts at frequent intervals until sufficient organic material has accumulated to act as the pool, which may not be for several years.

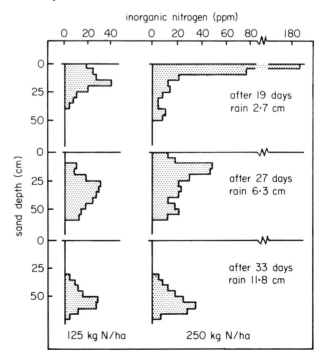

Figure 5.6. Leaching of nutrients, particularly nitrogen, can lead to poor growth: on china clay waste, where nitrate fertiliser was added at time of sowing, plant roots would have had difficulty in growing fast enough to keep up with the downward movement.

67

5.6   ACIDITY

In some derelict land materials there may be very considerable acidity, with the pH between 2 and 4. It is nearly all attributable to the presence of iron sulphide, pyrite, which when it weathers produces sulphuric acid by the action of water and oxygen on the sulphide, which is aided by the activities of microorganisms.

$$2FeS_2 + 2H_2O + 7O_2 \rightarrow 2FeSO_4 + 2H_2SO_4$$
$$4FeSO_4 + 2H_2SO_4 + O_2 \rightarrow 2Fe_2(SO_4)_3 + 2H_2O$$
$$Fe_2(SO_4)_3 + FeS_2 \rightarrow 3FeSO_4 + 2S$$
$$2S + 3O_2 + 2H_2O \rightarrow 2H_2SO_4$$
$$Fe_2(SO_4)_3 + 6H_2O \rightarrow 2Fe(OH)_3 + 3H_2SO_4$$

All these reactions occur concurrently. The essential end products are the sulphuric acid (H_2SO_4) and ferric hydroxide ($Fe(OH)_3$).

Pyrite is most common in sedimentary materials laid down under the anaerobic conditions found in swamps. It is therefore very common in coal deposits particularly in the soil accumulated with the plants making up the coal, which, when the coal is mined, is thrown out as spoil. But it is also common in some non-ferrous metalliferous deposits, especially those in which the non-ferrous metal is itself present as sulphide ore.

The pyrite problem is not easy to overcome. Unless it has all been oxidised there is a store of acid-generating material, so that even if the acidity is corrected by the use of lime, it may well return later (Figure 5.7). A corollary of this is that newly mined materials may not be acid to begin with, but only develop acidity as time goes on.

The sulphuric acid itself will get leached by rain, so that in the end the material may lose its acidity. But in doing so the acid water draining from the mine waste with a value of less than pH 2 can cause serious effects in neighbouring streams and lakes, which are difficult to remedy.

Figure 5.7. Acidity can be a serious problem on some waste materials containing pyrite: in this colliery spoil high levels of ground limestone were applied yet acidity returned because of oxidation of further pyrite.

Chapter 5: Derelict Land Problems

Some materials may be excessively alkaline with a pH above 10 due to the presence of hydroxides of calcium, magnesium, sodium and potassium. These are produced by various chemical processes and by the lime industry. Sodium and potassium hydroxide are soluble and will leach away. But calcium and magnesium hydroxides will not. However, the more common calcium hydroxide gradually absorbs carbon dioxide from the air to form calcium carbonate and so becomes neutralised, at least on the particle surfaces.

5.7   TOXIC MATERIALS

A great deal of derelict land is associated with mining for metals. Some of these, notably copper, zinc, lead and nickel, are extremely toxic to plants. They may kill the plant completely, but since their main effect is on root growth they may also make the plant susceptible to damage by drought.

The object of mining operations is to remove all the valuable metal ore from the mined materials. Modern separation techniques have vastly improved the completeness of extraction, but even so about 0·2 per cent of the metal can be left behind, quite sufficient to be toxic. A large proportion may be locked up in mineral particles but sufficient can be available to cause toxicity. In older materials 1 per cent was often left behind: this is very toxic and can totally prevent colonisation by plants (Figure 5.8). There may also be toxic levels of accessory metals which were never extracted.

Other materials may have toxic levels of other elements. Pulverised fuel ash contains high levels of boron and soluble salts: mine tailings may contain high levels of various toxic salts from the water in which the ore separation was carried out.

Figure 5.8. Heavy metal toxicity can prevent plants establishing on mine waste: the lead and zinc in these tailings at Trelogan, Clwyd, have prevented any growth since the mine stopped working 40 years ago.

5.8   SALINITY

Some waste materials particularly those produced by mining for heavy metals, but also some colliery spoils, contain sulphides such as pyrite and also carbonates particularly of calcium and magnesium. When the pyrite oxidises to give sulphuric acid it is neutralised by the carbonates to give calcium and magnesium sulphates. Neither of these are at all toxic at normal concentrations. But they are soluble and in arid climates may accumulate and cause salinity in the surface layers of the waste as the soil moisture evaporates. In some materials such as colliery spoils there may be sodium chloride in the ground water which behaves in the same way.

It is perfectly possible to find salt concentrations in some mine wastes of 2 per cent, as high as in sea water, concentrations which are lethal to plants. There may even be an accumulation of crystalline salts on the surface (see Chapter 8). The critical level for normal plants is when the conductivity of the soil solution reaches 8 mmhos/cm (4 mmhos in the saturation extract). In humid climates the problem does not arise so frequently because the salts are leached away as they are formed.

5.9   APPROPRIATE SPECIES

There is one other reason why an area of derelict land may be bare of vegetation—the plant species that could grow on it are not present in the vicinity and so are not available to colonise it. Plants have a wide variety of means of dispersal, and we perhaps imagine that any species can get anywhere in the course of a year or two. There are species such as dandelions (*Taraxacum officinale*), and sowthistles (*Sonchus asper*) which have spectacular capacities for dispersal: but these are not adapted to grow on poor soils—they are at home on fertile ground. There are species which are adapted to grow on the different extreme soils of derelict land, such as wavy hair grass (*Deschampsia flexuosa*) on acid soils, and gorse (*Ulex europaeus*) on dry sands: but these have limited powers of dispersal.

So although nearly all derelict land sites become colonised in the end by plants of one sort or another, the processes may take time, and on newly deposited materials the absence of plants need not be an indication that the material is completely inhospitable.

5.10   AFTERCARE

Rome was not built in a day; neither can a self-sustaining soil/plant ecosystem be rebuilt in a single act. The process of restoring the chemical, physical and biological functions of a soil takes time. If a soil is being made from raw waste the restoration will obviously take a very long time. But even if a soil is removed from an area and replaced almost immediately it will take time to recover. The vegetation which will have been completely destroyed will take several years to be properly restored, unless the land is being used for annual crops.

Aftercare will therefore be a problem in all land restoration, and failure to realise this has been the cause of failure of very many reclamation schemes. What actually is at fault and what will require greatest attention will depend on the material being reclaimed. Sometimes structure will be imperfect. It can be restored by cultivation and the growth of plants. But it will take several years for the plants to exert their maximum effect in breaking up soil aggregations by root growth and contributing sufficient organic matter to lighten the material. Until this has occurred the material will need to be treated with care or it could rapidly be damaged.

A considerable input of nutrients is always necessary. This cannot be done in one operation without providing more than the plants can take up, so that a great deal will leach away and be wasted. The need is a moderate input continued for a number of years. Yet this is often forgotten, and after the initial application no more is provided. This can lead to serious regression of vegetation which was looking very promising. If aftercare is not given, all the money and effort expended on the reclamation can be wasted. It will be necessary to find out what aftercare is needed, but a simple fertiliser experiment will usually show this very clearly (Figure 5.9).

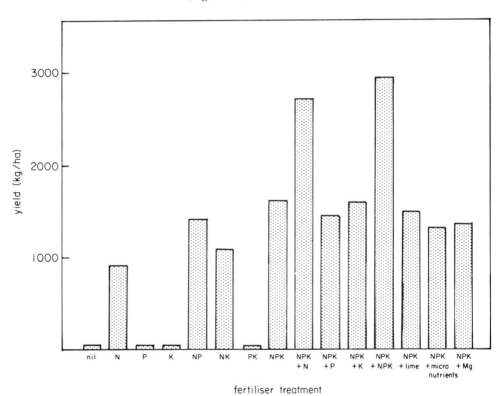

Figure 5.9. In reclamation, aftercare is essential: this grass sward on china clay waste was completely moribund but application of different fertiliser shows that if nitrogen is added growth is restored.

Aftercare is therefore as real a problem as all the other problems to be faced. Like the other problems it can easily be overcome if the right steps are taken. But it must be planned and budgeted for properly in the first place.

FURTHER READING

Brown L.J. (ed.) 1971. *Landscape Reclamation*. London: IPC Science and Technology Press.

Aftercare

Chadwick M.J. & Goodman G.T (eds.) 1975. *The Ecology of Resource Degradation and Renewal*. Oxford: Blackwell.

Gemmell R.P. 1977. *Colonisation of Industrial Wasteland*. London: Arnold.

Goodman G.T. & Bray S.A. 1975. *Ecological Aspects of the Reclamation of Derelict Land*. Norwich: Geo. Abstracts.

Goodman G.T., Edwards R.W. & Lambert J.M. (eds.) 1965. *Ecology and the Industrial Society*. Oxford: Blackwell.

Hackett B. (ed.) 1978. *Landscape Reclamation Practice*. London: IPC Science and Technology Press.

Hutnik R.J. & Davis G. (eds.) 1973. *Ecology and Reclamation of Devastated land* (2 vols.) New York: Gordon and Breach.

Jones M.T. (ed.) 1974. *Minerals and the Environment*. London: Institution of Mining and Metallurgy.

Schaller F.W. & Sutton P. (ed.) 1978. *Reclamation of Drastically Disturbed Lands*. Madison: American Society for Agronomy.

Whyte R.O. & Sisam J.W.B. 1949. *The Establishment of Vegetation on Industrial Waste Land*. Aberystwyth: Commonwealth Bureau of Pastures and Field Crops.

'The improvement of soils when pursued upon scientific principles is simple to understand and when practicable, easy to accomplish: but when extraneous, and accidental bodies are conceived to form a part of the soil, there is not only much difficulty created but also much uncertainty.'

WILLIAM GRISENTHWAITE

A New Theory of Agriculture. 1819.

6   Derelict Land Solutions

Because derelict land includes such a wide variety of materials the methods of reclamation have to be tailored to the specific problems of each material. However, there are a number of principles which are relevant to all derelict land, which we should consider.

6.1   AIMS

The aim of reclamation must be to restore the original qualities of the environment. We begin with a degraded or ruined ecosystem in which normal biological processes are at a standstill. These processes must be restored so that a normally functioning ecosystem of soil and plants is achieved, in which the natural processes of nutrient release, plant growth and nutrient cycling go on at a normal rate.

The natural development of such an ecosystem takes a long time even on natural materials. On glacial moraines in Alaska, although vegetation begins to colonise the bare material within five years (Figure 6.1), a proper vegetation cover and soil do not develop for 40 years and some attributes of the soil (e.g., bulk density which is a measure of soil structure and organic matter) are not properly developed for more than 100 years (Figure 6.2). This development is only achieved in situations where the alder, *Alnus crispa*, is present, which is able to fix atmospheric nitrogen and accumulate it in the soil/plant ecosystem at about 20 kg N/ha/yr. However, some other plants in the same situation (such as mountain avens *Dryas drummondi*) also fix nitrogen, but at a lower rate.

This illustrates that the key to improvement is upgrading all the activities of the soil component of the ecosystem by

Figure 6.1. Invasion by alders, which are nitrogen-fixing, is an important step in the development of a well-developed soil/plant ecosystem on glacial moraines: a) alders just invading 62 years after glacial recession; b) the exact view 26 years later, at Glacier Bay, Alaska.

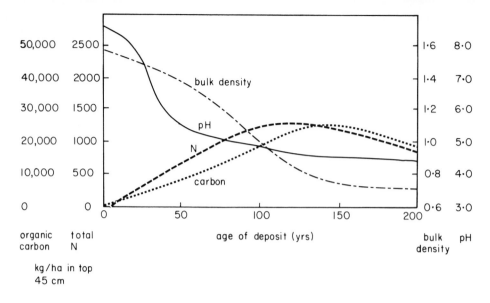

| organic carbon | total N | | | bulk density | pH |

kg/ha in top
45 cm

Figure 6.2. As a glacial moraine becomes colonised by alders and other plants, major changes take place in the material: in particular nitrogen increases to about 1000 kg/ha and bulk density decreases.

the input of those materials which are in short supply. These materials would occur as a result of the natural processes of weathering and accumulation. But if the soil ecosystem is to be charged up quickly, they must be added. This can be done in two ways: either directly, with nutrients increased by use of fertilisers, or indirectly, with organic matter build-up by the growth of plants.

When the soil ecosystem is properly charged, it has the nutrients and the physical properties which permit healthy plant growth and development. The plants are able to grow vigorously and the cycling of materials can begin: a self-sustaining ecosystem results.

The input of organic matter with satisfactory nutrient content and carbon/nitrogen ratio encourages the growth of microorganisms such as fungi and bacteria, which causes the organic matter to decompose. Because the spores of microorganisms are extremely widely distributed, they enter the system immediately. At the same time the development of populations of micro-invertebrates such as millipedes (*Diplopoda*), woodlice (*Isopoda*), as well as the smaller spring-tails (*Collembola*) and mites (*Acarina*) will be encouraged. All these break up and consume organic matter, encouraging its rapid decay. These animals are an important and often forgotten component in the developing ecosystem (Figure 6.3), more important than earthworms which are very slow at invading derelict land materials.

This ecosystem then accumulates further nutrients in surface layers by bringing them up from lower soil horizons and by collecting dust from the air. As a result the surface layers of the soil acquire appreciably higher concentrations of available nutrients than the subsoil (Figure 6.4). Nitrogen accumulates by the activities of nitrogen-

Chapter 6: Derelict Land Solutions

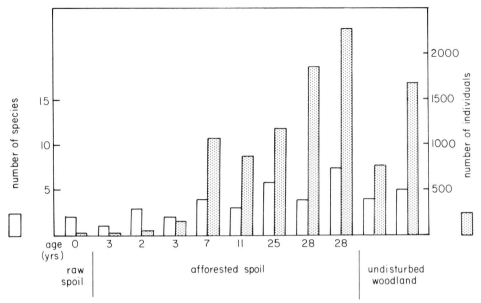

Figure 6.3. In afforested colliery spoil there is considerable increase in wood lice so that after 28 years there are as many as in normal soils: wood lice are important for the breakdown of organic matter.

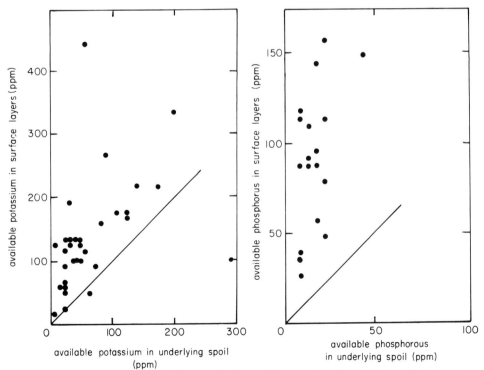

Figure 6.4. The enrichment of nutrients in the surface layers of colliery spoil: the amounts in surface layers in different afforested heaps in the Ruhr is higher than the amounts in the underlying spoil.

fixing microorganisms. The soil structure improves because of the input of organic matter and the activities of the soil microorganisms.

But all this takes time. Natural development of a soil ecosystem on derelict land materials, for instance on ironstone, certainly does not occur quickly (Section 8.5). If artificial restoration is undertaken soil ecosystems cannot be restored in one operation unless techniques (using top soil) are employed. Usually the aim must be to upgrade the ecosystem progressively over several years.

6.2   TOP SOIL CONSERVATION

The most obvious solution to the problem of derelict land is prevention rather than cure. If an area is to be disturbed by surface mining or tipping, the fertile surface layers of soil, the top soil (30 cm) and sub soil (60 cm) have to be removed separately and stored, and replaced later where disturbance has finished, so that the original soil is restored immediately.

This is particularly easy to do in a progressive, strip-mining operation where the extraction operation moves quickly over the area taking a relatively thin layer of material, such as coal, bauxite or sand, lying under overburden. To expose the initial working face the top soil, sub soil and overburden must be dumped. Thereafter the overburden can be removed and replaced where extraction has finished, followed by subsoil and finally top soil, in one operation, with consequent savings in handling, in a continuous, progressive operation (Figure 6.5).

Figure 6.5. A well-planned strip-mining operation in which the overburden and top soil are continuously replaced so that only a small area is withdrawn from agricultural use: a cement works at Dunbar in Scotland.

Chapter 6: Derelict Land Solutions

The top soil loses very little and providing care is taken to avoid consolidation, agricultural crops and other vegetation can immediately be re-established without difficulty. In areas of natural vegetation such as in the mineral sand extraction regions in Australia (Chapter 12), the seed and vegetative fragments carried over in the top soil may enable the native species to re-establish without any further assistance. In this operation an added refinement is that the extraction is continued back to the starting point so that the original heaps are used to fill the final hole.

In a lot of sites the depth of working may be considerable and the area small, so progressive replacement is not possible and the top soil has to be stripped at the outset, stored and then replaced later. Top soil stored in a large heap tends to lose its structure and some of its fertility. Nevertheless if it is removed and replaced carefully, during dry conditions without being mixed with other materials, the texture is quickly restored. The British National Coal Board have so refined their techniques that it is virtually impossible to detect the sites where open-cast mining has taken place three years after the operations have finished (Figure 9.9, pages 166–7). The only clues are the lack of trees and the new fences.

In nearly all modern progressive operations top soil replacement will soon be standard practice and should be required by authorities permitting mining developments. However, in modern large-scale strip-mining it may be difficult and expensive to transfer the topsoil across the working face to the replaced overburden. It is possible that the overburden with a little improvement can form a better soil than the previous top soil. This has been shown to be true in regions as far apart as the Bowen Basin coalfield in Australia, and in the chalk quarries of N. Kent in England. In the Bowen Basin the overburden shales weather rapidly to give a productive soil; in N. Kent the overburden is silty loams of the Thanet Beds, capable of forming land of grade 1 agricultural quality, much better than the superficial clay with flints.

6.3   TOP SOIL APPLICATION

It may be possible to obtain good soil from a site which is being developed for other purposes and spread it over an area of derelict land from which the top soil has been lost. This provides in one operation a fully developed soil, of good structure and texture containing an adequate store of nutrients. The organic matter and nutrients constitute a buffer against any extremes of toxicity or other adverse factors which may be present in the derelict land material, and the good structure ensures satisfactory water retention even if the waste material underneath has a poor water-retaining capacity.

As a result, establishment and growth of plants when top soil is used as a covering material, are excellent. Planting can be carried out over a wider period of the year than with raw waste materials. Growth after the period of establishment is also good since the soil has a store of nutrients which are released only slowly. Aftercare, in the form of fertiliser additions, may not be necessary. There is usually no need to know what is wrong with the material making up the derelict land since the top soil provides a totally new environment in which the plants can grow.

As a result, top soil is an obvious and widely recommended solution. It is one that appeals to many people, especially those who believe erroneously that top soil has a unique quality which cannot be reproduced.

If this is so, why is it not the universal solution? The simple answer is cost and availability. To be effective the layer of top soil must be at least 10 cm thick. This will be sufficient only to provide a good seed bed and a moderate store of nutrients for subsequent growth. Plants will have to be able to root into the underlying material and obtain much of their water and nutrients from it. To be totally self-sufficient a grass sward will need at least 25 cm. Trees will need far more than this.

A layer of 10 cm over one hectare is 1000 cubic metres, over an acre it is over 500 cubic yards. Loading, hauling and spreading such quantities, even with modern machinery, at present cost considerably more than £1000 per ha (£500/acre) and will cost much more when the soil has to be carried more than one or two kilometres. Where such costs cannot be met out of immediate income in an active industry, and the land is therefore truly derelict, such costs may be prohibitive. Even if money is provided from central government sources, people will ask whether it is appropriate to spend money in this fashion when it might be put to other aspects of the restoration such as the establishment of playgrounds, or even building houses or schools.

There are many situations, such as areas where there is a large amount of derelict land, where even if the money is available the top soil is not. In the Lancashire coal field the use of top soil would mean that other areas would have to be made derelict in order to acquire the top soil. The same is true in remote country districts and national parks where there is no constructional work which would provide top soil. However, where a large heap of waste is being reduced in height and spread over a larger area than it originally occupied it is often practicable to remove the top soil from the areas where the heap will be and then spread it back thinly over the whole heap (Figure 6.6).

The best part of a soil profile is the top soil (see Section 3.6). Since top soil is usually in short supply there will be a temptation to scrape up and include as top soil the deeper B horizon layers down to 30 cm. The result is that the top soil

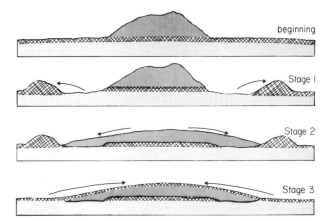

Figure 6.6. Finding top soil: stages in spreading out an old waste heap and covering it with adjacent material.

is adulterated with subsoil material, which may be of poor quality, and so spoilt. If the subsoil has a good texture it may at least not affect the physical qualities of the top soil. But the usual result is that top soils commonly available can be of dubious quality with regard to both nutrients and texture (Figure 6.7), and may be little better than the materials they are being used to cover.

Although top soil usually allows the nature of the underlying material to be disregarded, there will always be a limit to the depth of the soil that can be applied. The underlying material will be part of the rooting medium of the plants and its character therefore cannot be totally disregarded. If it is toxic or impermeable the plant roots will be restricted to the layer of top soil. As a result the plants will be very susceptible to drought and will soon exhaust the nutrients in the top soil and trees will be unstable. Although growth may be splendid for the first year there may be considerable deterioration later.

Figure 6.7. Top soil provided by contractors is variable in quality: the growth of grass on different samples of top soil being used for reclamation in N. England compared with growth on three good soils and two poor materials.

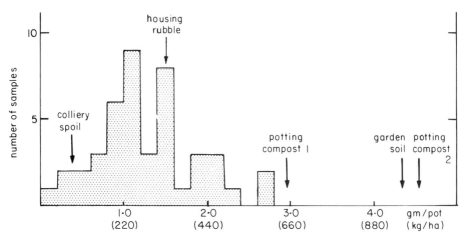

Top Soil Application

Impermeability of the underlying material can be overcome by ripping the material beforehand, though it will often not be possible to do anything about toxicity. Some materials such as chemical wastes are not only toxic in themselves but can release soluble substances which will poison the soil on top of them (Chapter 11). In these circumstances a deeper layer of soil will be necessary as a covering. It may be valuable to cover the material first with a deep layer of subsoil, which is easier to obtain (Figure 6.8).

Figure 6.8. Chemical waste successfully revegetated by using 50 cm of subsoil and 10 cm of top soil as a covering: most of this area at Widnes, Cheshire, is now a golf-course.

Top soil has to be spread by heavy machinery and as a result becomes consolidated. If it is good quality, containing a large amount of organic matter it will suffer less than if it is poor quality, but some form of heavy cultivation will be necessary.

In general, top soil is therefore not quite the universal remedy it first seems to be. It is most valuable in small sites where high-quality rapid solutions are required: it is also valuable where it is necessary to restore as faithfully as possible the original soil and vegetation, as has already been discussed. It is also valuable where the waste materials are inhospitable to plant growth. But it will always be very expensive if bought in specially.

6.4 OTHER MATERIALS

The idea of using one waste product to deal with the problems of another is appealing. There are many materials which are waste products from our society which are good media for plant growth, besides top soil. Although they have different origins they are similar in being non-toxic and water- and nutrient-retaining, as well as usually containing appreciable quantities of nutrients. Their properties are summarised in Table 6.1.

Chapter 6: Derelict Land Solutions

Sewage sludge is produced in large quantities by most sewage works as a fairly dry crumbly material, after a thorough fermentation and digestion of sewage solids. It is organic and contains reasonable levels of plant nutrients. It can also contain metals such as zinc and lead from industry. It is uncommon for these metals to be at levels high enough to cause toxicity, although repeated use of sewage sludge for many years can cause accumulation of metals to toxic levels. This would not occur in reclamation since the material would only be used once, on establishment. The structure and nutrient content of sewage sludge make it ideal as a covering material. The organic matter provides a slow release of nutrients. It also acts as a buffer against toxic metals in subsoil below, since most metals are complexed and rendered innocuous by organic material. Problems may arise sometimes over the release of nitrogen and other nutrients if the carbon/nitrogen ratio is too high and the bacteria using the carbon lock up these nutrients, but this can be overcome by addition of complete fertiliser.

Mushroom compost is a by-product available in some areas. It is a well-decayed mixture of cow and pig manure and straw. It can be extremely valuable; it contains a higher nutrient content than sewage sludge, especially of nitrogen, and has an even better water-retaining quality.

Peat is not usually a waste product but is dug purposely for horticultural and other use. However it can sometimes be available cheaply where deposits have had to be removed to clear ground for road-building etc. It varies in quality depending on the conditions under which it was formed. But it is usually a valuable ameliorant providing not only

Table 6.1. Many waste products can be used in reclamation work: the typical nutrient contents of organic and other materials that can be valuable

| material | composition (%) | | | | special problems |
	N	P	K	organic matter	
farmyard manure	0·6	0·1	0·5	24	can be toxic direct on plants
pig slurry	0·2	0·1	0·2	3	high water content
poultry manure (broiler)	2·3	0·9	1·6	68	high levels of ammonia
(battery)	1·5	0·5	0·6	34	high levels of ammonia
sewage sludge (air dried)	2·0	0·3	0·2	45	possible toxic metals and can have high water content
peat (partly dried)	0·1	0·005	0·002	50	variable, especially calcium content
mushroom compost (dried)	2·8	0·2	0·8	95	none except high lime content
domestic refuse (municipal)	0·5	0·2	0·3	65	miscellaneous objects
straw	0·5	0·1	0·8	95	adverse C/N ratio
building rubble	0·05	1·8	2·0	0·5	brick and pieces of masonry
colliery spoil	0·03	0·04	0·4	0	possible high levels of pyrite causing acidity
pulverised fuel ash	0	0·05	2·2	0	high boron

Other Materials

nutrients but also a better water-holding capacity than most other materials.

Farmyard manure and pig slurry are produced by modern intensive farming systems in such large amounts that they cannot always be used on farmland. They are usually very fresh, contain high levels of ammonium and other organic compounds which are toxic to plant growth, and may be liquid. They cannot be used as a covering material in which plants grow direct, but must be incorporated into the surface layers of the soil in small amounts to act as a slow release source of nutrients. Used in this manner they do not provide as much organic matter as high bulk materials, but their contribution to soil structure is not negligible.

Poultry manure is similar. It is always dry and is therefore easy to handle and spread. But because it is produced by birds, it contains large quantities of uric acid and ammonium compounds and is very toxic until these compounds are broken down. It must be used like farmyard manure as a source of nutrients rather than for its bulk. But it has the advantage of being particularly rich in the crucial element, nitrogen, twice as rich as farmyard manure. It was used very successfully to restore the colliery shale areas left after the Aberfan disaster in South Wales.

Domestic refuse is now produced in vast quantities and makes its own serious disposal problem. It obviously contains a large proportion of inert awkwardly shaped material such as plastic bottles and pieces of iron. But it is mainly a mixture of soil, cinders, organic matter and coarser materials such as building waste. It therefore has high bulk, a satisfactory texture and adequate nutrients. So unless toxic materials have been included it is a satisfactory material for plant growth. The weeds on any town rubbish dump are good evidence of this. It can be used as a deep inert cover, but the awkward rubbish within it may make it produce more trouble than it solves. This can be overcome if the topmost layers are of screened and pulverised material. In some countries wood wastes are available. These have too low a nutrient content and high C/N ratio to be used by themselves, but can be valuable physical ameliorants.

Pulverised fuel ash produced by electricity power stations which burn coal has its own reclamation problems, because of its temporary boron and other toxicities and lack of plant nutrients (Chapter 11). But these can be overcome and it does have its own value as a uniform fine-textured material with a high pH and so some neutralising capacity, which may be available in some areas in large quantities at low cost. It is very deficient in nitrogen and even if this is added it may still be difficult to get a good plant growth. But as a covering to use over difficult toxic materials such as chemical wastes or over extremely coarse rocky materials or as land fill it can be very valuable.

Subsoil and other similar low-grade materials such as *build-*

　　　　　　　Chapter 6: Derelict Land Solutions

ing rubble are hardly materials which would normally be considered as useful materials since they present their own reclamation problems (Chapter 13). But like pulverised fuel ash they can be very valuable where there is a particularly intractable toxic area of derelict land which needs some sort of inert covering.

Colliery shales and other similar mine wastes may in some situations be valuable covering materials, especially those which do not contain pyrite and therefore can readily be made to carry vegetation with minimal lime and fertiliser treatments (Chapter 8).

Chemical wastes are rather specialised materials, but they can be extremely valuable, even although they can present reclamation problems when in bulk. The reclamation of highly alkaline toxic sites containing chromate has been made possible by the addition of ferrous sulphate which is a waste from titanium processing. The ferrous sulphate reduces the toxic chromate in the waste and renders it unavailable to plants (Chapter 11). Acid colliery shales can be ameliorated with lime wastes produced by the alkali industry. There is an infinite variety of chemical wastes, ranging from organic materials high in nitrogen and other nutrients to individual inorganic compounds with very specific properties, which may be very valuable.

We are beginning to realise that the profligate days when all waste materials could be thrown away are over. But it is not always easy to find the best uses for them. The restoration of land is one major outlet, not because it is somewhere that the wastes can be dumped, but because they can be of considerable direct value to the restoration process. The wise disposal of waste materials requires further consideration by society.

6.5   HYDRAULIC SEEDING

One of the major problems of derelict land is in the initial establishment: considerable effort has been made to find methods which are an improvement on traditional practice. Hydraulic seeding, or hydromulching is a technique in which seed and nutrients are sprayed over the ground in the form of a slurry. Extravagant claims have been made for it. It has even been held to be a substitute for top soil, but it is only a seeding technique.

The normal agricultural technique for sowing seed and spreading fertiliser is by means of a drill which trickles the seed and fertiliser into shallow furrows in the soil, or by means of a spinner which scatters them from a spinning disc. They must usually be covered and consolidated subsequently by harrowing or rolling. The advantage of agricultural techniques is that they are cheap and well-developed. The disadvantages are that the seed can only be spread where a tractor can go, and that the soil must have a texture fine enough to allow the passage of a drill or a harrow to bury the seeds. Derelict land materials may not always permit this.

The hydraulic technique is intended to provide the answer to these two problems. The seed is suspended in an aqueous mixture. This can then be sprayed over distances of up to sixty metres from a machine that does not have to pass over the ground (Figure 6.9). When the seed hits the ground it is carried into crevices by the liquid. Because it is difficult to keep a mixture of this sort properly mixed, even in a tank which is kept agitated, alginates, starch derivatives, latex or oil-based emulsions are added to give the mixture a higher viscosity. These have a second important advantage in causing the seeds to adhere better to the ground when they land: the latex and oil-based emulsions have the greater stabilising effect forming a definite crust which is nevertheless porous: the alginate does not do this so much but is supposed to give the seed a water-conducting pathway to the soil through the gelatinous alginate.

Seeds falling on the surface of the ground even if they tumble into crevices are still at the mercy of drying winds and sun. In an attempt to get over this problem, some light, high-bulk particulate material is usually added to the mixture which will lie on the surface and provide minute shady moist sites where the seed can germinate and the seedlings

Figure 6.9. Hydroseeding in progress: seed and fertiliser is sprayed onto the ground in a mulch of peat or woodfibre with water.

Chapter 6: Derelict Land Solutions

establish easily. The materials used can be peat, chopped straw, wood pulp or even shredded plastic foam or glass wool. The soft fibrous materials are usually the most effective. With the help of wood pulp or the latex or oil-based emulsions the coarse materials such as chopped straw can be prevented from blowing or washing away. Whether these materials have the effect intended is, however, not very clear with the amounts commonly used (page 90).

Adequate nutrients and lime must be provided or else the seeds may germinate well but fail to establish due to lack of nutrients or occurrence of acidity. The nutrients can be provided either by fertiliser or by a liquid manure such as pig slurry. But these materials are toxic in high concentrations and so only small amounts can be added to the mixture containing the seed—not more than 200 kg/ha of a compound fertiliser, containing about 30 kg/ha of nitrogen, phosphorus and potassium. Usually more than this is necessary; so the fertiliser must be spread separately either in suspension or mechanically. 10 000 kg/ha of lime may be required on acid soils: about half of this is the limit of what can be put in the slurry. So this must be spread separately too.

An example specification of the technique is given in Table 6.2. It appears simple and logical, but it has a number of problems. Perhaps the greatest is the cost. The machinery and materials are all more complex than in traditional methods, so that the normal cost is about £400/ha instead of about a sixth of this.

The second problem is that it does not guarantee seedling establishment. Despite many components of the mulch the seeds are still more vulnerable to variations in climate than if they were buried by traditional methods. Several stabilisers have been found to be toxic to germinating seedlings. With hydraulic seeding the contractor has to be prepared to come back again: this is one reason why the cost is so high.

Table 6.2. Hydroseeding is a useful technique in some situations: an example specification for the establishment of grass/legume cover in a temperate climate

material	application rate
Grass seed mixture appropriate for situation[1]	70 kg/ha
Wild white clover or other legumes inoculated, and pregerminated if necessary[2]	10 kg/ha
Mulch: wood fibre, chopped straw or glass wool	1–2 t/ha
Stabiliser: alginate, PVA or latex[3]	depends on stabiliser
Fertiliser: complete 15:15:15[4]	200 kg/ha—followed by
or	300 kg/ha after 8 weeks
dry organic manure	500 kg/ha
Lime[5]	0–5000 kg/ha

Notes
1 Include nurse crop in exposed situations.
2 Pregerminated clover should not be included in same mix as fertiliser.
3 Include only if likelihood of very severe erosion: latex least satisfactory: wood fibre mulch is good stabiliser by itself.
4 Slow release N fertiliser valuable if legume not included.
5 Include if soil pH requires it: may have to spread separately.

Hydraulic Seeding

The third problem is the need for adequate fertiliser and lime on acid soils. It was originally thought that the barrier to seedling establishment was at germination and not in subsequent growth. While this may be true in arid climates, the reverse is true in moist temperate ones. For this reason many hydraulically seeded areas have started well only to fail later. From bitter experience it has now been realised that it is always necessary to come once, twice or often more times in the same or subsequent seasons to provide further nitrogenous fertiliser dressings. This can be true also of normal seeded areas as well. Clover or other legumes provide the answer. If they are included in the seed mixture, extra nitrogenous fertiliser dressings will not be necessary although some lime and phosphorus may be if the material was originally very deficient, for example on china clay waste (Chapter 9).

This raises problems, because the success or failure of a hydroseeding project may well depend on getting a good legume establishment, and more often than not the legumes fail to establish although they were included in the original mixture. This is partly because legumes are rather slow to germinate and therefore remain vulnerable for longer. It may be worthwhile soaking the seed for a few days before seeding until the radicle is about to emerge. But it is also because germinating legume seedlings are very sensitive to the sort of concentrations of solutes particularly involving nitrogen and phosphorus which are produced by normal amounts of fertilisers lying on the soil surface (Figure 6.10). If fertilisers are left out of the original mix, legume germination is excellent. The mineral fertiliser should then be applied about 3–6 weeks after the initial hydroseeding.

Figure 6.10. The deleterious effect of fertilisers on seedling establishment in hydroseeding: legume germination is almost completely inhibited.

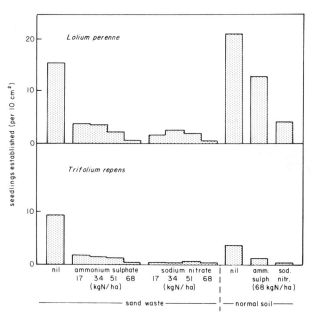

Chapter 6: Derelict Land Solutions

On balance then, hydraulic seeding is by no means a panacea: it is expensive and the technique is not yet fully reliable for all situations unless applied with great care. But it does have value on steep inaccessible slopes or where there is an extreme erosion problem requiring the use of a soil-binding material.

6.6 DIRECT IMPROVEMENT

The methods of reclamation suggested so far are omnibus techniques in which the limiting factors are overcome by something which is intended to eliminate all problems at once. They are appealing since, except for hydraulic seeding, they can be used on a wide variety of sites and materials without much attention as to what is wrong. But they have a common disadvantage of high cost, particularly when compared with agricultural seeding costs.

Is there any alternative? The answer must lie in using agricultural techniques themselves since these have been developed over a long period of time to be the cheapest and most effective methods. It is obvious that normal agricultural techniques cannot be applied directly to derelict land materials because of the particular and individual problems of the materials. But it should be equally obvious that if these problems could be dealt with directly and individually, as they present themselves during a normal agricultural type of approach, the chances are that the whole process of derelict land reclamation could be achieved effectively and cheaply.

This is indeed the essence of the modern approach to the reclamation of derelict land. Over the last few decades

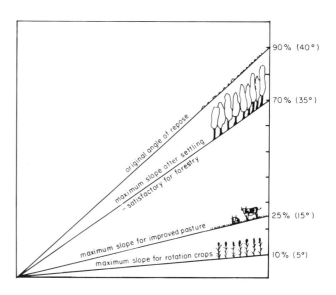

Figure 6.11. Slope not only restricts severely the restoration process but also the ultimate land-use: the diagram shows the maximum slopes at which particular land-uses are possible, but in each case a lesser slope is preferable.

Direct Improvement

practically minded agriculturalists and scientists, faced with the job of getting the reclamation done as cheaply and effectively as possible, have discovered that there are simple ways round almost any problem that derelict land can present.

Landform such as the hill and dale land left by strip-mining can seriously hinder reclamation and limit after-use, even if a land-use appropriate for steep slopes, such as forests, is adopted, there will be serious problems subsequently for thinning and extraction. Modern equipment, however, can soon deal with the earth-moving required. If properly planned and related to the ultimate land-use (Figure 6.11) the amount of earth-moving can be kept to a minimum.

Structure can be very poor, usually in the direction of excessive consolidation. In these cases cultivations can usually restore an open soil structure. This restoration can be long enough for plants to become established, after which time they will maintain the structure themselves by their root growth and contribution of organic matter. The most usual operation is ripping, where the surface is broken up to a depth of 50 cm by heavy hook-shaped tines mounted on a crawler tractor (Figure 6.12). In very difficult situations, organic matter can be incorporated. Structural problems will be reduced at the outset if earth-moving and levelling

Figure 6.12. A crawler tractor being used to rip the surface of overburden being replaced after strip-mining for coal in England: cultivations to a depth of 50 cm alleviate compaction.

Chapter 6: Derelict Land Solutions

are carried out by crawler tractors fitted with straked tracks: smooth-tracked or rubber-tyred machines cause extreme surface consolidation. If the material is too coarse with excessively large spaces between rock fragments the material can be blinded, treated with finer materials which run down the cracks and provide a rooting zone. For trees, fine material can be introduced into individual pockets.

Stability can be a problem on steep slopes, particularly where the material does not allow rain to infiltrate easily. But with the earth-moving that has to accompany most reclamation, slopes can be left at not more than 1 in 20. This will prevent serious erosion particularly if ripping has been carried out to allow rain water to penetrate rather than run off the surface. Mulches of a fibrous material such as chopped straw, shredded bark or wood pulp are widely used to protect the surface temporarily where there are heavy rain storms. Once a sward is established, erosion is no longer a problem. Sandy soils are rather special since they can blow away, but if seeding is done at a time when there will be rapid germination and growth, such as April or May, in northern temperate regions, the grass will have established itself before serious erosion has occurred. In extreme situations, such as coastal sands, special precautions may have to be taken, by the laying of brushwood or the erection of temporary fences (Figure 6.13). But these are only necessary for a short period if steps have been taken to ensure the rapid and continued growth of the sward. An alternative is a latex or plastic soil stabiliser sprayed on after seeding. There are a great variety of stabilisers and

Figure 6.13. Plastic fencing and brushwood being used to stabilise areas after mineral sand extraction: lines of Spinifex sown for six months in North Stradbrooke Island, Queensland will have covered the area within a year.

Direct Improvement

mulches: the most commonly used are listed in Table 6.3. A biological method of ensuring stability is to include in the seed mixture a small proportion of a rapidly growing stemmy plant such as sorghum (*Sorghum vulgare*) to act as a nurse crop: this will not only offer protection while it is growing, but for one or two seasons afterwards.

Water can be present in excess or deficiency. If it is present in excess, the area should be drained. Drainage is one of the prime requisites for most types of derelict land. In many cases the whole drainage system may have to be replanned and rebuilt to take account of changed topography. On heavy soils, if there is absence of soil structure normal percolation will not occur. The installation of permanent drains will not be possible until the ground has stabilised. Usually it will be simplest to arrange that drainage is by controlled surface run-off. Level sites should be left slightly convex like a bowling green with large open drains not more than 100 m apart (Figure 6.14). Shortage of water is usually not a problem in moist temperate climates,

Table 6.3. Surface stabilisation can be important: mulches and stabilisers suitable for derelict land reclamation

material	rate (tonnes/ha)[1]	persistence	stabilisation	soil water retention	nutrient	to
mulches						
excelsior	4	OO	OO	OO	o	
wood shavings	4	OO	O	O	o	
wood chips	10	OO	O	OO	o	
bark shredded	4	OOO	O	OO	o	
peat moss	2	O	O	O	o	
jute netting	–	OO	OOO	O	o	
corncobs	10	OOO	O	O	o	
hay	3	O	O	O	O	
straw	3	OO	O	O	o	
fibreglass	1	OOO	OO	O	o	
stabiliser/ mulches						
wood cellulose fibre (as slurry)	1–2	OO	OOO	O	o	
sewage sludge (as slurry)	2–4	O	OO	O	O	
stabilisers						
asphalt (as 1:1 emulsion)	0·75	O	OO	O	o	
latex (as appropriate emulsion)	0·2	O	OO	o	o	C
alginate or other colloidal carbohydrate (as emulsion)	0·2	OO	OO	o	o	
polyvinyl acetate (as 1:5 emulsion)	1	OO	OO	o	o	C
styrene butiadene (as 1:20 emulsion)	0·5	OO	OO	o	o	C

OOO high   O low   o nil

[1] rates can be varied depending on circumstance—will affect soil w capture and retention and seedling establishment

Chapter 6: Derelict Land Solutions

Figure 6.14. Drainage is critical in reclaimed land: open drains and a convex land surface in an area of colliery spoil newly reclaimed for agriculture in the Lancashire coalfield.

but it may be in drier climates. But there is usually sufficient water below the surface that plants, if encouraged to grow properly, will soon root down to wetter soil horizons where there is no water shortage. This may entail arranging special water-retaining pockets by which surface drought can be overcome, as on slate waste (Chapter 10), or even temporary irrigation in arid areas (Chapter 8).

Surface temperatures are only high in the absence of plants The obvious answer therefore is to ensure that plants are established during a cool period, and then grow sufficiently quickly to ensure a complete ground cover by the time intense solar radiation occurs. This means that attention must be paid to other factors which reduce growth. In those cases where the plants being established are slow to establish, a nurse crop that grows rapidly but survives for only a single season, such as sorghum or short rotation ryegrass, can be valuable.

Nutrients, particularly nitrogen are universally deficient in derelict land materials, and are the principle cause of failure. Now a wide range of artificial fertilisers are available to get over this, both simple and compound (Table 6.4). It is very easy, after determining the particular nutrient deficiencies (Chapter 7), to add them in appropriate amounts, either by choosing the appropriate compound fertiliser or using mixtures of simple fertilisers. Modern compound fertilisers come in such a variety of formulations, and are so cheap and convenient, that they are usually preferable. The levels required may be greater than in normal agricultural practice but this will add little to costs. Nitrogen is the most difficult deficiency to overcome, since it is needed in large amounts and is quickly lost by leaching from most derelict land materials. It can be provided either by fertilisers, or by leguminous plants since these, if inoculated, provide adequate supplies of nitrogen. Although nitrogen applied as a fertiliser is leached readily, a number of special slow-release fertilisers have recently been developed: unfortunately they are usually expensive and so for large-scale work legumes are preferable.

Toxicity can be the factor most difficult to overcome by specific treatment. Excess acidity can be readily overcome by the use of lime: even when applied at 20 tonnes/ha it is not an expensive commodity. In some circumstances acid-

Table 6.4. Correct fertilisers should be chosen to suit individual problems: nutrient contents of fertilisers commonly available

fertiliser	composition (%)				special characteristics
	N	P	K	other	
fast release					
N ammonium nitrate	35	0	0		nitrogen balanced $NH_4 + NO_3$
nitrochalk	25	0	0		contains lime
P superphosphate	0	8	0		
K potassium sulphate	0	0	41		
balanced 17:17:17	17	8	14		
high N 25:10:10	25	4	8		many other formulations available
high P 10:25:25	10	10	12		
high K 15:15:35	15	7	20		
slow release					
sulphur coated urea	32	0	0		rather fast release
magnesium ammonium sulphate	5	10	8	Mg 10	satisfactory release
urea formaldehyde	38	0	0		release slow and dependent on bacterial action
isobutylidene diurea	31	0	0		expensive
Osmocote	18	4	7		other formulations available—expensive but effective
rock phosphate	0	13	0		phosphorus only released in acid soils— cheap
basic slag	0	7	0		variable
hoof and horn	14	0	0		
bone meal	4	10	0		

Chapter 6: Derelict Land Solutions

ity can be washed out (Chapter 8). However, in some materials, such as colliery spoil containing high levels of pyrite, acidity may regenerate rapidly and it may be impossible to control it by liming or any other treatment. Toxic metalliferous waste and saline materials can sometimes be treated with ameliorants: salinity can be removed by leaching. Where there are no simple ways of removing toxicity it may be possible to find plant species or varieties, which possess tolerance to the toxic factor concerned. These may take some trouble to find but can provide a complete answer (Chapter 8).

If selective methods are adopted, the effort and energy that would be spent pointlessly overcoming apparent problems, which are not in fact important for the site, can be directed to overcoming the significant problems. In this way the real difficulties can be dealt with properly and the ultimate success of the project ensured. Money spent on using top soil, for instance, could be wasted if as a result insufficient money is spent on drainage; on an acid colliery spoil, money spent on a sewage sludge treatment is unlikely to give a reclamation as successful as if it were spent on adequate amounts of lime and fertilisers only.

6.7   GRASSES AND LEGUMES

One of the commonest component of all reclamation schemes is a grass cover, usually containing a legume. In Britain alone, which has a very restricted range of plant species, there are over 140 different species of grass, and about 70 different species of clover or other legumes found growing in grassy places. So which are valuable and should be used in reclamation schemes, and what are the best methods of sowing them?

Choice of species. The grasses and legumes of Britain are only a small fraction of the grasses and legumes of the world, and they are adapted to the British moist temperate climate. It would be valuable to look at the grasses suitable for derelict land on a world scale, but this is not practicable. However, the British species are a good illustration of the problems of choice and the principles that must be adopted, and since much of the world's derelict land is in temperate climates they are of widespread value outside Britain.

There are as many different types of species as there are environments, but from our point of view it is their adaptation to soil conditions that matters: so they are therefore classified in this manner in Table 6.5. Most of the species are readily available commercially since they are used for agricultural purposes, but there are a few which are not readily available since they have no place in agriculture. But they should not be disregarded since they can be very

grass species	fertility demand	pH tolerance	drought tolerance	temperature tolerance	cultivars
Agrostis gigantea (red top)	M	NC	M	CW	few
Agrostis stolonifera (creeping/ bentgrass)	M	NC	L	CW	few
Agrostis tenuis (bentgrass [brown top])	L	AN	M	CW	many
Alopercurus pratensis (meadow foxtail)	M	NC	M	CW	few
Dactylis glomerata (cocksfoot [orchard grass])	H	NC	M	CW	many
Deschampsia caespitosa (tufted hairgrass)	M	NC	M	CW	wild species
Deschampsia flexuosa (wavy hairgrass)	L	A	H	CW	wild species
Festuca arundinacea (tall fescue)	H	NC	L	CW	many
Festuca ovina (sheep's fescue)	L	ANC	H	CdCW	few
Festuca rubra (red fescue)	L	NC	H	CdCW	many
Festuca pratensis (meadow fescue)	M	NC	M	CW	few
Lolium perenne (perennial ryegrass)	M	NC	M	CW	many
Phleum pratense (timothy)	M	NC	M	CW	many
Poa compressa (Canada bluegrass)	L	ANC	H	CdCW	many
Poa pratensis (smooth-stalked meadow grass [Kentucky bluegrass])	L	ANC	H	CdCW	many
	(low, medium or high)	(acidic, neutral or calcareous)	(low, medium or high)	(cold, cool or warm)	

Table 6.5. Grasses are an important tool but must be chosen carefully: species particularly suitable for derelict land in temperate regions

important in particular situations, and seedsmen may often carry small stocks.

Within each species there are usually many different varieties, cultivars, with different characteristics of hardiness, winter greenness, adaptation to soil and climate, etc. It is worthwhile spending time finding the most appropriate cultivars because the correct choice can make all the difference to the permanence and ease of maintenance of the end product.

Legumes are a crucial component in almost all grass mixtures because they contribute and maintain adequate nitrogen supplies and ensure the build-up of an adequate capital of organic nitrogen in the newly forming soil. They eliminate the need for aftercare treatment of nitrogen by increasing the amount of mineralisable nitrogen (Table 6.6). The choice again depends on soil conditions and on climate. Usually the most valuable legumes are those that are used in agriculture since they have high rates of nitrogen fixation. A classified list of useful legumes on a world basis is given in Table 6.7. Most productive legumes presently available require reasonably high levels of calcium and phosphorus for growth and nitrogen fixation. But

Chapter 6: Derelict Land Solutions

there is an enormous range of legumes in the world and a great deal of work is going on at present to develop new species and cultivars for agricultural use with greater tolerance to low nutrient conditions. So anyone anxious to find the best legumes should get in touch with his local agricultural advisory service.

Legumes are only valuable if they possess their appropriate strain of *Rhizobium*. In soils where the species has already been growing, the appropriate *Rhizobium* will already be present. But in soils being formed out of waste or other difficult materials they may not be, or there may only be a strain inefficient at fixing nitrogen. The proper *Rhizobium* may be attached to the legume seed, but this cannot be relied upon and the seed should be inoculated with the correct *Rhizobium* culture. This can be purchased in most countries at little cost: the address of suppliers will be available from the agricultural advisory service. The inoculum will either be in the form of a live culture or dried in a suspension on peat. In either case the culture is wetted and mixed with the seed, which is a simple operation. In some situations there may be no supply available. Soil from the region where the legume has been growing successfully will contain the appropriate *Rhizobium*. So if it is damped and mixed with the seed it will usually act as a substitute inoculum.

The value of a nurse crop for protection has already been discussed. The choice of species depends on the environment and the job that the nurse crop has to do. If the problem is a shortage of nutrients then a nurse crop will merely exaggerate the problem because it will compete for the nutrients. But for protection against other factors a nurse crop can be important if correctly chosen, for example on coastal sand (Chapter 12). Since the nurse crop must

Table 6.6. Clover is better than fertilisers in providing nitrogen gradually and continuously: a comparison of methods of aftercare on a grass sward established on limestone waste in Yorkshire

		aftercare treatment		
	none	N only (ammonium nitrate 40 kg/ha)	NPK (complete 17:17:17 300 kg/ha)	white clover (with superphosphate 250 kg/ha)
productivity (kg/ha/yr)	176	1594	1456	321
organic matter (%)	0·96	3·24	2·55	2·55
total nitrogen (%)	0·01	0·03	0·02	0·02
mineralisable nitrogen (ppm after 14 days' incubation)	+0·9	+2·7	+4·5	+14·3
sward cover (% at end of season)	20	70	70	40
sward colour (after treatment)	1	5	5	4
(at end of season) (1 brown—5 green)	1	1	1	2

Grasses and legumes

Table 6.7. Legumes are an essential part of land restoration practice: perennial legumes particularly suitable for derelict land

legume species	soil preference	climate preference
Amorpha fruticosa (indigo bush)	NC	W
Centrosema pubescens (centro)	AN	W
Coronilla varia (crown vetch)	AN	CW
Desmodium uncinatum (silver leaf desmodium)	AN	W
Lathyrus sylvestris (mat peavine)	NC	W
Lespedeza bicolor (lespedeza)	AN	W
Lespedeza cuneata (sericea lespedeza)	AN	W
Lespedeza japonica (Japan lespedeza)	AN	W
Lotus corniculatus (birdsfoot trefoil)	NC	CW
Lupinus arboreus (tree lupin)	ANC	CW
Medicago sativa (lucerne [alfalfa])	NC	CW
Melilotus alba (sweet clover [white])	ANC	CW
Melilotus officinalis (sweet clover [yellow])	ANC	W
Phaseolus atropurpureus (siratro)	ANC	W
Stylosanthes humilis (Townsville stylo)	AN	W
Trifolium hybridum (alsike clover)	ANC	C
Trifolium pratense (red clover)	NC	C
Trifolium repens (white clover)	NC	CW
Ulex europaeus (gorse)	ANC	C
	(acidic neutral or calcareous)	(cool or warm)

allow light to the associated plants it must nearly always be sown at low density and be a grass: the growth habit of grasses allows good light at ground level, species such as short rotation ryegrass (*Lolium italicum*), cereal rye (*Secale cereale*) and sorghum (*Sorghum vulgare*).

Establishment from seed. Agricultural methods are nearly always best. So the normal practice of cultivation, seeding and consolidation should be followed wherever possible, using normal agricultural machinery. It is sometimes necessary to employ specially strong cultivators to cope with material of poor texture. Similarly seed drills may give trouble, in which case it is better to broadcast. On some steep sites it may be impossible to use any machinery for seeding: in this case the old-fashioned art of sowing by hand, perhaps with a fiddle, is not out of place: it can be very effective, and cheaper than hydroseeding.

One or two special machines are beginning to appear particularly for reclamation work. There are combined cultivator–seed drills specially designed for difficult materials, and stone-picking machines. These may or may not offer advantages commensurate with their extra expense, but in some situations they may be invaluable.

Seeding rates should differ according to the species and the site, but again agricultural practice should be followed. This is important, because in horticultural practice it is quite usual to sow seed at 1–2 oz/sq yd or 500 kg/ha, yet in agriculture seed rates of 40 kg/ha are normal. It is an absurd extravagance to follow horticultural practice, yet it is often done in the belief that a high seed rate will ensure success. This is not true; only correct growing conditions will ensure this. So for grass establishment, seed rates should normally be 50–100 kg/ha in temperate climates and less in tropical climates.

The cultivation before seeding and the consolidation afterwards should follow agricultural practice, although it may be necessary for the cultivation to be more thorough. The consolidation after seeding can be omitted in many instances because the seed will become buried naturally by the effects of rain, and perfect establishment may be sacrificed for savings in cost.

Fertilising and liming. These and other ameliorative treatments must be carried out with great care. The amounts will depend considerably on the material and site being reclaimed but the critical nutrients will nearly always be nitrogen and phosphorus. This point is considered in detail in relation to individual situations later. Normal methods of application can be used.

Vegetative propagation. In some situations where seed establishment is difficult this is an important alternative method. Marram and beach grasses for instance (*Ammophila arenaria* and *breviligulata*) used for stabilising coastal sand areas, are normally planted by hand, using small clumps of three or four tillers, set out at about 30 cm centres. The material can easily be obtained by splitting up existing clumps. Where clonal material specially adapted to particular conditions, such as are found in metalliferous tailings, has been identified, vegetative propagation can be a very effective method of establishment and ensures that the genetic characteristics of the material are preserved (Chapter 8).

Vegetative material will require just as much care in the soil-ameliorative treatments as seed material. Although the starting material is bigger and has a greater store of nutrients in the short term, in the long term it will require the same supply of nitrogen and other nutrients as seed.

6.8   TREES AND SHRUBS

The alternative to sowing grass is to establish trees or shrubs. Trees may be able to provide a commercial crop, if the right species are chosen. They can be planted on ground where agriculture is impossible such as steep-sided heaps and old strip-mined land left as hill and dale. They can disguise man-made contours and provide positive contributions to the landscape. And they make attractive wild areas suitable for recreation even in the middle of industrial areas (Figure 6.15). They are, however, less effective than grasses in stabilising soils against erosion.

Figure 6.15. Trees can disguise man-made contours and provide a positive contribution to the landscape: a mature forest of black locust on colliery spoil in the Ruhr.

Choice of species. Just as with grasses the choice of species suitable for planting on derelict land is immense on a world scale. It is necessary to choose species known to be well-adapted to the local environment, using the advice of the local forest service. In general the most valuable species are those that are natural pioneers. For temperate climates it is possible to identify the species which have been found to be particularly well-adapted to the nutrient-deficient, difficult conditions which exist early in natural successions and also in derelict land. But as with grasses, the species must be chosen in relation to the particular qualities of the sites such as pH and climate (Table 6.8).

There are a number of leguminous trees, notably black locust (*Robinia pseudoacacia*) in cool climates, and wattle and other members of the genus *Acacia* in warm climates, which are very valuable because they have the same capacity to fix nitrogen that is possessed by herbaceous legumes. Some trees (species of alder (*Alnus*) are an example) which are not legumes also fix nitrogen. These species can grow relatively quickly without assistance from nitrogenous fertilisers (Figure 6.16) and are useful restoration tools, although they can be demanding of other nutrients.

The choice of shrubs is immense. Since there is no question of commercial use, the species to use will be those of

tree species	fertility demand	pH tolerance	moisture tolerance	climate tolerance
Acer pseudoplatanus (sycamore)	M	NC	D	CW
Alnus glutinosa (black alder)	L (N)	ANC	W	C
Alnus incana (grey alder)	L (N)	NC	W	C
Betula papyrifera (birch)	L	ANC	WD	W
Betula pendula (birch)	L	NC	WD	C
Betula pubescens (birch)	L	ANC	WD	C
Coriaria arborea (coriaria)	L (N)	AN	D	CW
Eleagnus sylvatica (Russian olive)	L (N)	NC	D	CW
Eleagnus umbellulata (autumn olive)	L (N)	NC	D	CW
Fagus sylvatica (beech)	M	ANC	D	C
Fraxinus americana (white ash)	M	NC	WD	W
Fraxinus excelsior (ash)	M	NC	D	C
Juniperus virginiana (eastern red cedar)	L	ANC	D	CW
Larix leptolepis (Japanese larch)	L	ANC	D	C
Pinus banksiana (jack pine)	L	AN	D	C
Pinus echinata (shortleaf pine)	L	AN	D	W
Pinus nigra (Austrian pine)	L	ANC	D	CW
Pinus rigida (pitch pine)	L	AN	D	CW
Pinus strobus (white pine)	M	ANC	D	CW
Pinus sylvestris (Scots pine)	L	ANC	D	CW
Pinus taeda (loblolly pine)	M	AN	D	W
Pinus virginiana (Virginia pine)	L	AN	D	W
Platanus occidentalis (western plane)	M	NC	W	CW
Populus tremula x *tremuloides* (hybrid aspen)	M	ANC	W	C
Robinia fertilis (bristly locust)	L (N)	ANC	D	CW
Robinia pseudoacacia (black locust)	L (N)	ANC	D	CW
Salix caprea (goatwillow)	L	ANC	WD	C
Salix cinerea (sallow)	L	ANC	WD	C
Salix daphnoides (violet willow)	L	NC	W	C
Salix purpurea (purple willow)	L	ANC	W	C
Salix viminalis (osier)	M	NC	W	C
Sorbus aucuparia (rowan)	L	ANC	D	C
Thuja occidentalis (northern white cedar)	M	NC	WD	C
	(medium or low) (N fixing)	(acidic, neutral, or calcareous)	(wet or dry)	(cool or warm)

Table 6.8. Trees improve landscapes and provide timber: species particularly suitable for derelict land in temperate regions

Figure 6.16. Leguminous trees such as this *Acacia saligna* (*cyanophylla*) can grow extremely quickly: these on Trojan nickel mine tailings in Rhodesia are only 18 months old.

Trees and Shrubs

the region which are particularly adapted to derelict land and degraded soils. Nitrogen-fixing bushes such as gorse (*Ulex* sp.) and autumn and Russian olive (*Eleagnus* sp.) are particularly valuable.

Establishment methods. There are three major ways in which trees and shrubs can be established, by seed, young seedlings or transplants, and by standards. Each of these has their place in land restoration. The most usual method is by young *seedlings* or *transplants*, trees or shrubs one to three years old, 10–30 cm high, which have been raised in a nursery. These can be planted quite rapidly by hand, using a spade or mattock (about 60/hr). These transplants are bare-root—they have no soil with them, and so they must not be allowed to dry out even for very short periods before being planted. The roots should be covered with the best material available. An alternative method is to use seedlings less than a year old grown in small fibre tubes or other containers. These are often easier to handle and establish more readily because the roots are protected.

In certain places *standards*, or slightly younger trees known as *whips*, 100–200 cm tall, can be used to provide an instant effect or to avoid damage from vandalism or animals. Planting these trees will be expensive because they need holes dug at least 30 cm square (up to 1 m square for full standards) and secure rot-proof staking matching the size of the tree. Because of their expense it is common practice to ensure satisfactory growth by filling the planting holes with good soil brought in from elsewhere. This is easier to do when, as with standards, fewer but bigger trees are being planted. But care must be taken to ensure that the soil is satisfactory and nutrient-rich (Figure 6.7) otherwise the effort and expense will have been wasted.

There is now machinery that allows large, *semi-mature trees*, 4 m or more in height, to be moved. Where an instant effect is needed, for instance near a building, the method is valuable, but elsewhere it is a great waste of money. Experience shows that after five years has elapsed, a younger tree will overtake the semi-mature tree because it has suffered less in transplanting.

In the restoration of derelict land, the ground often starts by being almost bare of vegetation. As a result, trees and shrubs can in some cases be successfully established by *direct seeding* because there is no competition from accompanying vegetation. In commercial forestry, direct seeding is widely used, particularly in N. America, as a means of establishment, and it has been applied to derelict land very effectively, although it is only likely to be successful where conditions for seedling establishment are good. Seed is scattered by hand or cyclone seeder or by helicopter, at a rate of about 1 kg/ha for pine. If the seed does not germinate quickly it is likely to be eaten by animals, etc., so slow-germinating seed should have its dormancy broken by stratification. Seeding must be done at the end of the winter or dry season, but the exact date must be determined by experience. In some cases, seed can be obtained from natural vegetation merely by laying seed-carrying branches on the ground at the appropriate season (Chapter 12) or by passing the branches through a wood-chipping machine to make a mulch. The soil surface can either be in its original state, or it can be ripped or cultivated to provide micro-sites into which the seeds will fall and germinate.

Planting density must be a compromise between achieving an early cover and a stand that requires excessive thinning. 2000 trees/ha is a good compromise leading to a stand closure when the trees are 5–10 m high. But the essential point is not the number of trees planted but a stand of trees which will grow properly over a long period.

Fertilising and liming. These are just as important for trees as they are for grasses and legumes. If the nutrient deficiencies and pH are not corrected at the outset, and then maintained properly afterwards, growth will be poor. Ultimately the trees may root far enough to tap better nutrient supplies, but poor early growth can lead to death by vandalism or animals, or by competition from surrounding vegetation. Since properly grown planting stock will be well-fertilised and carry its own supply of nutrients for the first year, the main need will be in the second and subsequent years. The critical nutrients will nearly always be nitrogen and phosphorus as with grasses.

Accompanying vegetation. Since trees are established at low densities and a lot of ground is left unprotected, a ground cover may be important. Where the ground is flat, ground cover will probably not be required, but where there is likely to be erosion a cover may be essential. This can be a grass/legume mixture or pure legume: legumes are valuable because of the nitrogen they contribute. But a ground cover will compete for nutrients and water with young trees, and even for light if the trees are small. So the species must be chosen with care and the seeding rates kept very low, much lower than for areas without trees. Even so it may be necessary to control the vegetation around the young trees by cutting or spraying herbicide during the second and third years.

6.9   WILD SPECIES

Wild material of both grasses and legumes may sometimes be very important. Legislation may require that the native vegetation is restored: or it may be that wild species are particularly well-adapted to the extreme characteristics of a site, better than commercially available species. It is also possible that cultivars of a species are already available commercially, but that wild populations would be better. Within all species, local populations exist which are specially adapted to their own environments: such populations may have characteristics which make them better than commercial material for reclamation purposes. Metal-tolerant grass populations are a good example (Chapter 8).

Wild material may also be used to add diversity of species to a site, important if the site is going to be used for amenity or nature conservation. In this case, the choice of material is very wide indeed and depends on the particular characteristics of the site being reclaimed. The potential of reclaimed sites as refuges for wild species must not be forgotten (Chapter 2).

Wild material cannot usually be bought. But it can always be collected at the right time of year. Even if only small quantities of seed can be gathered it can form an inoculum from which the species can be spread. In certain situations, whole branches or shoots bearing seeds can be harvested and spread as a mulch after being passed through a chipping machine (Figure 6.17). Alternatively,

(a)

(b)

Figure 6.17. To reinstate natural scrub vegetation in dry regions, the ground can be ripped and mulched with seed-bearing branches of native species put through a wood-chipping machine: land, a) after treatment; b) after four years at Kambalda nickel mine, Western Australia.

seed and plant material can be carried over in top soil. If top soil is being used for this purpose, care must be taken to find out where the species are and the manner in which they will persist during the operation. Seed is often only in the top few centimetres of the soil, as in heather moorland (Figure 6.18). In this case, this layer must not be mixed and spread with the lower layers, or seed will be diluted and buried: it must be scraped off carefully and replaced in the final earth-moving operation. Many plants will carry over in vegetative fragments; these will be killed if the soil is stored for too long a time, or is consolidated too heavily by earth-moving equipment. A nurse crop will be important to protect the young material and prevent erosion. But on no account must it be too competitive.

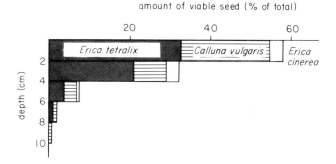

Figure 6.18. In most natural soils such as this heather moorland the seed of wild species lies mostly in the top 5 cm so the surface layer must be removed and replaced carefully if the wild species are to re-establish successfully.

Contrary to some opinion, fertiliser will almost certainly be necessary. While it is true that many native species are adapted to low nutrient levels and will be used for this reason, most derelict land materials will be far too deficient in nutrients for satisfactory growth. So fertiliser will be necessary. Even when top soil is being used to re-establish wild species, some nutrient additions will be necessary at least to replace the nutrients lost in the land disturbance. Nitrogen will usually be the most important nutrient to add—it has the advantage of not having long-lasting effects: but phosphorus will often also be required. The amounts must be determined by experiment.

The subsequent management of areas of wild species needs some thought. It will be necessary to apply the same management as the species receive in their natural habitats. This could be, as on moorland dominated by heather (*Calluna vulgaris*), intermittent burning and only light grazing; or it could be, as for grassland on limestone rocks, heavy grazing. In shrub- and tree-dominated areas, grazing must be carefully excluded.

6.10   LOCALISATION OF DAMAGE

When a mine or quarry is first established, it is just a small hole, with a small pile of waste. A decade later it will be a

103

larger hole and a larger pile of waste. But it will be more than that, for around the workings an area of degraded or spoilt land will have accumulated, where rubbish has been dumped, vehicles parked, or farming prevented. When concentrators and refineries are built the worst degradation of the surroundings may take place at the beginning, because of movement of construction machinery and temporary dumping.

Mining towns will bring their own trail of degradation, not at the beginning when they are being constructed, but when they are established and cause pressure on their surroundings from wood-cutting, grazing and recreation. At Broken Hill, Australia, as well as the loss of amenity, the degradation of the surroundings has caused as much dust pollution as the mines themselves.

This effect on the surroundings is not to be under-rated. It is obvious in arid areas where the degradation leads to complete destruction of the normal vegetation, as at Kalgoorlie and Broken Hill. But it is just as pernicious in temperate regions where mining operations, for instance in the Lancashire coal field and the china clay area north of St. Austell, Cornwall, have lead to degradation of surrounding areas equal to more than a quarter of the area of the mining sites themselves.

The solution is easy. It is proper control of operators and people and maintenance of existing land used wherever

Figure 6.19. One simple precaution is to preserve the natural vegetation of a site from unnecessary damage: curbing put down at Kambalda nickel mine, Western Australia, to preserve native vegetation near the concentrator.

Chapter 6: Derelict Land Solutions

possible. If areas are properly defined at the outset, and marked out on the ground, operations can be restricted to appropriate places, and areas which would otherwise be spoilt can be maintained in their original state. It may be important to provide proper fences or even curbing. One of the most outstanding examples of this policy is at Kambalda, Western Australia, where the natural vegetation has been preserved within 20 m of the mine plant and buildings by careful curbing (Figure 6.19): it is in complete contrast to the neighbouring Kalgoorlie.

Where damage has occurred it can be put right by tidying up and suitable planting. At Kambalda steps have been taken to re-establish the natural vegetation to preserve the character of the area. It may be important to establish a protected zone around a town or mine site in which access and grazing is restricted or prevented. The 2-mile zone round Broken Hill established 40 years ago has led to the natural re-establishment of vegetation and elimination of dust and other problems.

FURTHER READING

Aims

Crocker R.L. & Major J. 1955. Soil development in relation to vegetation and surface age at Glacier Bay, Alaska. *J. Ecol.* **43**, 427–48.

Leisman G.A. 1957. A vegetation and soil chronosequence on the Mesabi Iron Range spoil banks, Minnesota. *Ecol. Monogr.* **27**, 221–45.

Top soil conservation

Department of the Environment 1978. *Joint Agricultural Land Restoration Experiments*. London: Department of the Environment.

Knabe W. 1965. Observations on world-wide efforts to reclaim industrial waste land. In: *Ecology and the Industrial Society*, ed. G.T. Goodman, R.W. Edwards and J.M. Lambert. 263–96. Oxford: Blackwell.

Other Materials

Cooke G.W. 1967. *The Control of Soil Fertility*. London: Crosby Lockwood.

Johnson M.S., McNeilly T. & Putwain P.D. 1977. Revegetation of metalliferous mine spoil contaminated by lead and zinc. *Environ. Pollut.* **12**, 261–77.

Gemmell R.P. 1976. Revegetation of derelict land polluted by a chromate smelter. Part 2. Techniques of revegetation of chromate smelter waste. *Environ Pollut.* **6**, 31–7.

Hydraulic seeding

Hanson A.A. & Juska F.V. (eds.) 1969. *Turfgrass Science*. New York: American Soc. Agronomy.

Sheldon J.C. & Bradshaw A.D. 1978. The development of a hydraulic seeding technique for unstable sand slopes. I. Effects of fertilisers, mulches and stabilisers. *J. Appl. Ecol.* **14**, 905–18.

Kay B.L. 1976. *Hydroseeding, straw, and chemicals for erosion control*. Agronomy Progress Report 17. Davis: Univ. California.

Direct improvement

Downing M.F. 1978. Drainage. In: *Landscape Reclamation Practice*, ed. B. Hackett, 70–84. London: IPC Science and Technology Press.

Dudeck A.E., Swanson N.P., Meikle L.N. & Dedrick A.R. 1970. Mulches for grass establishment on fill slopes. *Agron. J.* **62**, 810–12.

Jeffrey D.W., Maybury M. & Levinge D. 1974. Ecological approach to mining waste revegetation. In: *Minerals and the Environment*, ed. M.J. Jones. 371–85. London: Institution of Mining and Metallurgy.

Toms A.H. 1948. The effect of vegetation on the stabilisation of artificial slopes. In: *Proceedings of Conference on Biology and Civil Engineering*, ed. Institution of Civil Engineers. 99–112. London: Institution of Civil Engineers.

Townsend W.N. & Gilham E.W.F. 1975. Pulverised fuel ash as a medium for plant growth. In: *The Ecology of Resource Degradation and Renewal*, ed. M.J. Chadwick and G.T. Goodman. 287–304. Oxford: Blackwell.

Younkin W.E. (ed.) 1976. *Revegetation Studies in the Northern Mackenzie Valley Region*. Canadian Arctic Gas Study Ltd. Alaskan Arctic Gas Study Co.

Species

Hutnick R.J. & Davis G. (eds.) 1973. *Ecology and Reclamation of Devastated Land* (2 vols.) New York: Gordon and Breach.

Natural vegetation

Brooks D.R. 1976. Rehabilitation following mineral sand mining on North Stradbrooke Island, Queensland. In: *Landscaping and Land Use Planning as Related to Mining Operations,* ed. Australasian Inst. Min. Metall. 93–104. Adelaide: Australasian Inst. Min. Metall.

Gillham D.A. & Putwain P.D. 1977. Restoring moorland disturbed by pipeline installation. *Landscape Design*. **119**, 34–6.

Localisation

Morris M. 1939. Plant regeneration in the Broken Hill district. *Aust. J. Sci.* **2**, 43–9.

Verschuer J. 1976. Landscape architecture—policy into practice. In: *Landscaping and Land Use Planning as Related to Mining Operations*, ed. Australasian Inst. Min. Metall. 281–8. Parkville, Victoria, Australia: Inst. Min. Metall.

'They receive their nourishment from the external elements; they assimilate it by means of peculiar organs; and it is by examining their physical and chemical constitution and the substances and powers which act on them and the modification they undergo, that the scientific principles of Agricultural Chemistry are obtained.'

SIR HUMPHERY DAVY

Elements of Agricultural Chemistry 1813.

7 Techniques of Investigation

Early work on the restoration of land from waste materials relied heavily upon agricultural and forestry experience or the accumulated wisdom of parks and gardens departments. The waste material on which it was desired to establish vegetation was regarded as a soil—a peculiar soil certainly, but one that could have routine soil analyses applied to it, normal seed mixtures sown, and trees planted that originated from forest nursery stock. On occasions this approach produced spectacular successes. Unfortunately however, initial establishment successes were often followed by the vegetation dying and the appearance of bare patches that became the nodal points for erosion and gullying. So the necessity for detailed site investigation to precede full-scale reclamation work has become appreciated.

These investigations form a progressive series—*site inspections*, *laboratory analyses* of the waste material, *pot experiments* away from the site (in a controlled environment room, greenhouse, laboratory, yard or garden), *experimental field trials* on the site and finally *site monitoring* to follow the success of particular restoration treatments. Not all of these will be appropriate for any one type of waste material or for every specific reclamation site, but they are each important for one situation or another.

7.1 SITE INSPECTION

Almost everyone who has been connected with scientific advisory work in the course of reclamation projects will have experienced at some time the arrival of one or two bags of 'material for analysis' in their laboratory! This is usually a most unsatisfactory way to begin any investigation and we would urge that the start is a proper site visit.

Not only should general site characteristics be recorded, but also any obvious signs of variability in the material. Indications of erosion, by run-off water or wind, give useful information of the physical characteristics of the material: any evidence of waterlogging or drainage problems should be noted.

The natural regeneration of vegetation can be a very useful guide to the potential of the material for revegeta-

107

tion and also point to the remedial treatment required. The vegetational features that must be taken into account include:

degree of vegetational cover
number of species
species composition
annuals : perennials

percentage of woody species
extent and depth of rooting
plant vigour
deficiency or toxicity
symptoms

There are pitfalls. For example, the degree of plant cover and the range of species will depend not only on the nature of the waste material as a medium for plant growth, but also on whether the waste contained plant propagules when it was originally dumped or is close to vegetation producing seeds. Species composition can be used as an indicator of substrate conditions, but it depends on accurate identification. Toxicity and deficiency symptoms are a snare to all but the specialist observer, as *toxicity* symptoms can resemble phosphorus deficiency and iron deficiency chlorosis may be mistaken for nitrogen or sulphur deficiency and so on.

Nonetheless, a number of principles do hold good sufficiently generally to be of use in making site assessments based on vegetational criteria:

(a) the absence or sparseness of colonising plants is usually indicative of a waste material with toxicity, deficiency or physical problems; conversely, a high degree of plant cover generally indicates a reasonable potential for plant growth.

(b) a high number of species (high floristic diversity) indicates a higher potential for reclamation than a lower number: this effect can be related to site age, but is generally more closely connected with substrate factors.

(c) species composition can be a good guide to the nature of the substrate: many species have well-defined ecological tolerances and can be used as indicator species (Table 7.1).

(d) plant vigour and the general appearance of vegetation can be instructive guides to site conditions: usually plants that are unhealthy are light green, or yellow, or show purple hues, mottling or brown tips to the leaves.

(e) excessively long, sparsely-branched roots are often an indication of insufficient water supply: very shallow rooting indicates waterlogging or soil toxicity.

7.2   SAMPLING

After the initial survey, the sampling programme for subsequent analysis of the material must be worked out. Inadequate or faulty sampling can give a completely wrong assessment of the nature of the material, which will in turn lead to inappropriate remedial procedures.

One important decision is whether to sample before or after earth-moving and landscaping works. Sampling a site in its initial condition can give useful information about the nature of the material, which can be incorporated into the earth-moving specifications and landscape design. If particularly adverse material can be identified it can be buried underneath amenable material. Generally, however, it is more satisfactory to carry out a sampling programme on the landscaped site: even if it is possible to keep track of material during earth moving, it is likely that its chemical and physical features will have become altered during the movement.

Both the number of samples to be taken and the distribution of samples over the site are important as well as depth of sampling. Waste material is nearly always more variable than soil because extraction methods have often altered with time, or the material tipped may have had different origins (washery waste and unwashed debris on a coal tip; toxic and inert material in waste heaps for metal mining). Therefore 'the more samples the better' is a good maxim but, of course, practical difficulties will limit the number. It is essential to weigh the amount of extra work involved

Table 7.1. Associations of flowering plants can be used to indicate substrate characteristics: species commonly associated with particular habitats in the United Kingdom

Acidic
Agrostis canina (brown bent)
Agrostis tenuis (bent grass)
Betula pendula (birch)
Deschampsia flexuosa (wavy hair grass)
Digitalis purpurea (foxglove)
Galium saxatile (heath bedstraw)
Pteridium aquilinum (bracken)
Rumex acetosella (sheep's sorrel)
Ulex europaeus (gorse)
Vaccinium myrtillus (bilberry)

Calcareous
Achillea millefolium (yarrow)
Brachypodium pinnatum (torgrass)
Briza media (quaking grass)
Festuca rubra (red fescue)
Fraxinus excelsior (ash)
Helictotrichon pratense (oat grass)
Trisetum flavescens (yellow oat grass)

Neutral
Agropyron repens (couch grass)
Aira caryophyllea (silver hairgrass)
Anisantha sterilis (sterile brome)
Arrhenatherum elatius (false oat)
Bromus mollis (soft brome)
Atriplex hastata (orache)
Chamaenerion angustifolium (willow herb)
Cirsium arvense (creeping thistle)
Cirsium vulgare (spear thistle)
Hordeum murinum (wild barley)
Poa annua (annual meadowgrass)
Poa pratensis (smooth stalked meadow grass)
Tussilago farfara (coltsfoot)

Waterlogged
Agrostis stolonifera (creeping bent)
Alnus glutinosa (alder)
Caltha palustris (marsh marigold)
Deschampsia caespitosa (tufted hair grass)
Filipendula ulmaria (meadow sweet)
Juncus articulatus (jointed rush)
Juncus effusus (common rush)
Phalaris arundinacea (reedgrass)
Phragmites australis (reed)
Salix atrocinerea (sallow)
Salix fragilis (crack willow)
Typha angustifolia (reed mace)
Valeriana dioica (marsh valerian)

Saline
Agropyron junceum (sea couch)
Atriplex littoralis (orache)
Cakile maritima (sea rocket)
Festuca rubra (red fescue)
Hippophae rhamnoides (sea buckthorn)
Honckenya peploides (sea purslane)
Puccinellia maritima (sea poa)

Heavy metals
Agrostis tenuis (bent grass)
Agrostis stolonifera (creeping bent)
Festuca ovina (sheep's fescue)
Festuca rubra (red fescue)
Minuartia verna (spring sandwort)
Silene vulgaris (bladder campion)

Sampling

against the increase in accuracy that may accrue. Some guidance can come from plotting running means cumulatively against increase in sample number for the samples already available (Figure 7.1) as techniques based on comparative variance calculations are difficult to apply with very heterogeneous waste materials. The distribution of the samples over the site may well have more effect than the number of samples taken.

Figure 7.1. The number of samples to take when the substrate is variable can be given by plotting mean values: for colliery spoil from a site in Yorkshire 40 samples were sufficient.

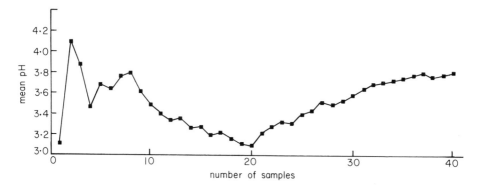

Samples may be taken over the site at *random* (the position of one sample in no way influences the position of any other), *regularly* (equally spaced over the area or along a transect) or *clumped* (aggregated in areas that are presumed to be different and about which information is particularly sought). Figure 7.2 illustrates three sampling regimes on part of a recently landscaped site. *Random* sampling allows an estimate of the accuracy of the mean value to be obtained but may lead to the under-representation of some areas of the site within the total number of samples: positional differences are also less easily recognised. *Regular* sampling covers the whole site equally, but does not allow estimates of accuracy to be made and may miss particularly

Figure 7.2. Sampling schemes may take a number of forms: three sampling regimes on a site all employing 24 samples, in relation to the presence of four distinct sub-areas.

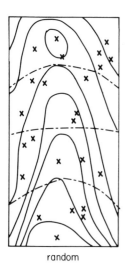
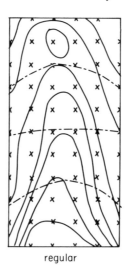
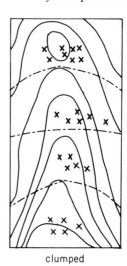

random   regular   clumped

Chapter 7: Techniques of Investigation

significant areas: a transect, say from the bottom to the top of a waste tip, allows variation with position to be detected if it exists. *Clumped* sampling, within areas that have previously been recognised, allows particular areas of waste material to be assessed: it does not, however, allow accuracy estimates to be made unless sampling is at random *within* each area.

It may be valuable to compare areas covered with vegetation with those without. An example for two colliery spoil sites is given in Table 7.2. Whereas one spoil shows that acidity (and associated toxicities and deficiencies) is preventing the growth of vegetation, the other shows it is a deficiency in the level of some nutrient elements. This method provides a direct indication of the causes of plant growth failure.

Table 7.2. Sampling vegetated and unvegetated waste material can indicate factors which inhibit vegetation growth: difference in colliery spoil chemical characteristics from vegetated and unvegetated areas of two contrasting spoils (significant differences underlined)

		deficient spoil		toxic spoil	
		vege-tated	unvege-tated	vege-tated	unvege-tated
pH (in 0·01 m Ca Cl$_2$)		2·38	2·43	4·49	2·93
conductivity (mmhos/cm)		0·30	0·19	2·7	3·2
Ca		16·6	12·6	100	95
Mg		8·2	7·2	55	45
K		4·1	3·4	1·22	0·75
Na	available	2·4	2·0	3·3	3·6
Zn	(ppm)	0·18	0·12	0·14	0·49
Fe		0·36	0·11	0·15	0·65
Mn		0·34	0·24	1·37	4·1
Cu		0·05	0·04	0·09	0·22
Al		5·3	5·7	5·5	27

The depth of sampling should be related to the depth of rooting of the plants it is hoped eventually to establish. Certainly it cannot be assumed that the characteristics of the waste material of the top 10 cm will be representative of material at a greater depth. This is particularly true where the top layers are subject to chemical changes that do not occur lower down (Figure 8.14, page 136).

7.3 PHYSICAL ANALYSIS

Waste material can be analysed for its physical or chemical characteristics, either by taking measurements in the field or by working on samples that have been brought back to the laboratory.

Of all the physical measurements, those that give some idea of the water status of the waste material are most important. Water content, water availability and the moisture characteristics of the material will have direct effects on plant growth and indirect effects arising from the fact that chemical reactions take place in an aqueous medium.

The water content of waste material, expressed as percentage moisture, can be determined simply by the mass (weight) of the sample before and after the removal of water by drying at 105° C. But this measure has a number of shortcomings. The value, particularly in surface layers, will vary considerably from one position to another and from time to time as rain or evaporation occurs, so a single mean value for a site is meaningless.

An even more important drawback is that percentage moisture is not a measure of water availability. Material with the same percentage moisture can have different amounts of water availability (Chapter 3). One way of overcoming this difficulty is to make use of *tensiometers*. A tensiometer is a porous ceramic cup filled with water, connected to a vacuum gauge, and inserted in the waste material in such a way that the water in the capillaries of the material are connected to water in the porous cup. As water is depleted or added to the waste material, changes in the reading of the tensiometer gauge, measuring water potential, will indicate water availability (Figure 7.3).

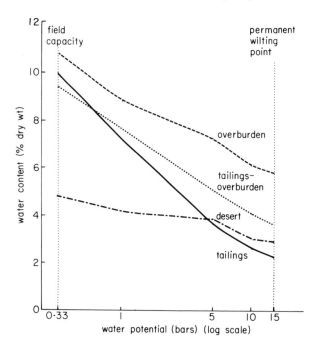

Figure 7.3. Available water capacity can be measured by the difference in water content at field capacity and at wilting point: in a copper mine in Arizona the tailings have the highest water capacity.

Infiltration, the rate of water movement through material, can be of extreme importance in waste materials, especially where these are already dumped or shaped into mounds. The entry of water into the soil, its movement to plant roots, drainage and evaporation obviously all affect plant growth. Measurements can be made in the laboratory by maintaining a constant head of water above a sample in a tube and collecting the percolate beneath, or more simply by measuring the rate of fall of a standard height of water, added on top of a sample which is contained in an open tube. Measurement in the field can be made very simply by inserting a metal ring into the ground and determining the rate of fall of level of water placed within it. In all cases it is essential that undisturbed samples of waste material are used.

Bulk density, the ratio of mass to volume, given an index of soil consolidation and lack of organic matter, can be used with other determinations to obtain porosity measurements. It can be determined by carefully excavating a known volume accurately and then weighing the material after drying.

Particle density may be determined by weighing the sample and then determining its water displacement to obtain its volume. From this *porosity* of a sample can be determined as:

$$\frac{\text{particle density} - \text{bulk density}}{\text{particle density}} \times 100$$

Porosity has a substantial effect upon infiltration and water-holding capacity.

Particle size analysis gives a key to the ultimate physical make-up of a material. It is determined after organic matter has been removed with hydrogen peroxide, and cementing materials and calcium carbonate dissolved by hydrochloric acid. Coarse grains are separated by sieving, and finer fractions by their different rates of sedimentation in water. The methods, however, for particle size analysis have been developed for soils and are only partly applicable to waste materials. Materials freshly excavated can be extremely coarse and bear no relation to the situation that will exist in the material a few months later. Weathering by the action of the rain and frost quickly reduces the size of larger lumps of material to relatively fine aggregates and particles.

The *temperature* relationships of spoil material in the field can have considerable effects on water content, plant growth, chemical reactions, physical weathering and microbial processes. Some form of continuous temperature recording, even if only for a limited period, is valuable if any realistic interpretation is to be made. The usual thermometer is not suitable for this. Thermistors which can measure accurately at a specific point and provide a continuous output are essential.

7.4   CHEMICAL ANALYSIS

Because nutrient and toxicity problems are so universal chemical analyses have been more favoured in waste material investigation and are indeed essential. It is not possible to give a universal checklist of chemical analyses that will yield useful information from a plant growth point of view for all waste materials since spoils will sometimes exhibit very specific chemical characteristics that give rise to special problems. Nevertheless there are certain basic analyses which are always necessary.

pH(hydrogen ion activity), of all the measurements, is certainly the most widely used (and misused) for waste material investigations. It is highly correlated with base saturation, lime requirement, calcium and magnesium levels, and toxicities (Al, Mn, particularly). It is usually measured electronically, with a glass electrode which is very sensitive. Measurements can be made on fresh material in the field or dried material in the laboratory. Spoil is mixed with 2 volumes of water or a weak salt solution (0·01M CaCl$_2$). The degree of dilution will influence the pH measured, this rising as dilution increases. The addition of a neutral salt releases the available hydrogen ions and although giving lower values is often preferred, as it is usually closer to the pH of the spoil *in situ*.

Exchange acidity allows account to be taken of all ionic forms that contribute to the total acidity of a substrate (aluminium and weakly dissociated acidic in groups in clay minerals and organic matter as well as hydrogen ions). It can be used to calculate the *lime requirement* of the spoil. A common method is equilibrium extraction with barium chloride-triethanolamine solution and neutralising the displaced acidic groups with free triethanolamine. The exchange acidity in the extract is determined by direct titration and the lime requirement calculated.

Pyrite and carbonate content of materials affect long-term trends in acidity (Table 8.4, page 131). Pyrite is difficult to determine and several methods are used. These usually involve a preliminary extraction to remove non-pyrite sulphur followed by an oxidising extraction which brings the pyrite iron and sulphur into solution for subsequent measurement. Carbonate can be measured by treatment of the ground material with dilute hydrochloric acid and back titration with alkali to determine the amount of acid neutralised.

Cation exchange capacity is normally determined by saturating the exchange complex with a cation: this is subsequently leached out and the amount determined. If ammonium ions are used to saturate the exchange complex the *total exchangeable bases* can be determined in the course of this procedure.

Soluble salt may be extracted with water. The greater the dilution the more easily this is accomplished, but it may not then give an accurate indication of the level experienced by the plant roots even though corrections are made for the dilution. For this reason a saturation paste extract is often used or 1:1 or 1:2 material/water extracts (Table 7.3). The soluble salt content may also be quickly estimated by using a measure of the electrical conductivity of the extract.

The *extraction procedure* for individual ions should obviously give an indication of the concentration of ions available to plants and also the capacity of the material to keep supplying ions to the solution once some have been removed by the plant roots. This is not easy as elements behave differently and are differentially affected by other features of the material. Thus extraction procedures differ from material to material and from element to element. Commonly used methods of extraction are water, dilute acids (hydrochloric acid, acetic acid), salt solutions (potassium chloride, ammonium acetate), EDTA and many others. Water removes that which is immediately in solution: the acid and salt extracts give a better correlation with plant yield response over a period of time.

Table 7.3. Salinity effects can be determined by measuring the electrical conductivity of spoil extracts: the relationship between electrical conductivity (millimhos/cm) and salinity effects on plant species growing on colliery spoil

	saturation paste extract	1:1 spoil: water suspension	1:2 spoil: water suspension
salinity effect negligible—may indicate nutrient deficiency	2·0	0·9	0·6
level for most well-fertilised spoils—salt sensitive plants may be injured	2·0–4·0	0·9–1·8	0·6–1·2
increasing indications of salinity effects— growth may be severely restricted	4·0–8·0	1·8–3·6	1·2–2·4
only tolerant species will grow satisfactorily on colliery spoil— postpone sowing	8·0–16·0	3·6–7·2	2·4–4·8
injury will occur to all species—long periods of leaching required	16·0	7·2	4·8

The *concentration* of the element in the extract will usually be determined by titration, colorimetry, flame spectrophometry or by atomic absorption spectrophotometry. The presence of ions in an extract can interfere with the detection of other ions and to avoid complicated removal procedures, methods like atomic absorption spectrophotometry have been developed and can be used successfully for a large number of cations.

However, one problem is particularly acute—it is only possible to detect the elements that have been looked for. The early attempts to grow plants on pulverised fuel ash floundered in this way. Originally low fertility, particularly phosphorus was blamed. In fact, boron was a major cause

115 *Chemical Analysis*

of poor growth, but had never been measured. Total elemental analysis by X-ray emission spectrography or optical emission spectrography may therefore be worth using in initial studies despite their expense.

The two major plant nutrients, *nitrogen* and *phosphorus* present special problems. Although inorganic (mineral) nitrogen can be easily determined by extraction with KCl, this measure may not have had much biological significance as it fluctuates seasonally, daily and even hourly at any one site. It should be accompanied by a digestion procedure to determine total nitrogen, and an incubation technique to give an indication of the supplying power of mineral nitrogen by the material.

For phosphorus it is necessary to determine levels of labile phosphorus to get some indication of the potential phosphorus-supplying power of a material—usually by 0·5 M sodium bicarbonate extraction. But the sodium bicarbonate soluble phosphate level is not a good predictor of plant response to applied phosphate on substrates of very low phosphate status, as are so many waste materials. Hence some measure of the phosphorus application required to raise the phosphate level in solution equilibrium to a predetermined level is found to be a better estimate of the P status of the substrate. This takes account of the phosphate sorbed by the substrate and how easily additions of phosphate fertiliser can change the level of phosphate in the substrate solution (i.e., buffering capacity). The amount of phosphate sorbed to give an equilibrium solution of 0·3 ppm P is usually determined.

Plant uptake presents an alternative to direct chemical analysis. If plants, not necessarily the same species as those to be grown on the waste material, are grown on the material in pots for a short period (2–6 weeks) they can be harvested and analysed out for a series of elements. This method has the virtue of revealing what is taken up naturally (see Table 7.6).

There is no reason why this method should only be used with material brought into the greenhouse or laboratory. Plants growing on material on site can be collected and subsequently analysed. This method—frequently termed *foliar analysis*—is used by foresters in particular to gauge the nutritional status of trees in plantations and on difficult

Table 7.4. Analysis of plant material growing on waste can give indications of its nutrient status: percentage nitrogen in birch leaves growing on a range of different colliery spoils

	Spoil	% N in leaves
1	high N	2·49
2		2·27
3		2·11
4		2·05
5		1·99
6	N deficient	1·19

Chapter 7: Techniques of Investigation

sites. It is a useful method of monitoring the progress of vegetation, particularly tree species, on reclaimed areas.

7.5   PLANT GROWTH EXPERIMENTS

Analytical procedures will give information, relatively quickly, that can be used to predict the potential of waste material as a growth medium for plants. The real test, however, is to see whether plants will grow on the material, and how it can be altered to improve growth. This can be done very easily by pot, box and small-scale field trials. If designed intelligently, and conducted correctly, they can yield precise information.

The reclamation officer who first scattered a few ryegrass seedlings on some spoil in a plastic tray was conducting a rudimentary experimental investigation into the potential of waste material for plant growth (Figure 7.4). Expanded in scope, this practice of bringing small amounts of waste material in from the field for use as an experimental plant growth medium in small pots or boxes is exceptionally useful for reclamation investigations. But trials in the field involving individual plots may be the ultimate test required. Whichever method is used there must be replication: no material under trial should be represented by a single sample and it is generally advisable to use areas or blocks as replicates. Within each block each sample or treatment should be placed at random whenever possible. Replication and randomisation will prevent misleading chance effects being given spurious biological significance. Any experiment is best conducted in a situation as environmentally uniform as possible.

Figure 7.4. Simple box experiments can be very informative: the growth of ryegrass sown on an acid colliery spoil shows that both lime and complete fertiliser are necessary.

Many waste materials will have one or all of the major plant nutrients (nitrogen, phosphorus and potassium) in short supply. If the investigation is aimed at establishing which nutrient is limiting then it is essential to ensure that

Plant Growth Experiments

the other two macronutrients are not limiting. Thus a series of treatments (additions to the spoil) would be

critical treatments			useful treatments	
no nitrogen	$N_0 P_+ K_+$	(1)	$N_+ P_0 K_0$	(6)
no phosphorus	$N_+ P_0 K_+$	(2)	$N_0 P_+ K_0$	(7)
no potassium	$N_+ P_+ K_0$	(3)	$N_0 P_0 K_+$	(8)
no additions	$N_0 P_0 K_0$	(4)		
complete	$N_+ P_+ K_+$	(5)		

Comparison of plant growth on (1), (2), or (3) with (4) and (5) will indicate the most seriously limiting macronutrient. But it may be better to have all possible combinations including (6), (7) and (8). Other nutrients may also be limiting growth so additions of any nutrient expected to be in short supply should be tried.

More usually it is not merely the overall limitation caused by an element that will require testing but how much and in what form it should be added, for instance nitrogen by nitrogenous fertilisers (Figure 7.5). Similar experiments, where the pH or toxicity of the material is thought to be at fault, might involve additions of different amounts of lime ($CaCO_3$) or organic ameliorant.

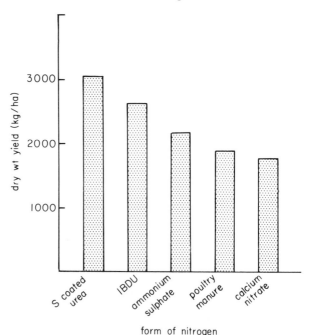

Figure 7.5. The form of a fertiliser has an effect on growth and may have to be tested: yields of herbage from plots given 250 kg/ha of nitrogen in different forms.

Since different species of plants respond in different ways to levels of macronutrients, micronutrients and toxic elements, pot and small-scale field experiments offer an economical way to make initial assessments of material and the most promising species and varieties to use for their reclamation (Figure 7.6).

Field experimentation on waste material and spoil heaps presents particular problems. Heterogeneity of substrate is

Chapter 7: Techniques of Investigation

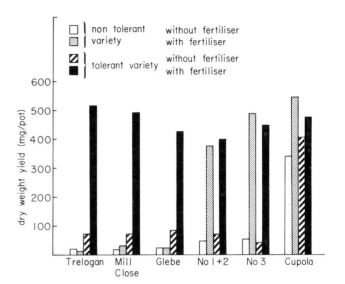

Figure 7.6. A biological assay of metalliferous wastes: on the older toxic wastes (left) growth is only obtained by metal-tolerant red fescue and fertiliser, on the rather unusual waste (right) growth can be obtained with normal material and no fertiliser.

Legend:
□ } non tolerant variety — without fertiliser
▨ } with fertiliser
◩ } tolerant variety — without fertiliser
■ } with fertiliser

y-axis: dry weight yield (mg/pot)

x-axis: Trelogan, Mill Close, Glebe, No 1+2, No 3, Cupola

Figure 7.7. Many forms of experimental design can be utilised: a replicated field trial on colliery spoil in which the main plots were given different fertiliser treatments and sub-divided with ten different grass varieties.

often a major problem and replication and randomisation becomes of prime importance. Small-scale plots can alleviate the difficulty but effects caused by the closeness of the plot edge can take over completely where plot size is reduced too far. Nevertheless, many factors such as cultivation and sowing methods can only effectively be investigated in the field. The only practical procedure may be to split plots for a second level of treatments (Figure 7.7); the designs for such experiments are well-established.

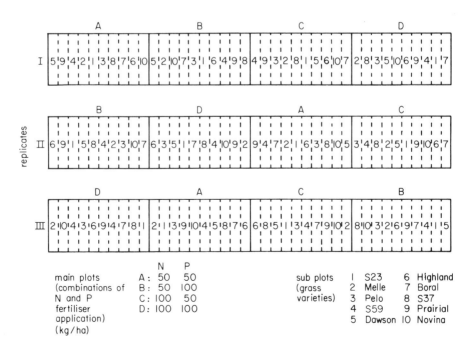

main plots (combinations of N and P fertiliser application) (kg/ha)	N	P
A:	50	50
B:	50	100
C:	100	50
D:	100	100

sub plots (grass varieties)		
1	S23	6 Highland
2	Melle	7 Boral
3	Pelo	8 S37
4	S59	9 Prairial
5	Dawson	10 Novina

Plant Growth Experiments

Pot, box and field trials represent a hierarchy of weapons in the reclamation expert's armoury which can be used in sequence. They can provide information applicable to many situations if established with care and the results analysed with precision and initiative. In agriculture, forestry, horticulture and ecology they form the back-bone of the science. In reclamation work, this store of information, which allows informed judgements to be made, still needs much adding to it.

7.6   AFTERCARE

The design and establishment phase does not mark the end of reclamation schemes but merely the beginning. With a building or piece of machinery, the designer or architect leaves and the construction is left to do the job for which it was designed. With land restoration, the biologist cannot do this. When vegetation is established on a reclamation site it will either develop healthily into a self-sustaining ecosystem or gradually regress until plants die and are not replaced, bare spoil material is eroded and the whole

Figure 7.8. Evidence for aftercare can come from curious sources: the greatly improved growth caused by dogs is evidence of a considerable nitrogen deficiency in a reclamation area in Liverpool.

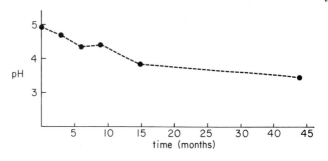

Figure 7.9. Regression after initial treatment can be gradual and can require monitoring over a long period: decline in pH after reclamation of colliery spoil at Bullcroft, Yorkshire due to weathering of pyrite.

Figure 7.10. Simple fertiliser experiments show what aftercare is required: on china clay waste combinations of macro- and micronutrients show that lack of nitrogen alone was preventing growth.

community deteriorates. This is why the site cannot just be left—it must be monitored and managed.

Not all monitoring procedures need to be highly sophisticated. Visual inspection will reveal the development of bare patches, signs of poor growth, die-back or obvious chlorosis. In the case of trees, annual extensions of shoots will give a quite accurate picture of growth that can be used comparatively. Regular inspections of this kind will show then when fertiliser applications are required. It may be possible to find the key to an aftercare problem by quite unpredicted pieces of evidence (Figure 7.8)!

However, on many sites a slow or progressive deterioration will not be so obvious and regular monitoring of spoil characteristics may be required. In colliery spoil, for example, gradual weathering of iron pyrites will lead to a fall in the pH of the material (Figure 7.9). Nutrient depletion can occur by leaching (especially nitrogen) or fixation in a form largely unavailable to plants (especially phosphorus). Here, leaf analysis, particularly of trees, may be a very useful tool for spotting the onset of nutrient deficiency (Table 7.4). But in many cases a simple field experiment will be the easiest and most direct way of discovering what is wrong (Figure 7.10).

FURTHER READING

Allen S.E., Grimshaw H.M., Parkinson J.A. & Quarmby C. 1974. *Chemical Analysis of Ecological Materials*. Oxford: Blackwell Scientific Publications.

Aftercare

Gee G.W., Bauer A. & Decker R.S. 1978. Physical analysis of overburden materials and mine land soils. In: *Reclamation of Drastically Disturbed Lands*, ed. F.W. Schaller and P. Sutton. 665–86. Madison: Amer. Soc. Agron.

Jackson M.L. 1958. *Soil Chemical Analysis*. London: Constable.

Ozanne P.G. & Shaw T.C. 1968. Advantages of the recently developed phosphate sorption test over the older extractant methods for soil phosphate. *Trans. 9th Int. Congr. Soil Sci.* **2**, 273–82.

Preese F. 1967. *Elementary Statistical Methods for Foresters*. Washington: USDA Forest Service.

Ridgman W.J. 1975. *Experimentation in Biology*. Glasgow: Blackie.

Stuart A. 1962. *Basic Ideas of Scientific Sampling*. London: Griffin.

Walsh L.M. & Beaton J.D. (eds.) 1973. *Soil Testing and Plant Analysis*. Madison: Soil Science Society of America.

'An episode of scientific discovery begins with the plain and unembroidered evidence of the senses—with innocent unprejudiced observation, the exercise of which is one of the scientist's most precious and distinctive faculties—and slowly builds upon it a great mansion of natural law.'

PETER MEDAWAR

The Art of the Soluble. 1967.

8   Deep Mines

Of all the categories of derelict and waste land, tips made up of waste from underground and deep pit mines for coal and metals are probably those most associated in the public mind with derelict land. Yet coal mining in Britain, for instance, accounts for something less than 20 per cent of the total area of derelict land. The trouble is that this sort of mining has attracted other industries and as a result is now situated in centres of high population.

Because of this many people are affected by the dereliction and land is sterilised in the very places where it is in shortest supply. Whole areas are degraded and economic development retarded.

As part of the mining process, rock adjacent to the coal seams or metal ore is brought to the surface, usually because the deposits are thin and working space is required. Although this is often inert silica it also contains clay and other minerals, including iron pyrite. Low-grade coal and ore is also discarded. The result is heaps of material that, after hundreds of millions of years underground, can suddenly become very active. Air, finding its way into the heaps, can cause spontaneous combustion of the coal; the pyrite and the metalliferous materials oxidise to form soluble acids and metal salts. The wastes become extremely acid: plants grow on them only with difficulty (Figure 8.1): the drainage water pollutes streams. The spoil heaps have an impact on their surroundings out of

Figure 8.1. Bare colliery spoil heaps cast a miserable shadow over their surroundings: but this large area near Bolton, Lancashire, is now being reclaimed to agriculture and public open space by the local authority.

all proportion to their area. So there is considerable incentive and importance in reclaiming them and putting them once again to productive use.

8.1   COLLIERY SPOIL

8.1.1   Considerable environmental problems

Throughout the world, coal mining is heavily concentrated in particular, populated, areas. In the Federal Republic of Germany it is in the Ruhr; in Poland it is found within a small area of Silesia; in the USSR it is concentrated in a relatively few areas, principally the Donbass region in the Urals coalfield area and in the Kuzbass coalfield; in the USA it is heavily concentrated in areas in Pennsylvania, West Virginia and Ohio (until the recent discovery of huge deposits in the Mid-western states); in Britain each major coalfield, such as in Staffordshire or South Wales, is in a major centre of population.

Most coal is gained from the Coal Measures, which are part of the Carboniferous system of rocks made of Carboniferous Limestone, Millstone Grit and the Coal Measures. These rocks represent three successive phases of material deposition in water. During deposition, subsidence was occurring and sedimentation kept pace with this. The limestone was formed in clear water but the Millstone Grit began to form as neighbouring land was uplifted and eroded so that mud and sand were deposited, usually in deltas. As the deltas became silted up, vegetation grew and vast forest swamps became established. Later, as further earth movements occurred, these were buried by further sediments.

As a result, the layers of organic matter give rise to coal seams interspersed between mudstone, shales, and sandstones. Because the rocks were formed under swampy anaerobic conditions, relatively high amounts of pyrite, FeS_2, were deposited with them.

When the coal is mined today, neither the low-grade carbonaceous material nor the inorganic rocks associated with the seams are wanted. These form the spoil tip (Table 8.1). The low-grade carbonaceous material, which is high in nitrogen, sodium and chlorine, is slow to weather and produces very little in the way of nutrients for plant growth.

Colliery spoil heaps may sometimes become colonised with vegetation naturally (Table 8.2). If the classic view of ecological succession is applied to colliery spoil then there should be an increase in the number of plant species on older spoil tips. But if we look at species number in relation to tip age in Yorkshire, no obvious age/species number relationship exists (Figure 8.2).

If, however, the number of species is compared with the acidity of the colliery spoil, it can be seen that as pH

Table 8.1. A small fraction of the total waste may exert an over-riding influence on the characteristics of a colliery spoil: summary of colliery spoil composition (excluding coaly fraction

mineral	amount (%)	components
Quartz	} 90+	SiO_2
Clay minerals		aluminosilicates
Ankerite		Fe, Ca, Mg, Mn; CO_3
Siderite	} 5	Fe; CO_3
Iron pyrite		FeS_2
Gypsum	} 1–2	$CaSO_4$
Jarosite		K, Fe; SO_4
Amorphous material	1–2	SiO_2, $Al(OH)_3$, $Fe(OH)_3$

Table 8.2. Colliery spoil has its own characteristic flora: occurrence of vascular plants on twenty-two colliery spoil tips in Yorkshire (expressed as %)

Grasses	Agrostis tenuis	68	Poa pratensis	23
	Dactylis glomerata	59	Festuca ovina	23
	Holcus lanatus	55	Deschampsia caespitosa	18
	Deschampsia flexuosa	50	Arrhenatherum elatius	18
	Festuca rubra	41	Festuca arundinacea	5
	Poa annua	32	Zerna ramosa	5
	Agrostis stolonifera	27	Agropyron repens	5
	Lolium perenne	23	Festuca gigantea	5
Legumes	Lotus corniculatus	27	Ulex europaeus	5
	Trifolium pratense	14	Cytisus scoparius	5
	T.repens	14	Trifolium dubium	5
	Vicia sativa	5	Lathyrus montanus	5
	Lupinus sp.	5	Anthyllis vulneraria	5
	Medicago lupulina	5		
Trees	Crataegus monogyna	36	Acer pseudoplatanus	9
	Quercus robur	36	Fraxinus excelsior	5
	Betula pendula	27	Ulmus procera	5
	Salix cinerea	23	Quercus petraea	5
Shrubs	Sambucus nigra	32	Corylus avellana	5
	Rubus fruticosus	27	Rosa canina	5
	Calluna vulgaris	5	R.pimpinellifolia	5
	Salix nigricans	5		
Herbs	Epilobium angusti-folium	74	Epilobium hirsutum	9
	Tussilago farfara	64	Digitalis purpurea	9
	Rumex acetosella	59	Senecio sylvaticus	9
	Cirsium arvense	59	Leontodon autumnalis	9
	Heracleum sphondylium	36	Potentilla erecta	9
	Taraxacum officinale	36	Polygonum persicaria	9
	Senecio viscosus	32	Artemisia vulgaris	9
	Hieracium pilosella	32	Atriplex hastata	9
	H.umbellatum	32	Dipsacus fullonum	9
	Leontodon hispidus	27	Urtica dioica	9

Table 2 continued

	Polygonum aviculare	27	Rumex acetosa	9
	Cerastium fontanum	27	Epilobium parviforum	9
	Rumex crispus	27	Spergularia rubra	5
	R.obtusifolius	27	Solanum nigrum	5
	Linaria vulgaris	22	Senecio erucifolius	5
	Achillea millefolium	22	Symphoricarpus rivularis	5
	Centaurea nigra	22	Tripleurospermum mari-timum	5
	Plantago lanceolata	18	Calystegia sepium	5
	Cirsium vulgare	18	Teucrium scorodonia	5
	Reseda luteola	18	Sonchus arvensis	5
	Ranunculus repens	18	Potentilla reptans	5
	Senecio jacobaea	18	Galium saxatile	5
	Matricaria matricarioides	18	Juncus effusus	5
	Solanum dulcamara	18	Reseda lutea	5
	Senecio squalidus	18	Ranunculus acris	5
	Convolvulus arvensis	14	Centaurea scabiosa	5
	Chrysanthemum leucan-themum	14	Polygonum arenastrum	5
	Atriplex patula	14	Sonchus oleraceus	5
	Stellaria media	14	Hypochaeris radicata	5
	Senecio vulgaris	9	Plantago major	5
	Plantago lanceolata	9		
Pteridophytes	Pteridium aquilinum	18	Equisetum arvense	9

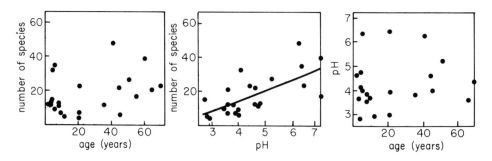

Figure 8.2. The number of plant species colonising a coal tip often does not show any clear relationship with age: it seems to be a function of the acidity of the tip material.

increases, the number of plant species also increases—pH seems to exert a greater influence than age. At the same time the spoil pH is not really related to the age of the tip. This variation in pH and capacity to support vegetation can be found within a single tip, or between tips. In Yorkshire and Lancashire in Britain there are many acid spoil tips, whereas in the Forest of Dean and South Wales spoil tips are usually less acid. So colliery spoil cannot be regarded as a simple material.

It is the components that are present in only small amounts that have a large effect on the nature of the spoil material, particularly the minerals ankerite, siderite and pyrite. The pyrite is responsible for producing the acidity: ankerite and siderite are carbonate minerals which are able to have a somewhat similar effect to lime (calcium carbonate). If any acidity is produced on the coal tip, they can neutralise it, producing secondary minerals like gypsum ($CaSO_4$) and jarosite (a complex sulphate mineral of potas-

Chapter 8: Deep Mines

sium). But if the acidity is produced in excess, free hydrogen ions accumulate and the spoil will be very acid (pH< 3).

The rate of pyritic breakdown and the acidity produced depends not only on the amount of pyrite but also on its grain size. The smaller the grain size, the more reactive the pyrite. Therefore, if we know only the overall pyritic content of spoil material, samples with a relatively high pyritic sulphur content can produce acid at the same rate as samples with a much lower pyritic content (Figure 8.3). However, if the pyritic sulphur content is multiplied by the percentage of reactive pyrite then something like the right prediction for acid production can be gained. Unfortunately it is time-consuming to carry out tests to show the form of the pyrite in spoil and thus predictions of the potential of spoil samples for acid formation are difficult to arrive at.

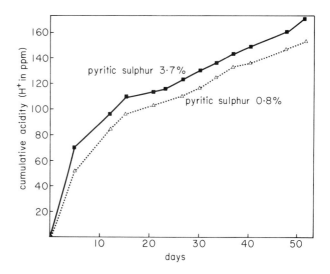

Figure 8.3. Similar acid production can occur in colliery spoils with different pyritic sulphur contents because of difference in form of the pyrite: acid production from contrasting samples of spoil.

Water and oxygen will affect the surface layers of spoil heaps first; it is here that acidity develops most strongly (Figure 8.4). This acidity is toxic in itself but also has detrimental effects on the spoil material which render it more inhospitable as a rooting medium. The cation exchange capacity of the material drops and it is able to hold less of

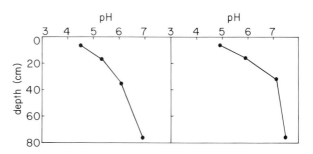

Figure 8.4. Colliery spoil can oxidise rapidly at the surface to produce a very acid substrate for plants: pH profiles of two colliery spoil tips.

127

Colliery Spoil

the beneficial ions against leaching. At the same time the clay minerals become degraded and some of their constituents, in particular aluminium, come into solution: even at very low concentrations, aluminium in solution is extremely toxic to plants. Under acid conditions the mineral ankerite releases manganese in solution: this again is toxic to plants in low concentrations.

Colliery spoil from different sites can be very different (Figure 8.5). Burnt spoil (e.g., Woolley) has usually lost much of its aluminium and manganese content and is not particularly toxic (although changes due to heat can make it physically difficult for plant growth). Spoils low in pyrite will usually lack toxicity (e.g., Hound Hill).

But all colliery spoils inevitably lack reasonable amounts of the major plant nutrients, nitrogen and phosphorus.

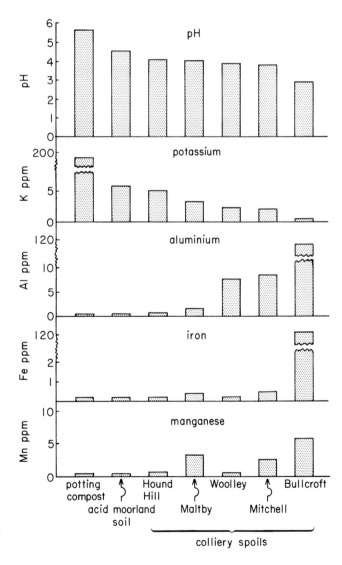

Figure 8.5. Colliery spoil suffers from acidity, lack of nutrients and high levels of potentially toxic elements: values for a range of colliery spoils.

This was demonstrated very simply in an experiment on spoil in Yorkshire (Table 8.3). The spoil was limed to correct the acidity. Then the area was split up and different fertiliser treatments applied. Two grass swards were sown—one of red fescue (*Festuca rubra*) and bent grass (*Agrostis tenuis*) and the other with perennial ryegrass (*Lolium perenne*). The plots receiving complete fertiliser outyielded the others and although the absence of potassium brought about a reduction in yield, this was not so great an effect as the absence of nitrogen or phosphorus. It is evident that in the species requiring high fertility, ryegrass, lack of phosphorus gave the biggest yield reduction. In the sward mixture containing the two less demanding species, red fescue and bent grass, lack of nitrogen or lack of phosphorus caused similar yield reductions.

Table 8.3. Phosphorus, nitrogen and potassium can all be important deficiencies in coal waste: yield of grass species given different fertiliser treatments on colliery spoil at Newmarket Silkstone, Yorkshire (in kg/ha)

grass mixtures		Fertiliser treatment (kg/ha)			
		no nitrogen	no phosphorus	no potassium	complete
	N	0	75	75	75
	P	50	0	50	50
	K	100	100	0	100
red fescue (*festuca rubra*) and bent grass (*Agrostis tenuis*)		222	229	560	920
perennial ryegrass (*Lolium perenne*)		363	179	996	2463

Some freshly deposited spoils show salinity problems due to a high content of water-soluble salts originating from groundwater. But salinity can also develop on weathering by the interaction of the acid from pyrite with carbonates in the spoil. It is usually due to salts of calcium, magnesium and sodium, mostly as sulphate and chloride (Figure 8.6). Fortunately, in humid climates, sodium and chloride ions are relatively easily leached from spoil material and salinity problems are fairly short-lived; but this will not be true in arid climates.

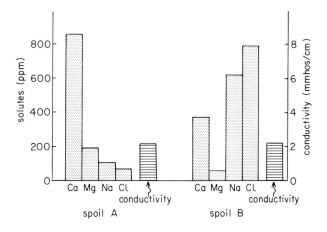

Figure 8.6. Colliery spoils with similar electrical conductivity differ in their salinity: comparison of saturation paste extracts from two colliery spoils from South Yorkshire.

Colliery Spoil

Although colliery spoil presents mainly difficulties of a chemical nature for plant growth, physical features also present complications. Particle composition may be reasonable, but lack of organic matter will lead to lack of structure. As a result, impervious surface layers may develop which reduce infiltration by rainfall so that there is lack of moisture. This can be compounded by high temperatures in the surface layers due to lack of plant cover and dark coloration. Water that does not infiltrate will run off the surface and erosion occurs, often resulting in deep gullies. This surface instability can be increased during cold periods by frost heaving. There may also have been compaction during tipping, or fusion of material when burning occurred, preventing proper root penetration.

There is one final complication—different spoil materials may vary considerably in their chemical characteristics. The variation within a single site can be as great as the variation between sites. This can result in very patchy plant establishment and growth (Figure 8.7). Vegetated patches and bare spoil can form a mosaic. When the levels of various elements in the spoil beneath vegetation and from bare patches are compared, it is discovered that vegetation fails to establish, for instance, on the spoil areas with lower pH values and low potassium status which are also the areas showing generally higher levels of toxic elements like aluminium (Table 7.2, page 111).

Figure 8.7. A patchy vegetation cover indicates variability in the spoil: here plants are colonising burnt areas which have lost their sulphur and so are less acid.

8.1.2 Permanent solutions

The first step in the establishment of vegetation must be an analysis of the material. This must give some indication of the acidity (and the likelihood of continued acid generation) and the level of major plant nutrients. Although it is not possible to make firm predictions of the future rate of acid generation from simple analytical determinations, pH and lime requirement measurements on weathered material will give some indications. In addition, spoils with relatively high pyrite and low carbonate contents are more likely to give extreme acidities than those with the reverse (Table 8.4); so these values will help to indicate long-term trends, although pH values will need to be checked during the first few years following reclamation. Since the material is so variable, the sampling must be carried out in a way which will reveal the extent of the variability. The methods have been discussed in Chapter 7.

Table 8.4. In colliery spoil acidity is related to pyrite and carbonate content: pyrite, carbonate, pH and the response of ryegrass to liming on contrasting colliery spoils

colliery	pyrite %	carbonate %	pH	response to liming
Florence	1·72	4·39	6·6	1·04
Bold	3·71	2·73	5·9	1·16
Heath	1·04	3·88	5·0	0·86
Sutton Manor	1·21	1·07	3·8	0·96
Littleton	0·58	0	2·3	2·31
Harrington	0·62	0	2·3	9·31
Silverdale	0·94	0·05	2·1	28

$$\text{response to liming} = \frac{\text{shoot dry wt. @ 20t/ha limestone}}{\text{shoot dry wt. @ 5t/ha limestone}}$$

Figure 8.8. Deep ripping of colliery spoil is essential: here the surface of the spoil has been loosened to 50 cm depth after liming to ensure that the lime is incorporated and the spoil is thoroughly open.

Restoration will begin with earth-moving to landscape the site and tidy it: drainage work will also have to be undertaken. Cultivations must then follow to relieve compaction. It may be necessary to rip to a depth of 50 cm at 40 cm spacing to ensure satisfactory infiltration of water and reasonable conditions for rooting (Figure 8.8).

Liming is carried out at this stage and incorporated to a depth of 20–50 cm by further deep ripping, shallower tining or rotovation. In highly pyritic spoil, 30–50 tonnes/ha may be required, lime being added above that required for the normally determined lime requirement. But very large amounts may fix phosphorus, accelerate loss of nitrogen and give rise to secondary growth problems affecting legumes in particular (Figure 8.9). It may be necessary to identify particularly acid spoil and bury it under less acid material during earth-moving operations. Alternatively, the spoil can be spread over a wider area, from which the

Figure 8.9. Liming is essential on acid spoils but excess may upset clover growth: but this effect is temporary and it is important to control long-term development of acidity.

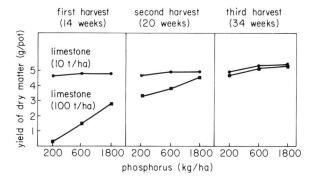

Colliery Spoil

soil has been removed, and then covered with this top soil (Figure 6.6, page 79).

Further cultivation must follow to obtain an adequate seed bed and it may be necessary to remove larger stones by hand. Tining to 20 cm followed by harrowing and light rolling are normally practised. Nitrogen and phosphorus fertiliser applications are phased in with these operations, as well as sowing the seeds mixture.

In spite of the fact that colliery spoil contains low-grade coal, fossil organic material, which contains appreciable amounts of nitrogen, little or none of this becomes available for plant growth on the tips, and so it must be added. Acid conditions do not favour the microorganisms that convert ammonium forms of nitrogen to nitrite and nitrate (*Nitrosomonas* and *Nitrobacter*) and thus nitrogen remains in the ammonium form. Less acid conditions favour the conversion from ammonium-nitrogen to nitrate. But nitrate is more mobile and more easily leached out of spoil and so is lost more readily than ammonium-nitrogen. This can be seen in two contrasting spoils to which nitrogen in the ammonium form was added with or without lime (Figure 8.10).

This work indicates not only the possible solution for upgrading spoil as a medium for plant growth, but also the dilemma posed by amelioration techniques. Raise the pH

Figure 8.10. Acid colliery spoil has a store of nitrogen not found in neutral spoil where ammonium-nitrogen is converted to nitrate and lost by leaching: neutral and acid colliery spoil incubated with various additions.

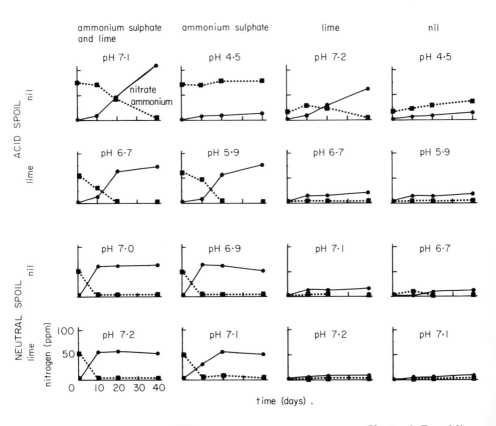

time (days) .

too high and the nitrogen (both natural or added as fertiliser) will be converted to the nitrate form and may be lost through leaching or run-off. Spoils must be adequately limed but it may be necessary to use top dressings of nitrogen as well as other fertilisers. It is wasteful to add excessive nitrogen initially, more than about 100 kg/ha, and better to add further nitrogen once the plants are established, when they can take up the nitrogen directly.

With phosphate the problem is really the reverse: in colliery spoils, added phosphorus rapidly becomes unavailable. When the pH is below 4·5, phosphorus is virtually completely unavailable. Even in spoils not at such a low pH, much of it is lost by absorption and fixation. This is why, when analytical determinations of spoil phosphorus status are to be made, both the phosphorus reserve (the capacity or total labile phosphorus) and the phosphate sorption capacity must be determined. If appropriate methods of determining P-status are used, good agreement can be obtained between levels of phosphorus additions that need to be made to spoil and levels of plant response (Table 8.5).

Table 8.5. Response to phosphate fertiliser is determined by the nature of the spoil: yields of *Lolium perenne* and phosphorus recovery for two spoils with different additions of phosphorus (all in kg/ha)

		phosphorus levels			labile phos-phorus	phos-phorus sorbtion index
		1·5	6·0	24·0		
Spoil A	yield	186	667	1927	0·9	33·3
	P recovered	0·33	1·23	3·20		
Spoil B	yield	2096	2463	2746	12·1	17·2
	P recovered	3·39	4·07	4·42		

Figure 8.11. A well-balanced sward of ryegrass and white clover on acid colliery spoil in Lancashire: very heavy dressings of lime (50 t/ha) and fertiliser (200 kg P/ha) were used to ensure satisfactory growth.

Fertiliser and lime requirements depend on the species being sown. Acid-tolerant, low-nutrient-requiring species such as wavy hair grass (*Deschampsia flexuosa*) can grow well on acid spoil with fertiliser and little or no lime, whereas ryegrass (*Lolium perenne*) requires both. Unfortunately, wavy hair grass is unpalatable and valueless for grazing, so ryegrass and similar demanding species have to be used where agriculture is intended.

Legumes are an essential ingredient because of their capacity to fix nitrogen. In the first season they may contribute little but in subsequent seasons a well-balanced sward (Figure 8.11) can contribute well over 100 kg N/ha, equal to a very heavy fertiliser dressing. But the most valuable legumes, particularly white clover (*Trifolium repens*), requires high levels of available phosphorus which may be difficult to provide when heavy liming is required (Figure 8.9). It may be better to use other legumes such as bird's foot trefoil (*Lotus corniculatus*) which are more tolerant of poor acid conditions, or species such as crown vetch

133

Colliery Spoil

(*Coronilla varia*) which has been used with great success in the USA. Certainly without legumes, swards established on colliery spoil quickly deteriorate, unless they are continually fertilised.

Trees are often incorporated into colliery spoil reclamation schemes (Figure 2.2, page 13). They can be established on steeper slopes, perform a screening function and mask angular shapes, act as shelter belts, and be planted for wood production. Tree species show less clear-cut responses to surface additions of fertiliser as these encourage the growth of grass, clover and other herbage species. This gives rise to competition for both nutrients and water with a consequent decrease in survival and growth of the tree species, particularly those not adapted to difficult soil conditions (Figure 8.12). This can create problems with tree-planting schemes as it is often necessary to establish a grass sward beneath trees to give some measure of erosion control. It can be minimised by the correct choice of tree species and the use of grass mixture of non-competitive species sown at a low density.

The addition of fertiliser can bring about an amelioration of nutrient deficiencies. However, loss through leaching and fixation of nutrients in an unavailable form may mean

Figure 8.12. Tree growth on colliery spoil is reduced if a grass cover is established at the same time as tree planting: the effect of grass on tree height on colliery spoil in West Yorkshire.

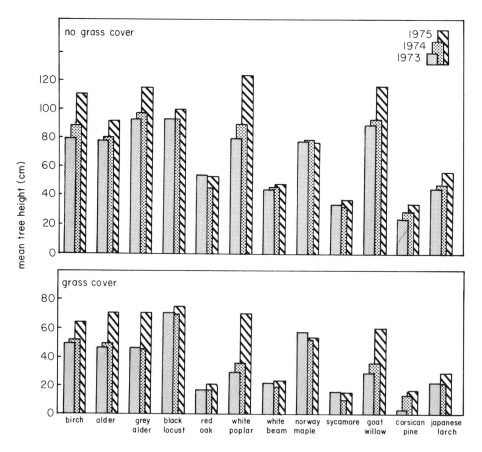

that their effects are only short-lived. In the early stages either fertiliser must be added frequently or an amendment employed that releases nutrients over an extended period of time. This has led to the suggestion that organic materials, often waste products, should be added to spoil. But many of these have proved disappointing because they have rather high ratios of carbon to nitrogen. Micro-organisms in the spoil utilise the carbon as an energy source but in doing so utilise and lock up nutrients that are also released from the organic material.

Salinity problems will usually disappear as a result of natural leaching which will be encouraged by cultivations. However, in more arid regions, salinity problems can be troublesome. It can sometimes be overcome by furrow grading which concentrates the rain in the furrows and permits sufficient leaching for satisfactory growth.

Aftercare will be essential. What is necessary is best tested by direct experiments. These show that on colliery spoil, apart from liming, there is an almost universal need for nitrogen (Figure 8.13).

Figure 8.13. Apart from liming, one of the most common aftercare needs on colliery spoil is nitrogen: the results of an aftercare fertiliser experiment on established grass sward in Lancashire.

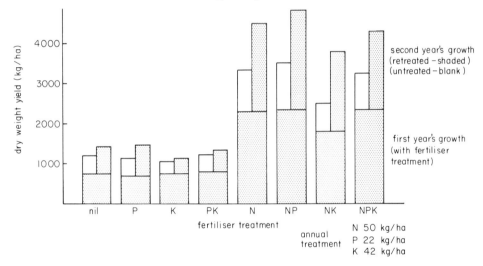

This can possibly be provided by the use of fertilisers that release nitrogen slowly over a period of time, maintaining growth over extended periods (see Table 6.4, page 92). Their effects can be measured by looking at the amount of regrowth of grass swards following an initial

Table 8.6. Form of nitrogen can be crucial: regrowth over two years after initial cutting of grass swards following application of 250 kg/ha of nitrogen to colliery spoil in different forms or sowing clover

fertiliser	yield (kg/ha)
IBDU (s.r.)	1091
$(NH_4)_2SO_4$	804
Gold N (s.r.)	800
$Ca(NO_3)$	714
Chiguano (s.r.)	324
White clover	100

s.r.—slow release fertiliser

Colliery Spoil

cut (Table 8.6). However, all slow-release fertilisers are very expensive. It can be seen that in the early stages, nitrogen had not begun to be supplied by clover (*Trifolium repens*) in significant amounts; but in the end it, or an equivalent legume, should be the cheapest and most effective means of supplying nitrogen. After longer periods of time, nutrients accumulate very well in the surface layers and a self-sustaining system is produced (Figure 8.14).

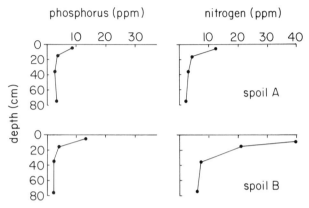

Figure 8.14. In good restoration, nutrients build up in the rooting zone due to continued fertilisation and the activities of plants: nitrogen and phosphorus profiles from two colliery spoil sites.

The performance of tree species can often be gauged by fairly simple chemical analysis of their leaves. The results of a comparison of similar leaves from birch trees (*Betula pendula*) growing on natural acid soils and spoil sites, for instance, revealed that the trees had elevated levels of iron, aluminium and manganese on spoil sites (Table 8.7). This was correlated with reduced leaf area and weight and indicated the need for liming.

Table 8.7. Accumulation in leaves can mirror spoil chemistry: concentration of elements in leaves of silver birch from heathland and two colliery spoil tips

	concentration (ppm dry tissue)		
site	Mn	Al	Fe
heathland	348	255	171
colliery spoil—Mitchell	737	312	374
—Maltby	1348	377	370

8.2   GOLD

8.2.1   Sand heaps and slimes dams

The gold-mining industry of South Africa on the Witwatersrand is based on the 'reef', a gold-bearing quartzite intrusion which stretches for a hundred kilometres, and carries gold to a great depth. Much of the mining is now carried on at a depth of 2000 m (over 1 mile). The rock which contains gold (not more than a few gm/tonne) is crushed finely and the minute quantities of gold extracted. The vast quantities of waste from the extraction are dumped at the surface.

Chapter 8: Deep Mines

Figure 8.15. The bright yellowish slimes dams which surround Johannesburg are a key to the wealth of the city: but they are a troublesome source of dust and silt.

In 80 years' life the gold mines have produced more than 8000 ha of waste, made up of 1200 ha of older sand dumps and 6800 ha of more recent slimes dams (Figure 8.15). Johannesburg grew up around the mines and the dumps and for many years it was the dumps which dominated the city, not just because of their conspicuous shape and yellow colour, but because they were a perpetual source of pollution. No plants would grow on them and every wind would lift off fine dust, stopping factories processing food from working on windy days and holding up traffic on main roads because of poor visibility. At the same time, rivers silted up and more than one lake was completely obliterated. In the early days the growing dumps signified the wealth of the city, but later on the inhabitants have come to realise these dumps have other attributes.

The dumps are made of quartzite, 95 per cent silica. The sand produced by the earlier, coarser crushing is in the coarse sand range: the slimes now produced are ten times finer. The processing leaves some cyanide in the waste but this decomposes in two months. What is more important is the complete lack of plant nutrients and the high pyrites content, 1·5–3·5 per cent FeS_2 (Table 8.8).

When initially deposited, the waste is alkaline (pH > 10), but this drops over a period of a few months to between 2 and 4 as the pyrite becomes oxidised. The material is unstable and very dry, at least on the surface in the dry season. With the acidity and the lack of nutrients it is scarcely surprising that there is very little vegetation. However, as the pyrite becomes completely oxidised and the resulting acid is leached away, the pH recovers, and there is a very gradual development of a vegetation, at least on the top of the heaps, which is tolerant to the acidity, exposure and low-nutrient conditions. The only other areas where vegetation is to be found are where soil and refuse has been deposited.

Table 8.8. Gold wastes are low in nutrients and high in pyrite: typical analysis of the material forming slimes dams produced by gold mining in South Africa

particle analysis (%)		> 0·2 m	0
		0·2–0·02	50
		0·02–0·002	30
		< 0·002	20
chemical analysis	pH		2·5–3·1
	P		13
	K	available	15
	Mg	(ppm)	110
	Ca		1400
	S	total (%)	0·2–0·4
	N		0·02

8.2.2 Establishment of a vegetative cover

The greatest problem to be overcome is the acidity caused by pyrite. This was found to require the addition of 1 tonne/ha of lime for every 2000 ppm of acidity or pyrite (measured in terms of H_2SO_4) to neutralise it. To begin with, therefore, heavy dressings of lime were used. However, these were not always effective and acidity returned in many areas because of an excessive pyrite content of the waste. But it was apparent that natural oxidation and leaching processes could cause the slow disappearance of the pyrite. This provided in the 1950s the key to the technique that has now been adopted.

Pyrite and acidity are leached out of the root zone by the application of water as a fine mist from a network of overhead pipes (Figure 8.16). During leaching, the acid water may move down through the waste material at a rate of 5

Figure 8.16. The key to the establishment of vegetation cover on gold mine waste in S. Africa is the removal of pyrite by leaching: the acidity is quickly washed downwards.

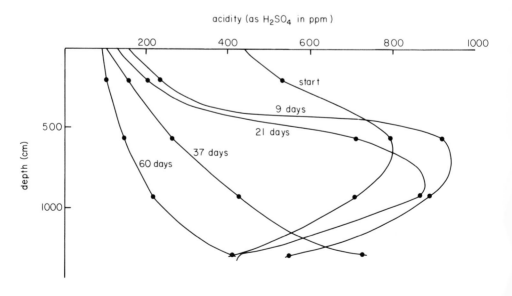

Chapter 8: Deep Mines

cm/day. If the leaching is stopped, there can be an upward rise of 1 cm/day. The leaching is therefore controlled so that the downward movement of water is continuous until the pyrite has been reduced to about 2000 ppm (measured in terms of H_2SO_4) at the surface, and the bulk of the acid has been leached down at least 3 m below the surface. This may take many months. The input of water for leaching is matched to the permeability of the slimes material.

On the slimes dams, the leaching process overcomes the two problems of drought and erosion by wind. But on the sand dumps, the material is so loose and so liable to wind erosion that it is necessary to erect temporary wind breaks of reed (*Phragmites australis*) stems 70 cm high (Figure 8.17). The sides of the slimes dams have their own particular problems; they may have become so encrusted with salts that the surface has to be broken by hand to allow the leaching to take place.

Figure 8.17. Sand waste heaps are liable to erosion by wind: fences of reed are erected by hand before grass is sown: the method is expensive but effective.

Lime is added to bring the pH to 6·5, the amount depending on the pyrite and acidity concentration. If the initial pH is greater than 3·5 and the total acidity and pyrite measured as H_2SO_4 is less than 3000 ppm, long-term leaching is not necessary. Otherwise leaching may continue for several months. A general-purpose grass mixture is sown, including various temperate grasses, perennial veldt grass (*Ehrharta calycina*) and weeping lovegrass (*Eragrostis curvula*), and some legumes, particularly alfalfa (*Medicago sativa*). Runners of kikuyu grass (*Pennisetum clandestinum*) and star grass (*Cynodon plectostachys*) are planted by hand against the wind breaks. General fertiliser giving about 20 kg/ha N, P and K is applied at seeding: subsequently, further dressings, of nitrogen in particular, are given. There is no obvious need for applications of micronutrients.

Figure 8.18. Leaching, by overhead sprays, is carried out while the grass is establishing: it irrigates the grass at the same time as it leaches the pyrite.

The result has been remarkable (Figure 8.18): there is immediate cover and when the irrigation is removed the vegetation settles down to a sward dominated by *Eragrostis* and *Ehrharta*. Some direct seeding of *Acacia baileyana* and *A. melanoxylon* has been attempted: it is usually unsuccessful, but where it does succeed, a good bush cover develops.

The method is very expensive and rather dependent on low labour costs. But it is an effective solution to a difficult problem. The shape of the heaps is not disguised, and leads to some of the high costs. It has been suggested that slimes dams should be constructed with sides at a slope of 18° instead of the present 30–45°. This would not only make the dams more aesthetically attractive, but it would also allow the use of agricultural machinery on the walls. It would, surprisingly, allow a greater dam height and the storage of more, not less, material.

There are some signs of regression after five years. This does not occur where legumes, particularly the alfalfa, persist in the sward: this suggests nitrogen shortage. In reclamation of similar mine wastes at the old Hollinger Mine, Ontario, bird's foot trefoil (*Lotus corniculatus*) has been very successful. There is a need to examine the processes of nutrient accumulation on the slimes dams, especially since small amounts of plant nutrients were added in the first place, followed by substantial leaching. The levels of nutrients need to be maintained more carefully, especially calcium and phosphorus, to ensure the legumes do not die out, or species must be chosen which are more tolerant of low nutrients.

Chapter 8: Deep Mines

8.3 HEAVY METALS

8.3.1 Serious ecological problems

It is difficult to imagine how the world could do without metals such as copper, lead and zinc. They play a critical part in modern society. Yet these and other heavy metals are the cause of some of the most difficult reclamation problems.

The early miners worked on a very small scale, usually with rich underground veins. As these deposits became exhausted, they worked lower-grade material and erected water-powered machinery to grind and concentrate the ore. The machinery was very crude and the tailings, the waste left after concentration, sometimes contained as much as 10 per cent metal. At the same time, quantities of waste rock were often produced, from the surrounding unmineralised rocks, and also from the vein itself.

Modern flotation techniques have reduced the concentration of metal left behind in tailings to as little as 0·1 per cent. This has meant that it is worth while mining rocks containing low metal levels (0·5 per cent) in areas where there is diffuse mineralisation. The result has been the development of mining on a scale which a century ago would have been inconceivable. The copper mine on the island of Bougainville in Papua, New Guinea, is more than 1 km across after five years' activity and produces about 85 000 tonnes of waste rock and 80 000 tonnes of tailings per day (Figure 8.19): at Magna, Utah, the tailings are deposited in a pond which is 20 km² in extent and rises 6 m per year. In an area with a longer mining history, the copper-rich zone south of Tucson, Arizona, $2·5 \times 10^9$ tonnes of waste rock have already been accumulated, and one million tonnes are added every day.

Strictly speaking, these new mines are not 'deep' mines, but they have the same problems. They produce the same

Figure 8.19. Modern metal mines produce enormous quantities of tailings: on Bougainville they fill the valley of the Jaba river and flow out to sea but are not sufficiently toxic to restrict vegetation.

Heavy Metals

dumps of waste rock and tailings ponds, as well as the deep pit. The heights of the two former are less than the depth of the pit and so together occupy considerably more land than the pit (Figure 8.20). The waste materials cannot usually be put back into the pit because they would prevent access to ores lying at a greater depth. However, in some new operations which have been planned to work progressively, for instance Mt. Gunson in south Australia, the waste rock is being returned behind the advancing front of the pit. This reduces the area of destruction enormously, but the tailings still have to be deposited in a separate area. A modern underground mine, such as Mount Isa, has no open pit and may produce no waste rock. About half the tailings is returned underground: but even so, the rest of the tailings have to be disposed of in great ponds.

Figure 8.20. An aerial view of modern open pit mining in Pima Co., Arizona: the terraced pit complex is in the top centre surrounded by pale dumps of waste rock and dark tailings ponds. Width of photograph covers 16 km (10 miles) approx.

It is, however, the metals remaining in the wastes which are the major problem of old and modern mining operations because many of them are toxic to plants, animals and human beings (Table 8.9).

When mining operations were crude, the water used was discarded into local streams and the tailings were deposited in unprotected heaps. As a result, whole river systems were wrecked, often in agricultural areas of outstanding beauty, such as the Rheidol and Ystwyth river valleys in Wales. This was a threat to farming during the period of operation and also later, because stock could ingest mud containing high levels of lead and zinc. In mid-Wales, metals can still be detected in the agricultural

142   *Chapter 8: Deep Mines*

Figure 8.21. The waste heaps of Captain's Flat mine in New South Wales polluted many miles of the Molonglo River above Canberra: note the overflowing catch ponds when the photograph was taken.

soils downstream and part of the Ystwyth is still devoid of fish. At Captain's Flat in New South Wales, Australia, the heaps of tailings from a lead/zinc mine were a constant threat to the whole river system above Canberra until measures were taken recently to stabilise them (Figure 8.21).

Some metals, notably zinc, are fairly soluble in water. These will disperse in drainage water even when there is

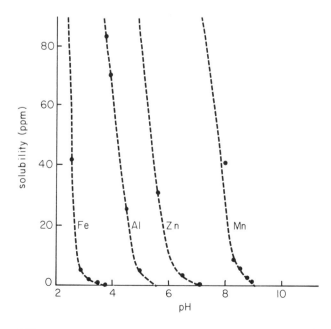

Figure 8.22. Solubilities of heavy metals at different pH: all are more soluble in acid conditions; nevertheless, in alkaline soils they can still be toxic.

143

Heavy Metals

Table 8.9. The common heavy metals are toxic to living organisms even at low concentrations: properties of the more environmentally important metals

	Cu	Zn	Pb
common weathering product of common mineral	sulphate	sulphate	sulphate
solubility of sulphate[1]	320	960	0·04
toxicity in solution to plants[2]	0·02	1·3	1·7
toxicity in solution to fish[3]	0·02	1·3	1·7
maximum concentration in drinking water[4]	1·5	15	0·1
maximum concentration in water for farm animals[5]	0·5	25	0·1
maximum concentration in irrigation water[5]	0·2	2·0	5·0

values in ppm
[1] or common weathering product if different
[2] concentration reducing growth (of roots of *Lolium perenne*) to 50%: will vary with species
[3] concentration reducing survival of rainbow trout (*Salmo gairdneri*) to 50% after 48 hrs (concentrations permitting long term survival and reproduction may be 10% of these values)
[4] WHO (1971) recommendations
[5] Environmental Protection Agency, USA (1972) Water Quality Criteria recommendations under natural conditions toxicities can be reduced by several factors, notably by the presence of calcium, phosphates, carbonates, hydroxides, organic matter and clay minerals.

Table 8.10. The effects of effluent from a heavy metal/ pyrites mine on the neighbouring river: pH and metal concentration (ppm) in the Bremer River above and below the Brukunga pyrites mine, S.Australia,

no movement of solid matter. For most metals, solubility is increased by acid conditions (Figure 8.22). Sulphide minerals are more rapidly oxidised in the presence of ferric sulphate. So pyrite-rich metalliferous wastes can be a very serious source of acid drainage water containing metals in solution (Table 8.10). The long-disused acid lead/zinc mine

	upstream 20 km	downstream 0·5 km	3 km	10 km	16 km	20 km	permissible levels
pH	7·9	3·4	3·3	3·45	6·4	7·35	4·8
Fe	1	35	40	5	< 0·3	< 0·3	–
Al	< 1	96	115	53	< 1	< 1	1·0
Mn	< 0·1	11	12	8·5	1·9	1·4	2·0
Ni	< 0·1	0·5	0·8	0·4	< 0·1	< 0·1	0·5
Cd	< 0·005	0·09	0·11	0·045	0·015	0·005	0·005
Zn	0·1	12·5	15	8	1·2	0·5	5·0
Cu	< 0·1	0·3	0·3	0·2	< 0·1	< 0·1	0·2
Co	< 0·1	0·3	0·5	0·3	< 0·1	< 0·1	0·2

permissible levels are from Australian Water Resources Council for water used continuously on all soils

Cd	Cr⁶⁺	Ni	Fe	Mn	Al	Hg
sulphate	oxide insol.	sulphate	sulphate hydroxide	hydroxide	hydroxide insol.	oxide
755		630	4400	0·002		0·053
2·1	3·8	0·18	9·3	0·05	0·93	6·6
2·1	120	30	250	100	1·5	0·02
0·01	0·05	–	1·0	0·5	–	0·001
0·05	1·0	–	–	–	5	0·01
0·01	0·1	0·2	5·0	0·2	5·0	–

at Cwm Ystwyth still discharges 35 tonnes of zinc in solution into the very small river every year.

Metalliferous wastes are also a cause of pollution by wind blow because they are finely ground. The physical aspects are unpleasant: mine wastes are coarser and more abrasive than normal dusts and can affect not only people but also machinery. The dust problems endured at Broken Hill, Australia, during the first fifty years, are almost legendary. But the metals contained in dust can be more serious. Not only is the surrounding land contaminated so that plants absorb metals from the soil, but the dust that falls on leaf surfaces can be ingested by stock directly (Figures 8.23 and 1.4, page 8).

Figure 8.23. Distribution of zinc around an old lead/zinc mine at Cwm Ystwyth, Wales: zinc in the soils has mainly moved down the valley carried by water but zinc held on plants has moved up the valley carried by wind.

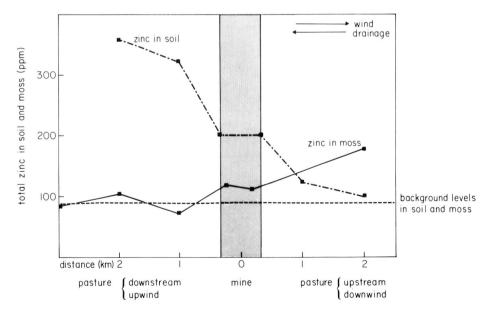

Heavy Metals

There are many different metals which can occur together. In the past, extraction may have been for one metal, such as lead, so that another metal, such as zinc, occurring in the ore at a considerably lower concentration, may end up with the highest concentration in the waste. Independently, pyrite may be present in abundance. At the same time, many different minerals (gangue materials) may be associated with the ore, calcareous minerals such as calcite, or inert, such as quartzite. There may also be a proportion of the surrounding (country) rocks.

As a result, it is difficult to generalise about metalliferous wastes, either in relation to their metal content, or in relation to the associated substances which will not only determine the amount of plant nutrients but also the availability of the metals. These must be analysed with great care. The sort of complete analyses that are necessary are given in Table 8.11. A full spectrographic analysis may

Table 8.11. Mine wastes have to be analysed carefully before their ability to support plant growth can be predicted: the characteristics of three calcareous lead/zinc tailings in Britain

	Trelogan	Parc	Cavendish
particle analysis (%)			
> 2 mm	6·7	0	0
2–0·2	14·6	52·4	1·0
0·2–0·2	29·7	17·8	53·3
0·02–0·002	24·8	12·8	30·4
< 0·002	24·2	17·0	16·3
chemical analysis (ppm) total (available in brackets)			
N	126 (2·4)	58 (6·7)	33 (7·0)
P	160 (0·3)	128 (0·9)	79 (2·6)
K	1070 (275)	688 (242)	1080 (242)
Mg	1500 (48)	1000 (68)	3800 (95)
Ca	138500	68800	119800
Pb	39800 (16200)	1300 (220)	6330 (1010)
Zn	95000 (35665)	2030 (390)	2020 (320)
Cd	267 (40)	93 (12)	11 (1·2)
Ni	87 (6)	49 (4)	30 (12)
Cu	205 (71)	188 (49)	32 (4·1)
F	185	395	174200 (5·1)
other characteristics			
pH	7·0	7·3	7·6
CEC (mEq/100 g)	2·8	3·9	3·4
conductivity (μ mhos/cm)	2280	3480	2520

Trelogan is very high in lead and zinc and is very toxic to plants: Parc and Cavendish, which are more recent, are less high in lead and zinc and because of the high pH are not very toxic to plants; but the high levels of fluoride in Cavendish together with the lead and zinc would give levels in established vegetation in all three sites high enough to cause problems for grazing animals: in all wastes nitrogen and phosphorus are very low but there are no problems from soil texture, acidity or salinity.

be necessary to ensure that no metals are missed and sulphide and carbonate determined if salinity is expected.

Physically, waste rock and tailings are opposites. Waste rock is a complex mixture of coarse pieces mostly more than 5 cm across. Tailings have been milled to a standard maximum particle size usually less than 2 mm. As a result, the physical characteristics of tailings are usually satisfactory for plant growth: there will usually be good water retention (see Figure 7.3, page 112) but liability to erosion by wind and water. Waste rock will be stable, but, unless there is a high proportion of fine material, it will be extremely permeable and dry.

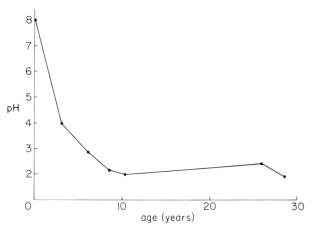

Figure 8.24. Tailings, containing pyrite, release acid on weathering: these copper tailings at Hurley, New Mexico, contain little calcareous material and so have become extremely acid.

Both materials are equally deficient in essential elements, especially nitrogen and phosphorus. There may or may not be deficiencies of other nutrients. But the critical problem will be the metal content. Although little of the metal will be exposed on the particle surfaces, weathering will allow it to be released slowly. In general terms, there usually has to be about 1000 ppm (0·1 per cent) of any metal in a waste for it to be toxic to plants. Metal availability depends on rate of weathering, pH and the presence of various cations and anions. But nearly all old wastes, as well as some newer wastes, contain toxic amounts of metal. Waste rock will usually contain higher levels of metal and be more toxic than tailings, since the cut-off point for metal content, below which it is uneconomic to process ore-bearing material, is always higher than the level of metal remaining in the tailings after extraction.

If there is pyrite, it will weather and oxidise to give ferric sulphate and sulphuric acid. This oxidation can be a very rapid process: the pH may be above neutral to begin with and, as at Magna, Utah, drop within a few months to pH 4 or less. But it can also be much slower (Figure 8.24). If carbonates are present, the acid will be neutralised, but a high level of soluble salts will be produced. In dry climates, evaporation will concentrate these at the surface as a saline crust, as at Mount Isa (Figure 8.25).

Figure 8.25. If tailings contain both pyrite and calcareous material, these can react to give large quantities of salts: in the dry climate of Mount Isa, Queensland, these accumulate on the surface and prevent vegetation establishment.

Heavy Metals

As a result, many metalliferous wastes are impossible for plant growth and have remained bare and liable to erosion for many years. However, on some older mine wastes, plants can be found, including some species which are rarely found on normal soils, such as the violet (*Viola calaminaria*) and alpine pennycress (*Thlaspi alpestre*). They were sometimes used as indicators of the presence of metals. There is a limited number of these species, metallophytes, which can grown on metalliferous soils (Table 8.12). On any site, the species occurring are determined not only by the presence of the metals but also the pH and calcium content of the waste and other factors such as climate.

Table 8.12. Metal contaminated areas have a characteristic native flora: examples of metallophytes from temperate and tropical regions

temperate	tropical
Agrostis stolonifera	Andropogon gayanus
Agrostis tenuis	Becium homblei
Anthoxanthum odoratum	Celozia trigyna
Armeria maritima	Combretum molle
Festuca rubra	Cynodon dactylon
Festuca ovina	Dicoma macrocephala
Holcus lanatus	Eragrostis racemosa
Mimulus guttatus	Fimbristylis exilis
Minuartia verna	Gomphrena canescens
Plantago lanceolata	Pogonarthria squarrosa
Silene vulgaris	Polycarpea glabra
Thlaspi alpestre	Tephrosia longipes

When these species have been examined carefully, a surprising fact has emerged; populations taken from a particular mine waste possess the ability to grow on the waste but populations of the same species found growing on ordinary soils do not possess this ability: if the latter are planted on mine waste, they die very quickly. It appears that the species found on mine waste have evolved metal-tolerant populations. When grown in soil or solution containing heavy metals, these populations continue root growth whereas the non-tolerant populations do not (Figure 8.26). The tolerance is more or less specific for individual metals, so that, for instance, a population of bent grass (*Agrostis tenuis*) from a copper mine will grow on waste containing copper but not on one containing lead and zinc, and vice versa.

However, the possession of metal tolerance by a plant is not enough to ensure it will be able to grow on a metal-containing waste. It will also depend on there being sufficient nutrients for plant growth, especially nitrogen and phosphorus. So plants are only found growing on the more fertile parts of mine wastes, and where there is adequate stability and moisture.

Figure 8.26. Metal tolerance in bent grass, shown by ability to root in solution containing 0·5 ppm copper: left—plants from the old Parys copper mine in N. Wales: right—plants from a normal pasture.

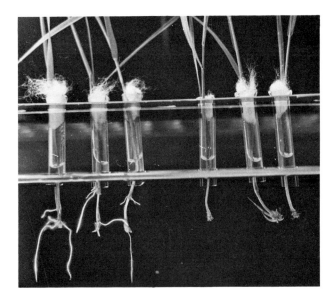

8.3.2 Physical and chemical treatment

Since metalliferous wastes are variable and restoration requirements diverse, there are several different approaches, each of which has its own advantages and disadvantages.

Since waste rock, gravel and sand are in demand for hard core and similar uses, this is one good way of getting rid of metalliferous wastes. But care must be taken because of the pollution problems which may arise. Farm tracks were surfaced with waste rock around the large old copper mine at Parys Mountain in the days before anything was known about metal pollution. An even less sensible use has been tailings as gritting material for frosty roads.

But the products of modern, large-scale operations produce far more material than can possibly be disposed of; and much of the material is too finely ground for many purposes. It must be stabilised where it is. Physical methods in which tailings are covered with materials such as crushed rock or granulated smelter slag have been widely used. These are effective, but they are expensive and may be impossible to apply to tailings which are soft. Chemical methods are an alternative. There is a wide range of materials (Table 6.3, pages 90–1) which can provide a temporary stabilisation. However, none of them offer a permanent solution. They are most valuable to fix the surface of one part of a tailings disposal area while another is being actively used.

None of these methods, of course, restore the land biologically or visually, so they must all be considered temporary solutions.

149   *Heavy Metals*

8.3.3 Direct seeding

Concentration of toxic metals in tailings may now be down to 0·1 per cent. At this level metal toxicity is unlikely, although it will depend on all the factors affecting availability, and the particular toxic metals involved. Waste rock may also not be toxic.

On these sites, providing there are no acidity or salinity problems, it is possible to establish a vegetation cover merely by the addition of fertilisers (400–800 kg/ha of a high-phosphate complete fertiliser) to supply the deficient plant nutrients and by sowing normal agricultural varieties of grasses and legumes. Liming should be carried out if the pH is below 5·5: it will relieve the acidity and render any metals less available. Growth is helped by addition of organic matter and higher amounts of phosphate than normal: these will provide essential nutrients and will again render some of the metals unavailable. Either normal agricultural sowing techniques or hydroseeding can be used. Some excellent examples of direct seeding are available, on nickel tailings at Sudbury, Canada, on lead/zinc wastes at Tynagh, Eire and on lead/zinc fluorspar tailings at Eyam, Derbyshire, U.K. (Figure 8.27).

Legumes must be included, for without them a continuous supply of nitrogen will not be provided. But they are more sensitive to heavy-metal toxicity than grasses (Figure

Figure 8.27. Calcareous tailings in Derbyshire containing lead and zinc, successfully treated by direct seeding: but since the vegetation contains lead, zinc and fluoride, the sheep may only graze for short periods.

Chapter 8: Deep Mines

8.28). Nevertheless, successful establishment of legumes has been achieved at Tynagh, Eyam and elsewhere and nitrogen fixation is known to be occurring.

Metal levels in the established plants should be checked if grazing is intended. Sufficient metal may get into the herbage to preclude use by grazing animals except on an intermittent basis. Under these conditions, it may be better to establish a tree or shrub cover. On copper tailings in an

Figure 8.28. Growth of white clover and ryegrass in sand to which metals have been added: legumes are more sensitive than grasses to heavy metals but the metals are different in their effects.

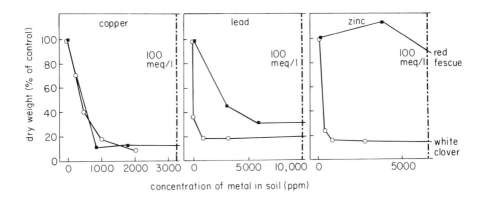

arid region at Tucson, Arizona, a mixture of grasses, such as lovegrass (*Eragrostis curvula*) and bermuda grass (*Cynodon dactylon*), with shrubs such as saltbrush (*Atriplex* spp.), creosote brush (*Larrea tridentata*), hopseed brush (*Dodonaea viscosa*), red gum (*Eucalyptus camaldulensis* ≡ *rostrata*) and *Acacia*, have done well, hydroseeded with processed animal manure slurry (Figure 8.29). This work shows that after the initial establishment phase, drought need not be a problem on tailings even in arid regions. Natural colonisation by shrubs can occur if appropriate seed parents are nearby, as at Broken Hill, Australia.

There are many sites in which the concentrations of metal or salt are sufficiently high to prevent the growth of normal plants. On these sites, plants, particularly grasses which have tolerant populations, can be established very successfully (Figure 8.30). Once nitrogen and phosphorus have been added, growth of tolerant material is as good as would occur on a normal site. The tolerant material roots deeply into the wastes and escapes the effects of surface drought. Some tolerant material is, anyway, more drought-resistant and tolerant of low-nutrient conditions than normal material.

Since metal tolerance is rather specific, material has to be found whose tolerance matches the toxicity of the site. Varieties tolerant to lead and zinc together have been produced, Merlin red fescue (*Festuca rubra*) and Goginan bent grass (*Agrostis tenuis*), adapted to temperate climates. Metal tolerance occurs in tropical and sub-tropical species, and in the next few years it is likely that we shall see the development of further metal-tolerant varieties.

Figure 8.29. Re-establishment of native species on a copper tailings dam at Cyprus Pima mine in Arizona: stabilisation involved spraying with an organic mulch fertiliser and native grasses and shrubs, followed by planting on trees and native succulents.

Problems of salinity can be overcome by the choice of salt-tolerant plant material. The advantage here is that there are not only salt-tolerant populations, but also salt-tolerant species that can be used, such as salt bush (*Atriplex nummularia*) and even a leguminous bush (*Acacia saligna* ≡ *cyanophylla*). Because it can fix nitrogen, *A. saligna* is capable of quite remarkable growth (Figure 6.16, page 99).

There is no reason why material should not be found which is tolerant to heavy metals and salt, such as the varieties of the grasses *Sporobolus virginicus*, *Dactyloctenium*

Figure 8.30. Metal-tolerant varieties are valuable on toxic, metalliferous wastes: on mine waste containing 1 per cent lead and 1 per cent zinc, normal red fescue (left) is compared with the lead- and zinc-tolerant variety Merlin (right).

Chapter 8: Deep Mines

geminatum, *Panicum repens*, *Paspalum virginatum* developed in Rhodesia. They can be established on tailings by hand planting: with appropriate fertilising they provide an excellent stabilising cover (Figure 8.31).

Figure 8.31. Tailings at the Trojan nickel mine, Rhodesia, planted with runners of selected tolerant perennial grasses: after three months with proper fertilising full cover is achieved—visible lower down the slope.

Metal-tolerant plants retain in their roots more of the metal they take up than ordinary plants. But enough gets into the shoots to make it dangerous to allow grazing on a regular basis, particularly if the tailings contain lead, zinc or cadmium. The areas must be fenced and left rough.

8.3.4 Surface coverings

On toxic wastes, an alternative approach is to ameliorate the surface of the waste sufficiently with materials such as sewage sludge, or domestic refuse or top soil so that normal plants can grow. The organic matter has the ability to complex soluble metals and render them unavailable to plants and is a long-term source of plant nutrients.

This method was pioneered in the Lower Swansea Valley: vegetation was very successfully established on a variety of metalliferous wastes, providing a layer of at least 10 cm was used. It has now been used widely, for instance at Anaconda mine in Montana and on steep-sided wastes heaps in England (Figure 8.32).

However, the rooting of vegetation is usually restricted to the organic layer and it may suffer from drought. The ameliorating effect of organic matter cannot be permanent, as it decomposes and becomes saturated with metal ions. The vegetation then begins to regress and may ultimately die altogether.

In one or two sites, notably Broken Hill, sewage effluent water has been distributed over the sides of tailings dams by a trickle feed system. The combination of water, nutrients and organic matter has permitted excellent growth of normal species. What is not quite certain, however, is

Heavy Metals

Figure 8.32. Toxic lead/zinc waste can be covered with sewage sludge: but this type of covering at Greenside Mine in the English Lake District, is likely to deteriorate eventually.

how this vegetation would survive if the water supply were withdrawn.

The problems of metalliferous wastes can be so great that it may be better to isolate them completely, particularly where there is excess salinity or acidity as well as metal toxicity, or when the vegetation is to be used for agriculture and must not contain high levels of metal.

It might seem best to use top soil, but this may not be ideal. It is nearly always difficult to obtain and to isolate the surface from toxicity; a substantial depth of material will be required. At the same time, the ability of top soil to retain soluble ions will be a disadvantage. In dry weather, evaporation will bring toxic ions up from below: in subsequent wet conditions, these will be retained by the top soil. If an open, porous material with low cation exchange capacity is used, the toxic ions will move down again and toxicity will not build up at the surface.

There are, therefore, good physico-chemical arguments for using inert, coarse inorganic materials. They will usually be easy to get hold of, often produced by the mining operation itself—overburden or non-metalliferous waste rock. At Mount Isa, Australia, the material used for covering the tailings is a by-product of the rock being quarried as a packing for the worked-out stopes. Pulverised fuel ash

Figure 8.33. When heavy metal wastes are extremely toxic, the only solution is to cover them with an inert material: here at Captain's Flat, New South Wales, the lead/zinc wastes shown in Figure 8.21 are being covered with a layer of rock surfaced with soil.

can also be used. In Wales, to prevent lead/zinc waste being a hazard for cattle and sheep, colliery shale, low in pyrite, from nearby coal mines, is being used.

The surface of the inert material will have to be upgraded with fertilisers, legumes and grasses in the usual way. But this will be easy. Where an extremely coarse material is used as the inert covering, it may be necessary to find something finer for the surface material, as at Captain's Flat in New South Wales (Figure 8.33).

This method is the only means by which trees can be successfully established on toxic wastes. But a substantial depth of material, of the order of 2 m, will be needed if the trees are to root and grow satisfactorily for more than a few years.

8.3.5 Aftercare

Vegetation cover not only prevents erosion but also reduces penetration of water through the waste. This occurs because the plants intercept and evaporate back a substantial proportion of the rainfall, even in a cool climate such as Britain, as much as half the precipitation. Pollution is therefore reduced in two ways.

Aftercare will be essential on such difficult materials, no matter how they have been treated, to maintain an adequate vegetation cover. Except where deep, inert coverings have been used, there will be no question of an agricultural use which would require high nutrient inputs. About 25 kg/ha/yr of nitrogen, phosphorus and potassium will be adequate to maintain growth after the initial establishment period. This should be continued for about six years. After this, recycling of the nutrients will begin to occur and further additions may not be necessary.

FURTHER READING

Coal

Brown L.J. (ed.) 1971. *Landscape Reclamation*. Vol. I. Guildford: IPC Science and Technology Press.

Brown L.J. (ed.) 1972. *Landscape Reclamation*. Vol. II. Guildford: IPC Science and Technology Press.

Chadwick M.J. & Goodman G.T. (eds.) 1975. *The Ecology of Resource Degradation and Renewal*. Oxford: Blackwell Scientific Publications.

Doubleday G.P. 1974. The reclamation of land after coal mining, *Outlook on Agriculture* **8**.

Fitter A.H. & Bradshaw A.D. 1974. Responses of *Lolium perenne* and *Agrostis tenuis* to phosphate and other nutritional factors in the reclamation of colliery shale. *J. Appl. Ecol.* **11**, 597–608.

Gemmell R.P. 1973. Colliery shale revegetation techniques. *Surveyor*, 6 July. 27–9.

Hall I.G. 1957. The ecology of disused pit heaps in England. *J. Ecol.* **45**, 689–720.

Hutnik R.J. & Davis G. (eds.) 1973. *Ecology and Reclamation of Devastated Land*. Vols. I & II. New York: Gordon & Breach.

Palmer M.E. 1978. Acidity and nutrient availability in colliery spoil. In: *Environmental Management of Mineral Wastes*, ed. G.T. Goodman and M.J. Chadwick, 85–126. Netherlands: Sijthoff and Nordhoff.

Schramm J.R. 1966. *Plant Colonisation on Black Wastes from Anthracite Mining in Pennsylvania*. Philadelphia: American Philosophical Soc.

Gold

Chenik D. 1960. The promotion of a vegetative cover on mine slimes, dams and sand dumps. *J. S. Afr. Inst. Min. Metall.* **60**, 525–55.

Clausen H.T. 1973. Ecological aspects of slimes dam construction. *J. S. Afr. Inst. Min. Metall.* **74**, 178–83.

Cresswell C.F. 1973. Changes in vegetational composition, nutritional status soils and microbial populations with the establishment of vegetation on gold mine dumps on the Witwatersrand. In: *Ecology and Reclamation of Devastated Land*, ed. R.J. Hutnik and G. Davies, vol. 2. 335–60. New York: Gordon and Breach.

Groves J.E. 1974. Reclamation of mining degraded land. *S. Afr. J. Sci.* **70**, 296–9.

James A.L. 1966. Stabilizing mine dumps with vegetation. *Endeavour* **25**, 154–7.

James A.L. & Mrost M. 1965. Control of acidity of tailings dams and dumps as a precursor to stabilization by vegetation. *J. S. Afr. Inst. Min. Metall.* **65**, 488–95.

Leroy J-C. 1973. How to establish and maintain growth on tailings in Canada. In: *Tailings Disposal Today*, ed. C.L. Aplin and G.O. Argall. 411–47. San Francisco.

Heavy metals

Alloway B.J. & Davies B.E. 1971. Trace element content of soils affected by base metal mining in Wales. *Geoderma*. **5**, 197–208.

Blessing N.V., Lackey J.A. & Spry A.H. 1974. Rehabilitation of an abandoned mine site. In: *Minerals and the Environment*, ed. M.J. Jones, 16–22. London: Instn. Min. Metallurgy.

Bradshaw A.D., Humphreys M.O. & Johnson M.S. 1978. The value of heavy metal tolerance in the revegetation of metalliferous mine wastes. In: *Environmental Management of Mineral Wastes*, ed. G.T. Goodman and M.J. Chadwick, 311–34. Netherlands: Sijthoff and Nordhoff.

Dean K.C. & Havens R. 1973. Comparative costs and methods for stabilizing of tailings. In: *Tailings Disposal Today*, ed. C.L. Aplin and G.O. Argall, 450–73. San Francisco.

Goodman G.T., Pitcairn C.E.R. & Gemmell R.P. 1973. Ecological factors affecting growth on sites contaminated by heavy metals. In: *Ecology and Reclamation of Devastated Land*, ed. R.J. Hutnik & G. Davis, 149–74. New York: Gordon and Breach.

Hill J.C. 1977. Establishment of vegetation on copper-, gold- and nickel-mining wastes in Rhodesia. *Trans. Inst. Min. Metall.* **86A**, 135–45.

Hunter G. & Whiteman P.C. 1974. Problems associated with the revegetation of metal mining wastes. *J. Austral. Inst. Agric. Sci.* Dec. 1974, 270–8.

Harris J.A. & Leigh J.H. 1976. Stability of mine residues in Broken Hill, New South Wales. In: *Landscaping and Land Use Planning as related to Mining Operations*, ed. Australasian Inst. Min. Metall., 151–66. Parkville, Victoria, Australia: Australasian Institute of Mining and Metallurgy.

Jeffrey D.W., Maybury M. & Levinge D. 1974. Ecological approach to mining waste revegetation. In: *Minerals and the Environment*, ed. M.J. Jones, 371–85. London: Institution of Mining and Metallurgy.

Johnson M.S. & Bradshaw A.D. 1978. Prevention of heavy metal pollution from mine waste by vegetative stabilisation. *Trans. Inst. Min. Metall.* **86A**, 47–55.

Johnson M.S., Bradshaw A.D. & Handley J.F. 1976. Revegetation of metalliferous fluorspar mine tailings. *Trans Inst. Min. Metall.* **85A**, 32–7.

Ludeke K.L. 1973. Vegetative stabilisation of copper mine tailing disposal terms of Pima Mining Company. In: *Tailings Disposal Today*, ed. C.L. Aplin and G.O. Argall, 377–408. San Francisco.

Nielson R.F. & Peterson H.B. 1972. *Treatment of Mine Tailings to Promote Vegetative Stabilisation*. Agri. Exp. Sta. Bulletin 485. Logan, Utah: Utah State Univ.

Peters T.H. 1970. Using vegetation to stabilise mine tailings. *J. Soil Water Cons.* **25**, 65–6.

Smith R.A.H. & Bradshaw A.D. 1972. Stabilisation of toxic mine wastes by the use of tolerant plant populations. *Trans. Inst. Min. Metall.* **81A**, 230–7.

'I walk in the way of Nature, till anon I shall fall and be at rest, yielding up my breath to that element from which I draw it day by day, and sinking into that same earth that gave my father his seed, my mother her blood, and my nurse her milk; that earth that has given me food and drink for many a year, and borne with me while I trampled her underfoot and abused her at will.'

MARCUS AURELIUS.
C3.

9   Strip Mines

The term 'mining' very often suggests an operation of tunnelling underground to get at the material required. Until quite recently all but the most superficial deposits had to be gained in this way because technological limitations prevented us from stripping away surface layers to any depth. In eastern Britain, Neolithic man practised underground mining for flints in order to manufacture his simple tools. For centuries men laboured underground in appalling conditions: for tin in Cornwall, for copper in Spain, for lead in Wales, for coal in many parts of Europe. However, technological advances have meant not only that we have been able to advance the scope of underground activities, to mine deeper and deeper but also that we can now strip away from the surface huge amounts of overburden material to recover minerals or fuel deposits without venturing underground at all. This operation is termed strip or opencast mining.

In the United Kingdom strip-mining for coal is undertaken where the ratio, by volume, of overburden to coal is 20:1 on bituminous coal sites and 30:1 on anthracite sites. As larger capacity earth-moving equipment becomes available these ratios may change and other factors like the nature of the strata and the site also have to be considered.

Strip-mining is now an extremely common practice for minerals, fuels and other materials. In particular bitumin-

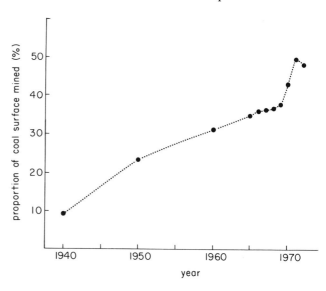

Figure 9.1. Surface mining is becoming more common as technological advances are made in earth-moving equipment: changes in the proportion of coal surface-mined in USA.

158

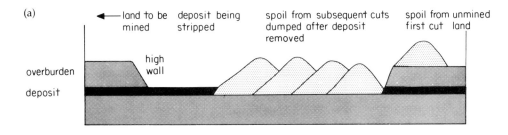

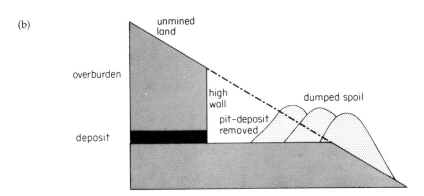

Figure 9.2. The type of surface mining depends on the relationship of the deposit to the surface: a) a shallow deposit in flat country exploited by area strip-mining; b) a deposit in hilly country exploited by contour strip-mining.

ous and brown coal (lignite) are being mined more and more in this way (Figure 9.1). Sometimes a single seam is exposed, sometimes it is a multi-seam operation. But minerals such as china clay, fire clay, manganese, iron ore and phosphorus are just a few of the materials gained in this way. Over 95 per cent of all the non-fuel minerals of the USA, for instance, are now strip-mined.

Strip-mining is basically practised in two ways: area strip-mining in flat or gently undulating country where the deposits are near to the surface over large areas: contour strip-mining in country with a more hilly topography where the deposits can only be worked for a short distance into, but for many kilometres along, the hill (Figure 9.2).

There are three phases: stripping off the overburden above the material required, removal of the mineral, fuel or other deposit (Figure 9.3), and, hopefully, replacement of the unwanted layers and restoration to biological productivity. The first has often been carried out in the past with considerable abandon, so that the soil and underlying rock strata have been completely mixed and large areas made sterile and derelict. Other operations have been carried out with considerable care and foresight. Mining for lignite in the Federal Republic of Germany, for manganese in Russia and opencast coal mining in the United Kingdom are model operations: the surface soil layers, on occasions the subsoil, and the rock strata have been care-

Figure 9.3. Area strip-mining on flat or gently rolling terrain can cover extensive areas of land: a view of strip-mining in operation.

fully separated for storage and subsequent replacement, so that we now have restored and productive landscapes.

A number of different methods of removing the overburden are used; a shovel, a dragline, a bucket wheel excavator or a combination of these (Figure 9.4). It is possible to design, with the appropriate combinations, very sophisticated operations in which the different layers of overburden are kept separate (Figure 9.5).

Failure to separate the components of the overburden—soil and the other strata—is not always due to carelessness. There are regions where sub-surface overburden deposits have been shown to have a higher fertility and potential for plant growth than the original top soil so that slavish adherence to sequential layer by layer removal and replacement is not always necessary (Figure 9.6). But is usually the direct cost that inhibits separate removal of top soil. It is estimated that in the Midwest States of the USA it would cost at least $8500 per acre to remove top soil and replace it on recontoured spoil, resulting in a total cost in these States of over $10 billion.

Area strip-mining has its form determined by the depth of the seam or seams, whether a single seam or several seams are being exploited, the overburden capacity, and

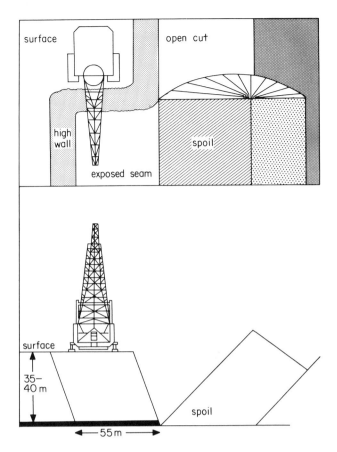

Figure 9.4. Area strip-mining for coal using a dragline: plan and section view of operations in USA: with modern equipment 50 m of overburden can be removed, but very high hill and dale results.

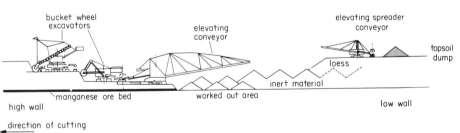

Figure 9.5. Area strip-mining can be very sophisticated: a manganese mine in the Ukraine with two bucket wheel excavators, where top soil and different overburden layers are conserved by being stripped and replaced separately.

whether or not top soil storage is taking place. A long trench (box-trench) is cut through the overburden to expose the mineral deposit and allow its removal. When top soil is to be stored separately it is removed by a bull-dozer or scraper and stacked; otherwise the total overburden (including soil) from the first cut is placed on unmined land. After the mineral deposit has been removed a second cut is taken and the overburden from this dumped in the trench created by the first cut. This continues until the last cut taken leaves a trench, which often fills with water, next to the final cutting face or high wall.

When left in this condition the area finally resembles a ploughed field on a massive scale, with huge ridges

Figure 9.6. Overburden can weather to give a satisfactory soil: shale in the Bowen Basin Coalfield, Queensland, disintegrating to give an easily cultivated, fertile material.

and furrows. Increasingly now the spoil is progressively smoothed and sown or planted. In the United Kingdom and Germany this has long been the practice, replacing the subsoil and top soil before planting.

Contour strip-mining takes place where the mineral deposits are beneath rolling or even very hilly country. The outcrop is located and then the overburden removed progressing along the hillside. The cut follows the contour line and the overburden is thrown down the hillside. The cut only goes into the hill a short distance and then is deserted (Figure 9.7). In the United States of America contour strip-mining for coal has devastated vast areas of the Appalachian Mountains; only recently have improved methods of mining become the rule.

Figure 9.7. A bite into the hill- contour strip-mining in W. Virginia: a cut like this can extend for many kilometres along the hill.

Chapter 9: Strip Mines

9.1 COAL

9.1.1 An enormous disturbance

The largest areas of strip-mining in the world are for coal. With increasing pressures on us to use coal instead of oil for a fuel, this state of affairs is likely to continue. So it is imperative that we understand how to cope with the results.

Where strip-mining follows a well-defined sequence of overburden removal and replacement, and is on a relatively small scale, there is usually little permanent alteration to the land-use patterns of the area. After mining, the spoil is recontoured, drainage works are undertaken, sub-soil and top soil are replaced and the area returned to its former land-use or a different but equally acceptable one. In Britain it is almost impossible to see where coal has been mined in this manner.

The same claim cannot be made for contour or area strip-mining without restoration as practised until recently on a vast scale in the United States of America. Original drainage patterns are destroyed; erosion of the spoil material occurs and siltation of water-courses follows. Where the spoil contains iron pyrite, as common in strip-mining as in deep-mining operations, weathering gives acid drainage water which pollutes streams and rivers. The original vegetation is destroyed and an often infertile and even toxic spoil substrate is substituted. With contour mining in particular, problems of stability arise and landslides can occur, often destroying vegetation not touched by the actual mining operation, as well as roads, farm land, reservoirs and buildings.

Progress of natural revegetation on land strip-mined for coal is very slow (Table 9.1). This is because the fertile top soil has been buried and usually covered with unweathered strata of overburden. This spoil is often low in nutrients, toxic (due to acidity or high alkalinity), physically of a coarse texture and often, due to mining over a large area, a considerable distance from a seed source.

Table 9.1. Return to nature after mining can be a long process: progress of natural colonisation of strip-mined land in Illinois

	Years since mining			
	2–3	10	40	55–65
percentage cover in:				
herb layer	24	84·6	89·3	98·3
shrub layer	0	35·8	57·4	51·2
tree layer	0	5·9	8·8	91·7
no. of species in:				
herb layer	12	24	35	18
shrub layer	0	11	16	12
tree layer	0	2	5	5
no. of bird species	5	18	32	32
no. of pairs per 100 acres	28	341	375	489

The cause of toxicity in many strip-mined spoils is the same as that shown by deep-mined coal spoil—oxidation of iron pyrite. Similarly, major plant nutrients are usually in short supply (Table 9.2). The pyrite causes the water draining from the mines to be very acid, high in iron and sulphate, as well as many other metals such as aluminium and manganese. These dissolved substances find their way from strip-mined spoil in to water-courses, completely changing their chemical nature (Table 9.3). The surface erosion which accompanies this drainage from ground surface devoid of vegetation, results in siltation problems which are often extremely serious (Figure 9.8).

Table 9.2. Spoil is highly variable: characteristics of three Pennsylvanian strip-mine spoils

| characteristics | | spoil | | |
		Brook-ville	Clarion	Lower Freeport
particle analysis				
> 2 mm		34	45	45
2–0·05 mm		33	16·5	18
0·05–0·002 mm	(%)	16·5	16	23
< 0·002 mm		16·5	22·5	14
chemical analysis				
pH		3·3	3·1	5·2
Ca		102	56	640
Mg		127	56	134
Fe exchangeable	(ppm)	24	47	17
Mn		13	6	58
Al		90	196	5
K		199	148	137
P extractable	(ppm)	3	5	25
N total	(%)	0·003	0·009	0·070

Table 9.3. Mining affects not only the land: chemical characteristics of a stream in Kentucky before and after surface mining (maximum values, ppm)

	conductivity mmhos/ cm	pH	Fe	Al	Mn	SO_4	Ca	Mg	Zn
before	73	7·0	0·27	0·05	0·12	12	6·6	4·4	0·80
after	334	7·5	3·80	0·15	1·20	132	30	24	1·20

Spoil material is often stony and lacking in silt and clay particles (Table 9.2) and has no organic matter apart from coaly material. Water-holding capacity is therefore reduced compared with a normal soil. However, physical factors do not often limit plant growth greatly.

9.1.2 Re-establishment of vegetation
Figure 6.5 (page 76) indicates what can be achieved by a well-planned strip-mining operation in which each layer of the unused overburden is replaced with care. Strip-mining for coal in the United Kingdom (usually called opencast

Chapter 9: Strip Mines

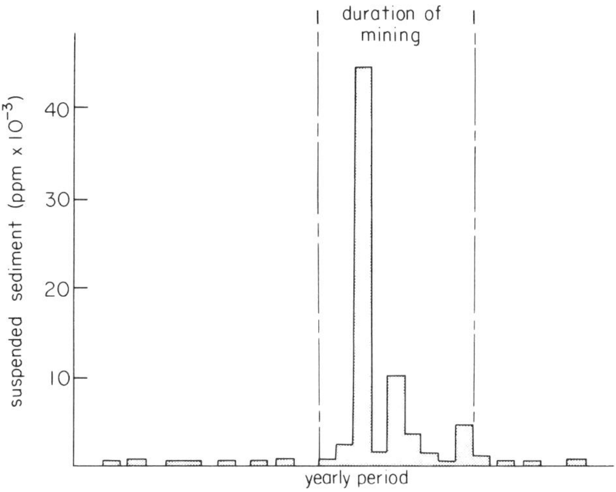

Figure 9.8. Surface mining can give a rapid increase in sediment burdens of streams: increase in the suspended sediment of a stream in a watershed during mining in Appalachia.

mining) is now not only planned to reclaim the areas currently being mined, but also to incorporate past dereliction such as old colliery tips from previous deep mines (Figure 9.9). Restored opencast sites in the United Kingdom have generally given good yields of arable crops and reasonable tree growth. Care has to be taken in the removal, storage and replacement processes. Cultivation to restore soil structure is very important. The restored and re-seeded land has sometimes needed high nitrogen dressings to the soil that is spread after storage in the dump, in order to obtain near normal yields of crops, because of losses in the dump by denitrification. However, the normal range of microorganisms persist in top soil dumps and eventually return to their original level as soil structure improves with plant growth.

In contour mining a similar careful replacement has now been shown to be possible, by the block cut (or haul back) method. After an initial section has been cut, the overburden from the next section is hauled back to fill the first section and covered with top soil. It is clearly going to be the main contour mining method in the future.

Unfortunately there are very large areas of strip-mining which have never been so treated. In area strip-mining, the land is often left in hill and dale. For this, the initial step must be some sort of levelling. The amount depends on the ultimate land-use intended (Figure 6.11, page 88). Although the operation may seem expensive, the amount of earth-moving is minute in comparison with the earth-moving already carried out, and full levelling represents little extra above partial levelling (Figure 9.10). It is therefore justifiable for it to be part of the mining process. Nevertheless until the development of new legislation all that was done in the major strip-mining areas such as Illinois was 'striking off' the crest of spoil banks by running a bulldozer along the ridge. Whether levelling

165   *Coal*

Figure 9.9. Current strip-mining operations can be planned to include the clearing of past dereliction: strip-mining restoration and colliery spoil tip clearance at Parkhouse, Derbyshire; *top* before; *below* after.

occurs or not, in this sort of mining, vegetation has to be established on the raw overburden.

Overburdens can sometimes be excellent for plant growth without the use of top soil. In the new Bowen Basin coalfield in Queensland, for instance, the surface soils are poor and leached, dominated with brigalow (*Acacia har-pophylla*). The rocky overburden exposed after mining breaks down rapidly to a structurally excellent neutral soil

Figure 9.10. Although complete levelling of hill and dale left by strip-mining appears costly, the extra earth-moving is a very small proportion of the total extra earth-moving required for an original 15 m of overburden.

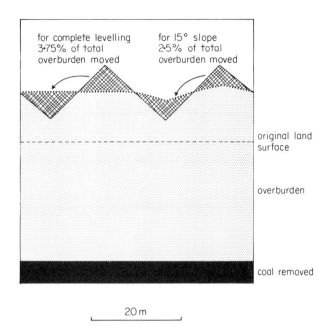

for complete levelling
3·75% of total
overburden moved

for 15° slope
2·5% of total
overburden moved

original land surface

overburden

coal removed

20 m

on which a productive sward of buffel grass (*Cenchrus ciliaris*), green panic (*Panicum maximum*) and rhodes grass (*Chloris gayana*) with the tropical legume siratro (*Macroptilium atropurpureum*) can be established with only a phosphate fertiliser (Figure 9.11). As a result restoration costs are only a few cents per tonne of coal produced.

In the United States of America strip-mined spoil from coal is very variable, but much has a high acidity and is toxic and even those not toxic are deficient in nitrogen and phosphorus. By analysing samples from the high walls, it is possible, early on in the mining operation, to gain some idea of the nature of the spoil that will be derived from the overburden and use this as a guide to reclamation pro-

Figure 9.11. Excellent restoration without the re-use of top soil: in the Bowen Basin coalfield in Queensland growth is better on the overburden than on the original leached top soil.

Coal

cedures. The analysis should cover pyrite and carbonate (Figure 9.12) as well as plant nutrients and texture.

With acid spoil material, grasses and legumes will still only establish a sparse cover even when lime and fertiliser are added to the spoil. The addition of a mulch, however, improves growth. Plant cover on spoil in Kentucky, for instance, sown with weeping lovegrass (*Eragrostis curvula*), grain sorghum (*Sorghum vulgare*), tall fescue (*Festuca arundinacea*), sericea lespedeza (*Lespedeza cuneata*), birdsfoot trefoil (*Lotus corniculatus*) and Kobe lespedeza (*Lespedeza striata*) was best when fertiliser, lime and shredded pine bark were applied (Table 9.4). Lime is required to neutralise acidity and correct spoil toxicity. Nitrogen and phosphorus must be supplied to provide adequate levels for

Figure 9.12. Predicting the characteristics of overburden material before stripping: overburden in West Virginia, above the Pittsburgh seam, analysed for pyrite and carbonate to indicate the ultimate lime requirements of the different strata.

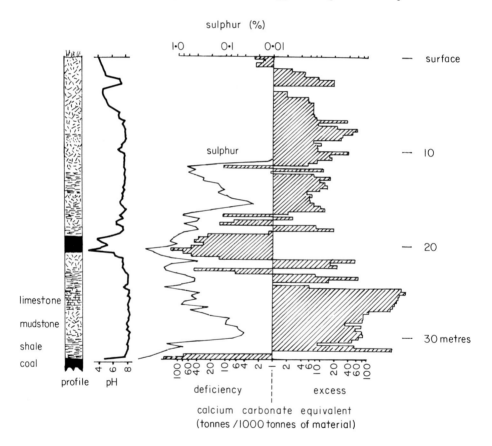

Table 9.4. Rapid establishment of a plant cover can require lime, fertiliser and mulch: percentage cover developed with different amendments on strip-mine spoil in Kentucky

amendment	1972	1973	1974	1975
none	0	0	3	3
fertiliser (75 kg N + 96 kg P/ha)	0	0	3	3
lime (15 t/ha)	20	10	30	35
fertiliser + mulch (189 m³/ha)	15	35	40	50
lime + fertiliser	35	50	65	75
lime + fertiliser + mulch	65	85	95	100

Chapter 9: Strip Mines

successful plant growth. The mulch provides surface steril-
ity, improves moisture infiltration, reduces evaporation,
maintains moisture levels in the rooting zone and aids
leaching of salts and toxic ions from the spoil.

A large number of grasses, legumes and shrubs have
now been tested for their suitability for growth on spoil of
different chemical characteristics (Table 9.5). Sowing them
may present difficulties on inaccessible steep terrain.
Hydroseeding may be valuable: in West Virginia several
thousand hectares have been seeded by helicopter.

Table 9.5. Choose species to suit the spoil: grasses, legumes and shrubs for planting on coal strip-mine spoil in the midwest and eastern USA

spoil pH	grasses	legumes	shrubs
5·6 or above	*Bromus inermis* (smooth brome)	*Coronilla varia* (crown vetch)	*Amorpha fruticosa* (indigo bush)
	Dactylis glomerata (orchardgrass)	*Lespedeza cuneata* (sericea lespedeza)	*Cytisus scoparius* (scotch broom)
	Festuca arundinacea (tall fescue)	*Lotus corniculatus* (birdsfoot trefoil)	*Elaeagnus umbellata* (autumn olive)
	Panicum virgatum (switchgrass)	*Medicago sativa* (alfalfa)	*Lespedeza japonica* (Japanese lespedeza)
	Phalaris arundinacea (reed canary-grass)	*Trifolium pratense* (red clover)	*Lonicera mackii* (Amur honeysuckle)
	Phleum pratense (timothy)	*Trifolium repens* (white clover)	*L. tartarica* (Tartarian honeysuckle)
			Robinia hispida (rose acacia)
			Salix purpurea (tall purple willow)
3·6–5·5	*Eragrostis curvula* (weeping lovegrass)	*Lespedeza cuneata* (sericea lespedeza)	*Amorpha fruticosa* (indigo bush)
	Festuca arundinacea (tall fescue)		*Elaeagnus umbellata* (autumn olive)
	Festuca rubra (red fescue)		*Lespedeza bicolor* (bicolor lespedeza)
	Panicum virgatum (switchgrass)		*Lespedeza japonica* (Japanese lespedeza)
	Phalaris arundinacea (reed canary-grass)		*Robinia hispida* (rose acacia)

Tree species planted on coal strip-mine spoil (Table 9.6),
will need treatments similar to those for land to be planted
with grasses and legumes. General fertiliser application
encourages the growth of herbs and sown grass, which is
important to give a stabilising cover. However, care must
be taken that this does not reduce tree growth (Figure 9.13).

Erosion and sedimentation control is important, particularly in contour mining. The establishment of vegetation
represents, after levelling, one important step in this control, but it is also necessary to plan the mining exercise
itself. Diversion ditches must be constructed above the
area being stripped, the first-cut spoil deposited at a low
outslope angle, part of the seam and overburden left as a
barrier, the second-cut spoil sloped to form a terrace, and
holes where coal has been removed by auger, properly
sealed (Figure 9.14, and compare with Figure 9.2, page 159).

The control of acid mine drainage water should be based on excluding oxygen from the pyritic material in the overburden and coal. Oxygen barriers, however (plastic film, bitumen or concrete), are costly to install and maintain. Surface sealants like lime, gypsum, sodium silicate and latex have been tried, but they also are costly and only partially effective. Consolidation may be the best answer. Where acid mine drainage water production cannot be prevented or the discharge controlled, then neutralisation must take place. The use of lime ($Ca(OH)_2$), limestone, anhydrous ammonia, sodium carbonate and sodium hydroxide have all been used with success, but there are problems of resulting water hardness, high levels of sulphate, high iron concentrations, sludge disposal and the increase

Table 9.6. Trees vary in their suitability for different spoils: species for coal strip-mined spoil in the eastern and midwest USA

species	pH range	compaction*
Acer saccharinum (silver maple)	4·0 – 8·0	lc
Acer saccharum (sugar maple)	4·5 – 8·0	lc
Alnus glutinosa (European alder)	3·5 – 7·5	c
Alnus incana (speckled alder)	3·5 – 7·5	c
Fraxinus americana (white ash)	4·5 – 8·0	lc
Fraxinus pennsylvanica (green ash)	4·5 – 8·0	lc
Juglans nigra (black walnut)	5·5 – 8·0	lc
Juniperus virginiana (eastern red cedar)	5·0 – 8·0	lc
Liquidambar styraciflua (sweetgum)	4·5 – 7·5	lc
Liriodendron tulipifera (tulip poplar)	4·5 – 8·0	lc
Pinus echinata (shortleaf pine)	4·0 – 7·5	l
Pinus rigida (pitch pine)	3·5 – 7·5	l
Pinus strobus (white pine)	4·0 – 7·5	lc
Pinus sylvestris (scotch pine)	4·0 – 7·5	l
Pinus virginiana (Virginia pine)	4·0 – 8·0	l
Platanus occidentalis (sycamore)	4·0 – 8·0	lc
Populus deltoides (cottonwood)	5·0 – 8·0	lc
Quercus borealis (red oak)	4·0 – 7·5	l
Quercus prinus (chestnut oak)	4·0 – 7·5	l
Robinia pseudoacacia (black locust)	3·8 – 7·5	lc

* lc – loose or compacted

Figure 9.13. Trees grow well on coal strip-mined spoil with additions of fertiliser, although underplanting with grasses and legumes may reduce this growth: height growth of four tree species in southeastern Kentucky.

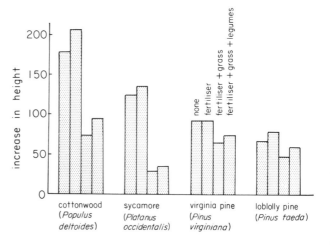

in total dissolved solids to be reckoned with. The most positive preventive method is good planning of the mining and restoration operation. As mining proceeds, backfilling and reclamation should keep pace with it. Watercourses should be diverted away from the mining area and erosion control practices followed.

Aftercare of reclaimed strip-mine sites is no less important than on other reclaimed sites. Until the full cycling of nutrients is restored, both fertiliser and limestone, to correct spoil reaction, may need to be applied from time to time—especially if hay or other crops are being removed from the site. The maintenance of legumes will be important to ensure the build-up of nitrogen. Maintenance will also be needed on waterways, acid mine drainage treatment plants and any sedimentation basins that remain.

Figure 9.14. Planning the removal and restoration of overburden, particularly when contour strip-mining, will alleviate many of the problems of stability, erosion control and stream pollution: section across a well-designed restoration scheme in Appalachia.

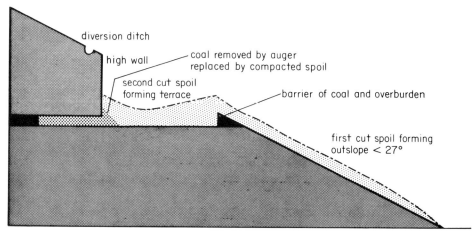

9.2   OIL SHALE

9.2.1   A developing problem

Oil occurs in porous sedimentary rocks. Normally crude oil flows and so can be pumped out of deposits, but there are also large deposits of more viscous oil, in oil sands and oil shales where the hydrocarbon is in a solid form known as kerogen. There are huge deposits of oil sands, little exploited yet, in Alberta in Canada, extending over an area of nearly 25 000 square kilometres, representing 300 billion barrels of oil (the annual consumption of the USA is 6–7 billion). Large deposits of oil shale are found in Colorado, Utah and Wyoming, USA, but these represent only about one-third of the recoverable oil deposits of the Canadian oil sands. They are, however, currently being exploited. Deposits of oil shale have been exploited for many years in the Estonian Soviet Socialist Republic.

Oil is derived from the kerogen in shale by thermal decomposition at about 500° C. At this temperature much of the sulphur and nitrogen is released along with a proportion of the hydrocarbon, but some carbon remains in the spent shale. For this reason, spent shale is sometimes ignited at higher temperatures to make use of energy from the carbon. The resulting product is shale ash.

Eighty to ninety per cent by weight of the excavated shale ends up as waste and indeed the volume may be greater than the original amount of shale because of the processing. As oil shale is increasingly exploited to supplement liquid oil resources, waste disposal and reclamation are likely to become major problems.

Spent shale has a high pH due to high concentrations of soluble salts. Electrical conductivity values are high, usually well above 4 mmhos/cm. The principle water soluble cation is sodium which may account for more than 75 per cent of the water soluble cations. The Ca:Mg ratio is often rather low, down to 0·24. Shale-ash usually shows the chemical characteristics of spent shale to an even higher degree (Table 9.7). As a medium for plant growth then, spent shale is unsatisfactory due to alkalinity, salinity and ion imbalance.

Table 9.7. Chemical characteristics of spent shale and shale-ash from Colorado, USA

Sample	pH	conductivity (mmhos/cm)	P	K	Ca	Mg	Na	cation exch cap. (meq/100 g)
				(available – ppm)				
spent shale 1	9·7	16·0	8·5	27	528	19	2852	7·6
spent shale 2	8·6	9·0	5·6	360	630	144	851	7·8
shale-ash 1	12·1	11·0	20	355	–	–	–	–
shale-ash 2	10·9	7·0	42	150	–	–	–	–

As might be expected in a material that had undergone considerable heating, nitrogen concentrations in the waste are low, indeed negligible in shale ash. Available phosphorus is low, but potassium rarely so. The cation exchange capacity tends to be rather low. At the high pH values encountered, it might be expected that some micronutrients might be deficient, but this has not been found.

The physical characteristics of spent shales are not particularly poor. Most of the spoil is in the normal soil particle range and its water-holding capacity satisfactory. However, materials coming from some extraction processes are extremely difficult to wet. Because of this, and the high pH, soluble salt content and low nitrogen and phosphorus status, little plant growth can occur without considerable alteration of the substrate. As the deposits are often found in areas of low rainfall (250–300 mm/yr in Colorado) there are a number of problems to be overcome.

9.2.2 Solutions are possible

Wetting of spent shale can be brought about by mechanically mixing water with shale. This can best be done as part of the disposal treatment following oil extraction. Further application of water will be required if excess salts have to be removed by leaching. This will only be accomplished if the bulk density of the material is not too high.

Soluble salts can be removed quite rapidly if sufficient water is applied. About 6 cm of water per 15 cm of shale need to be applied to remove 75–80 per cent of soluble salts. This still leaves the shale with a high proportion of the exchange capacity filled with sodium ions. Applications of gypsum ($CaSO_4$) have been suggested to alleviate this.

Attempts have been made to reclaim spent oil shale without leaching treatment by mixing it with soil and applying fertiliser. Two grass species, Russian wild rye-grass (*Elymus junceus*) and tall wheatgrass (*Agropyron elongatum*) showed only poor yields even when a 50:50 spoil:soil mixture was used and usually germination vigour was depressed.

All this suggests that a complete top soil cover is essential: if it is available it should certainly be used. It may be necessary to place a layer of overburden rubble between the shale and the soil to prevent movement of salts up to the surface. However, when spent oil shale has been previously leached, the addition of NPK fertiliser can give yields of Russian wild ryegrass and tall wheatgrass that equal production on soil. It has been found that additional micronutrients or a mulch applied with fertiliser does not improve on the yield obtained with NPK fertiliser alone. Indeed, all the evidence suggests that the potassium in the combined fertiliser is unnecessary.

In other areas where climatic conditions differ from Colorado, other species of plants will be more appropriate and if annual rainfall is higher, leaching with applied water may not be so necessary. Afforestation has taken place in Estonia using both coniferous and broad-leaved trees (Figure 9.15).

Sufficient experience has not yet accumulated on the long-term restoration of spent oil shale to be able to suggest management programmes for reclaimed areas. The low cation exchange properties and the ease with which leaching can be accomplished indicates the necessity for quite frequent additions of nitrogen and phosphorus fertiliser, or the use of slow-release materials. However, experience in Estonia shows that if less-demanding tree species are chosen, these can be grown satisfactorily in climates with sufficient rainfall.

9.3 IRON ORE

9.3.1 Dereliction and natural recolonisation

Recently, some of the world's richest iron ore deposits have been discovered in N.W. Australia in the Pilbara. These outcrop to the surface so that mining involves only removing the ore as it is wanted. But in other parts of the

Figure 9.15. Vegetation can be successfully established on spent oil shale: successful Pine establishment in Estonia.

world, iron ore has had to be mined from deposits lying underneath other material, using strip-mining techniques.

There are many of these areas. By now, the restoration techniques being used are often the careful methods already discussed. But in the past, no such care was taken and large areas of land were destroyed. Three examples, in England, the United States and Australia, show the breadth of the problems.

The opencast mining for ironstone in the English Midlands is a small operation by world standards. The total area exploited amounts to only 7500 hectares and the present rate of production involves only 50 ha/yr as the ironstone is replaced by richer and cheaper materials from overseas. But it is an interesting case-history because the mining has continued for several centuries and is in rich agricultural land.

Restoration was easy a century ago when the strata being mined were near the surface and there was not more than 5 m of overburden. The top soil was wheeled away in barrows, the sub soil overburden moved onto areas already mined, and the top soil then replaced on top of the overburden. Cultivation could quickly be resumed: the only sign now visible of this activity are productive agricultural fields that are curiously 2–4 m lower than their surroundings.

Chapter 9: Strip Mines

However, at the beginning of this century, steam-powered excavators began to be employed which were able to handle much greater depths of overburden. Agriculture was in a very depressed state and the profit from ironstone more than paid for the cost of acquiring the land. So there was no incentive to restore: the overburden was dumped in hill and dale, the top soil buried. The result was that by the end of World War II there was over a thousand hectares of totally derelict hill and dale land, in the middle of a rich agricultural region (Figure 9.16). Some attempts were made by the larger landowners to develop some sort of use for the land. The only possibility was rather low-grade commercial forestry.

Figure 9.16. Some of the derelict heavy clay hill and dale land once produced by large-scale mining for iron ore in England: now nearly all restored to agriculture (see Figure 9.19).

Then, as legislation was passed in Britain in 1947, giving planning control of mining and quarrying, the situation changed, and in 1951 an Ironstone Restoration Fund was established, based on a fixed levy from ironstone extractors, landowners and the Government, for every ton of ironstone extracted. With this, a programme of restoration was begun under the guidance of the Ministry of Agriculture. The major work was carried out by the County Council, but the subsequent management was carried out by the tenants who received subsidies for the extra cultivations and fertilisation involved. The result has been a reclamation programme which is still a model of its kind. The operation has more or less terminated because planning regulations now require the retention and proper reinstatement of top soil—a return to the approaches of earlier, more frugal, days (Figure 9.17).

Iron Ore

Figure 9.17. The only sign of open-cast mining for iron ore can be a lowered field level if the soil has been carefully replaced: a properly treated area in Northamptonshire.

Table 9.8. Measurable improvements can occur rapidly: characteristics of soils of ironstone spoil banks in Northamptonshire before and after reclamation with well fertilised lucerne or grass/clover ley for 10 years

The overburden consists of clays and limestones of the Jurassic period. The main material is a heavy clay little relieved by coarse particles (Table 9.8): the overburden is therefore a mixture of material of an overall heavy clay texture interspersed with lumps of limestone which vary in size from 5 cm diameter pieces to large boulders which disintegrate only slowly.

	site	pH	organic matter(%)	$CaCO_3$ (%)	P	K	sand	silt	clay
					(available ppm)[1]			(%)	
original	1	7·8	1·9	5·0	48	50	41	15	42
material	2	7·8	1·8	9·0	61	75	38	5	55
	3	7·6	1·4	11·0	48	149	29	10	60
reclaimed	1	7·8	4·7	8·0	1395	265	45	14	36
material	2	7·7	4·7	11·0	266	224	28	20	47
	3	7·4	9·3	10·0	610	896	36	18	37

[1] soluble in 1% citric acid P 60 low   125 high
                               K 75 low   250 high

There is a high level of calcium (pH>7) and low levels of phosphorus and potassium. There will be interaction between the calcium and both the phosphorus and potassium, rendering what little there is even more unavailable to plants. Although the top soil has been mixed into the overburden, the dilution is so great that the resulting material has effectively no organic matter and no nitrogen.

The result is therefore an inhospitable material. There are signs of anaerobic conditions below the top 10 cm, but gross waterlogging does not occur because of the hill and dale topography. Frost action keeps the surface loose and friable, but there is not a great deal of surface erosion because heavy rainstorms are unusual.

Colonisation by plants is not prevented but the lack of

Chapter 9: Strip Mines

major plant nutrients and the excess of calcium mean that growth is slow. The result is a specialised flora consisting of species which have good powers of seed dispersal and are able to tolerate the extreme soil conditions (Table 9.9).

Table 9.9. Colonisation of ironstone overburden is slow and there are opportunities for invasion by a wide variety of plants: species found in the early stages of colonisation of spoil banks in Northamptonshire

---

Agropyron repens (couch grass)
Calamagrostis epigeios (bush grass)
Cirsium arvense (creeping thistle)
Cirsium vulgare (spear thistle)
Crepis taraxacifolia (beaked hawks-
    beard)
Epilobium angustifolium (rosebay
    willow herb)
Festuca rubra (red fescue)
Hypochaeris radicata (cat's ear)
Lotus corniculatus (bird's foot trefoil)
Senecio jacobea (ragwort)
Trifolium repens (white clover)
Trisetum flavescens (yellow oatgrass)
Tussilago farfara (colt's foot)
Typha angustifolia (reedmace)

The vegetation remains open for many years (Figure 9.16). Shrubs such as hawthorn (*Crataegus monogyna*) and goat willow (*Salix caprea*) invade but they too find conditions difficult and grow slowly. There is a conspicuous lack of legumes, because of the low levels of phosphorus. The result is that natural soil development is slow, and from a pedological point of view, can hardly be detected in 20 years.

In the United States one of the major iron ore fields lies in the Mesabi Range in Minnesota. In 1950 it was providing one-half of the total production of the US. As a result, 27 400 ha were made derelict by 1965. Another similar area is in W. Virginia. Little has been reported about reclamation in these areas, except the tailings produced by concentration of taconite ore: the pits and strip-mined areas are left as they are. But the colonisation of the spoil banks left by the mining suggest that the situations are really very similar to that in England.

The overburden in Minnesota is glacial, consisting of sand, silt and clay layers, nearly neutral in pH unless limestone pebbles are present. The mining started in 1892 and has left a series of spoil banks of different ages showing the whole process of colonisation and soil development (Table 9.10). Invasion is by species, whether herbs or trees, which have good powers of dispersal. But prominent amongst the herbs are two legumes, clover (*Trifolium repens*) and sweet clover (*Melilotus alba*), which do not have particularly good powers of dispersal. Their success must be related to their ability to fix nitrogen. The trees appear only to be able to colonise in the early stages of the succession when there is no competition, and then only in years when climatic conditions are suitable.

Iron Ore

Table 9.10. A complete plant cover develops slowly: species succession on Mesabi iron-ore spoil banks (herbs as % frequency, trees as number per 100 m²)

species	2 yrs	13 yrs	21 yrs	32 yrs	51 yrs
			age of surface		
Trifolium repens	5	95	65	100	75
Poa pratensis		85	100	70	65
Fragaria virginiana		45	25	80	95
Sonchus arvensis		55	20	15	
Meliotus alba		45	95		
Achillea millefolium		30	10	40	15
Trifolium pratense		10	30		
Cinna latifolia		15			
Solidago nemoralis		20	15	40	20
Erigeron canadensis		10			
Rubus idaeus		10	30	15	75
Solidago gigantea		10	10		
Phleum pratense		5	35		75
Agropyron repens			15		
Cirsium arvense			15		15
Equisetum arvense			10		
Aster ciliolatus			5		15
Aster macrophyllus				15	
Diervilla lonicera				15	
Hieracium canadense				10	
Aralia nudicaulis					20
Bare substrate	100	55			
Litter		90	100	100	100
Populus tremuloides		2	12	92	49
Populus balsamifera			8	30	100
Prunus pennsylvania		3	4	2	
Salix sp.		3	4	7	

Figure 9.18. Natural soil development on iron ore spoil banks in Minnesota: organic matter and nitrogen accumulate to give a fully functioning soil/plant ecosystem: but the process takes many decades.

The impact of the vegetation on the soil is considerable (Figure 9.18). There is a continuous build-up of carbon and nitrogen in organic matter which has a direct and an indirect effect on the soil structure. As a result, the depth of top soil, the A horizon, increases with time. The carbon/nitrogen ratio is initially very high, the sort of organic matter which would decompose slowly; but as the legumes develop, the ratio falls quickly to levels found in better soils

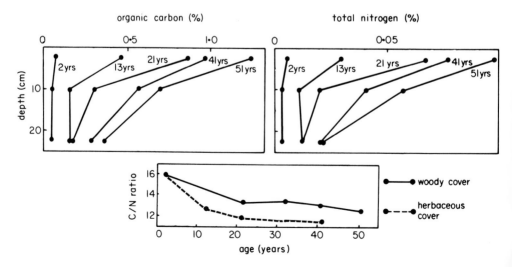

where there is good nitrogen cycling. In 50 years the total nitrogen content of the soil reaches 1400 kg N/ha. So the trees growing on the oldest banks grow faster than equivalent-aged trees on the younger banks.

This rate of soil development is matched very closely by the 100-year-old ironstone spoil areas in W. Virginia which have developed naturally into grassland and woodland. In 100 years 2500 kg N/ha has accumulated in the top 15 cm; this is a rate of 28 kg/ha/yr, the same as in Minnesota. The total is more or less equal to that found in the neighbouring soils (Table 9.11). The bulk density has not improved so completely, but it is clear that over this time-period, soils can develop which have very adequate biological and agricultural productive capacities.

Table 9.11. Eventually satisfactory soils develop naturally although bulk densities are still high: the characteristics of ironstone mine spoils and adjacent undisturbed soil in W. Virginia

site	estimated age (years)	present vegetation	bulk density (g/cm³)		nitrogen (kg/ha for 15 cm depth)	
			spoil	soil	spoil	soil
Chesnut Ridge	85–119	forest	1·48	0·90	2724	3188
Glen	72–83	forest	1·39	1·01	2839	3480
Johnson Hollow	85–131	forest	1·42	0·90	2130	2294
Massey	72–83	grass	1·58	1·12	1968	2319
Peters	72–83	grass	1·41	1·13	2733	3089
Quarry Run	85–119	forest	1·52	1·13	2825	2910
average			1·47	1·03	2536	2880

In the Pilbara, conditions are quite different. The climate is extremely hot and arid, with summer temperatures above 50°C (120°F). The vegetation is a semi-desert savanna dominated by spinifex (*Triodia* and *Plectrachne* sp.). So far, no areas have been worked out and there have been no opportunities for natural colonisation by spinifex. But the disturbance has encouraged the appearance of other species. This is important because there is already a need to know how to stabilise spoil banks and control dust.

9.3.2 Reclamation and aftercare

The earliest experiments in England showed that without any fertiliser treatment, growth of sown grasses was extremely poor. However, when a dressing of a complete fertiliser, 150 kg N, 70 kg P, 125 kg K/ha, was given, satisfactory growth could be achieved. When the effects of individual nutrients were tried, the response to phosphorus was particularly marked. The most successful plants were vigorous species with strong root systems (Table 9.12).

Full-scale reclamation involves levelling as the first operation. This can be carried out by bulldozers since no material has to be shifted very far. In this process large rocks are pushed out and buried. The whole area is then cross-ripped. This brings further large stones to the surface which would otherwise be an obstacle to subsequent cultivation, and also loosens the subsoil. The surface is then disced and harrowed to achieve a satisfactory surface, and sown by normal means. Good grass leys result (Figure 9.19).

Table 9.12. Normal agricultural grasses and legumes can be used: species for the establishment of grassland on levelled ironstone overburden in Northamptonshire

cocksoot	*Dactylis glomerata*	lucerne	*Medicago sativa*
meadow fescue	*Festuca pratensis*	alsike	*Trifolium hybridum*
ryegrass	*Lolium perenne*	red clover	*Trifolium pratense*
timothy	*Phleum pratense*	white clover	*Trifolium repens*

Figure 9.19. Hill and dale land restored to agriculture (compare with Figure 9.16): a grass/clover mixture has been sown and well-fertilised but aftercare is given to ensure effective restoration.

Figure 9.20. Lucerne (alfalfa) on heavy clay after grading hill and dale land in Northamptonshire: lucerne tolerates the heavy soil and fixes nitrogen, providing it is well-fertilised with phosphorus and potassium.

Surface consolidation can recur so rapidly that grass growth can become rather poor, despite fertilisation (visible in Figure 9.19). A more satisfactory sward is created by a mixture of lucerne (*Medicago sativa*) and cocksfoot (*Dactylis glomerata*) cut for hay or silage (Figure 9.20). The lucerne seems able to tolerate the heavy soil conditions and can give excellent yields if given adequate dressings of high-phosphate fertiliser. Cereal and root crops are possible but not really satisfactory, because of difficulties in wet weather. It is better to put the reclaimed areas down to a grass or lucerne ley for some years before attempting to grow arable crops.

Aftercare is crucial. The calcareous clay soils are very deficient in plant nutrients and require higher than normal amounts of fertiliser, particularly of phosphorus since this will be rendered insoluble and unavailable to plants. Phosphorus will only become readily available to plants when sufficient has accumulated in an organic fraction. Every year, for the first ten years, therefore, the amount of extra fertiliser required over normal is assessed for each reclaimed area, and the extra cost paid for by the Ironstone

Restoration Fund. The amount required is usually about twice that for normal land. There are few other situations where the aftercare requirements for reclaimed land have been so well appreciated, and budgeted for, and the results, therefore, so consistently successful.

In the period before the means of restoring the land to agriculture was understood, the only reclamation procedure possible was to plant trees. Blocks of forest trees were planted over a number of years from the 1920s, as a low-cost operation without levelling the hill and dale topography.

Planting was by hand, using 2–3 yr old transplants. Originally, no fertiliser was used, but it was later found that some is helpful. Quite a wide variety of species have been used, the most successful being sycamore (*Acer pseudoplatanus*) and larch (*Larix decidua*). Very good plantations have resulted. A forestry end point is not totally alien to the area, since there are large woodlands in the Rockingham Forest region on the limestone of the Great Oolite to the east.

In the Mesabi Range, most areas have so far been left to revegetate naturally. The rate of colonisation suggests that conditions are not so difficult as in the English situation. Nevertheless, when fertilisers were applied to young natural aspen (*Populus tremuloides*), very significant increases in growth rate (+60 per cent) were obtained when nitrogen, phosphorus and potassium were added together. This suggests that, just as in England, reclamation depends largely on proper supply of major plant nutrients. Many of the worked-out pits have been allowed to fill with water, creating over 1200 ha of lakes, which have become colonised rapidly by wild life of all sorts and are now a major recreational resource (Figure 9.21).

9.3.3   Stabilisation of tailings and waste
In the Mesabi region, low-grade taconite ore is concentrated by magnetic separation and the waste material, tailings, deposited, at an annual rate of 22 million tonnes, in basins covering 1000 ha which now require revegetation.

Figure 9.21. A lake formed from an old iron ore pit: a substantial addition to the environmental resources of the Mesabi iron ore region of Minnesota.

181

The taconite tailings are finely ground; the dam walls are formed from the coarser sand fraction, while the middle is much finer. The material has a pH of 7·4 or higher and consists of silica and inert iron compounds, with no phosphorus and nitrogen but adequate potassium.

Revegetation must involve overcoming the deficiencies of nitrogen and phosphorus. But apart from the lack of any proper soil texture, there are no other problems. A grass/legume mixture is therefore sown with lucerne (*Medicago sativa*) and birdsfoot trefoil (*Lotus corniculatus*) as legumes and either intermediate wheatgrass (*Agropyron intermedius*) and red fescue (*Festuca rubra*) or smooth brome (*Bromus inermis*) and ryegrass (*Lolium perenne*) mulched with hay or straw, tacked down with asphalt on the sloping dam walls. Fertilisation consists of 60 kg/ha of N to provide the initial nitrogen, the legumes providing the nitrogen subsequently, and 350 kg/ha of P, a heavy application intended to overcome problems of availability and long-term requirements of the sward.

The wetter areas are stabilised with reed canary grass (*Phalaris tuberosa*) and rye (*Secale cereale*), with lucerne and sweet clover (*Melilotus alba*), or sometimes only millet (*Pennisetum glaucum*) and barley (*Hordeum vulgare*). Both of these mixtures are attractive to wild fowl.

The outcome is an excellent vegetation cover and stabilisation, into which native species including trees such as aspen and birch are invading.

In the Pilbara, where conditions are so extreme, a technique of deep-ripping and the sowing of native species seems to be working well on the waste ore. Sometimes a short period of irrigation is needed in the early stages. The great problem is to find sufficient seed of the native species: it seems unlikely that agricultural species will be able to cope with the extreme climate.

9.4 BAUXITE

9.4.1 Extensive thin deposits

Aluminium is now one of the world's most important metals, and undoubtedly as other non-ferrous metals become scarcer, will be used more. As an element it is widespread in the earth's crust (about 8 per cent), in almost all important minerals. But it is very difficult to refine from most minerals, and modern production depends on using deposits in which aluminium has become specially concentrated.

In those parts of the world where temperature and humidity are high, base-rich rocks which are naturally high in aluminium, undergo a weathering process known as laterisation. The silicon and iron move down to lower layers and a more or less pure surface deposit of aluminium hydroxide, known as bauxite, is left behind, about 5 m

Figure 9.22. Extraction of bauxite involves removing a thin deposit, so large areas are disturbed: the mining operation at Gove in northern Australia.

thick, underneath a thin layer (<50 cm) of soil or over-burden (Figure 9.22).

This means that extraction is easy, but large areas must be used to provide the bauxite the world requires. The single area of bauxite at Weipa in northern Australia covers 2000 km². Fortunately most bauxite is in poor, unsettled tropical regions, but there are important deposits in Jamaica and in Guinea, West Africa, where the pressure on land is much greater. In Jamaica, where 160 000 ha, 15 per cent of the island possess bauxite, about 100 000 ha of arable land will have to be disturbed; this is over 20 per cent of the total arable land. But even in Northern Australia the terrain is the hunting-ground of aboriginal tribes, and in other regions the bauxite may be covered by important forest resources.

So the need to find ways of restoring the land to productive use is very great. Bauxite mining is a comparatively new industry, scattered throughout the world in a variety of situations, so that a variety of solutions is being examined. Nevertheless, because the properties of the lateritic deposits are similar, there is an overall pattern.

The soils produced by laterisation, latosols, are deep, and the bauxite deposits are part of the soil. Although the original rock was base-rich, the weathering has removed the minerals that could release plant nutrients. Much of the nutrients are therefore in the plants themselves (about 250 kg N/ha and 125 kg P/ha). There is little phosphorus in the soil (about 500 kg P/ha) and most of this is unavailable, bound to iron. But there is considerable nitrogen (about

2500 kg N/ha in the top 50 cm). The cation exchange capacity is very low (<15 meq/100 g). If the forest vegetation cover is destroyed, much of the nutrient store is lost: at the same time, the nutrients held in the organic matter are rapidly lost because the high temperatures and moistures cause breakdown of the organic matter. The soils are therefore not good for agriculture, which explains why there is little settlement in the areas where there are bauxite deposits.

The vegetation is characteristically rather open woodland or forest, visible in Figure 9.22. This is the reason why in N. Australia the areas form good hunting-ground for aboriginal tribes. There is a multitude of species all tolerant of the acidity and high aluminium content of the soils, such as guava (*Psidium guajava*) and screw pine (*Pandanus* sp.) in Hawaii, and *Eucalyptus tetradonta* and *Petalostigma quadriloculare* in northern Australia, together with the grass *Heteropogon triticeus*.

In the areas near to human settlements, such as in Hawaii and Jamaica, repeated burning and grazing have converted the woodland to an open mixture of trees and poor grassland containing species of *Paspalum* and *Sporobolus*, and scrub of *Haematoxylon campechianum*.

Underneath the bauxite deposits, the weathered lateritic deposits will often continue. But they may be indurated with the iron hydroxides leached from the bauxite layers above, to form hard ironstone, as at Weipa. In other areas, such as Jamaica, the original limestone rock which has not been weathered is found. In Hawaii, the underlying material is the original basalt, but this is partially degraded and soft.

9.4.2 Revegetation is not difficult
The bauxite is a very superficial deposit and the top soil itself may be where the highest aluminium concentrations occur. As a result, in some areas the top soil is removed with the rest of the bauxite. However, normally the top 50 cm is stripped separately and spread back over the site after extraction.

Since so little surface material is retained, the first essential is that the mined area is reshaped to make it suited for whatever use is proposed. This can be done by bulldozers, which at the same time can rip the mine basement to break up any hard rock. In Hawaii, where no top soil is retained, the ripping is followed by a series of cultivations which break down the basement material to a reasonable tilth.

It has never proved economic to carry out a two-level stripping of the overburden, so what goes back as top soil is in fact a mixture of all the surface materials to a depth of about 50 cm and can vary greatly in the amount of organic material and nutrients it contains (Figure 9.23).

The next steps, directed to re-establishing a vegetation cover, vary, since they depend on the end point required.

Figure 9.23. After mining, the top soil is spread back over the basement rock which has been ripped to break it down: this land in Jamaica is being returned to productive pasture.

In Gove, in Northern Australia, the indigenous vegetation must be replaced since the area is an aboriginal hunting area. The native vegetation re-establishes from seeds and vegetative pieces in the top soil, which is removed and spread on a stripped area in one operation. But where the top soil has been diluted with underlying material, the seed inoculum must be supplemented with seed collected by hand from the surrounding woodland. The aboriginals are expert seed collectors. This seed is scattered together with some rhodes grass (*Chloris gayana*) (6 kg/ha) and harrowed into the ground. Because the fertility has been depleted, fertiliser is applied, about 200 kg/ha of superphosphate, the amount adjusted to the quality of the soil cover. The whole operation is simple but effective (Figure 9.24).

Figure 9.24. Woodland re-establishing successfully in northern Australia: some of the trees come from dormant seed in the top soil, others are from seed collected from native trees by aborigines.

185

Bauxite

Commercial forestry demands more complex operations. At Weipa, two species of mahogany (*Khaya senegalensis* and *Swietenia macrophylla*) are being grown, in Jamaica caribbean pine (*Pinus caribaea*). These are planted by normal methods, often with quite substantial fertiliser dressings, (75 P, 200 N, 200 K kg/ha). Whether such heavy doses are cost-effective remains to be seen: it may be better to add smaller doses over a number of years since leaching is rapid through the lateritic material. The interplanting of leguminous and other nitrogen-fixing trees and shrubs, such as *Casuarina* and *Acacia* spp., as well as tropical forage legumes such as *Leucaena*, is being explored.

Grazing is an alternative, providing there are no husbandry problems. There are few problems of growing grass on latosols if the missing nutrients are replaced. Species such as pangola grass (*Digitaria decumbens*) and guinea grass (*Panicum maximum*) grow very well if fertilised and limed and can carry about 0·3 cattle/ha, yielding about 200 kg live weight gain/ha/yr. This is a good yield even from an established pasture on a poor soil (Figure 9.25). Legumes are being investigated.

Figure 9.25. Agricultural areas are mined in Jamaica and returned to full use afterwards: here is productive pasture—compare with Figure 9.23.

The final possibility is arable and plantation crops. Excellent yields of maize and other crops such sweet potato can be obtained in Jamaica on stripped areas which have only a 30 cm layer of soil replaced if adequate fertiliser or organic manure has been given. Although deeper layers give higher yields, they are not economically worthwhile because the yield advantage is so small (Figure 9.26). Now crops such as coffee, lime, pimento and avocado are being explored.

The weathering of the rocks that have given rise to bauxite deposits has usually been deep, so even if a large amount of material has been removed, it is still possible to create an effective soil out of what remains. The soil ultimately developed may be more fertile than the original. In view of the nature of bauxite deposits and the amount of exploitation which will inevitably take place, this is reassuring.

But aftercare will be necessary. Land restored to forest will require the least, especially if nitrogen-fixing tree, shrub or herbaceous species are present. But since lateritic soils have high phosphorus fixation capacities, some phosphorus addition will be inevitable. Agricultural land will require continued inputs of fertiliser, the amounts of individual nutrients depending on the crop. The need for aftercare and its benefits will be immediately apparent in crop yields.

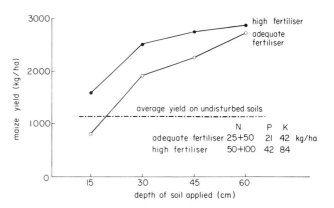

Figure 9.26. Yields on reclaimed land in Jamaica are excellent if sufficient fertiliser is applied—even without much top soil: this is important because the bauxite occurs close to the surface.

9.4.3 Red mud

Before bauxite can be used for the electrolytic extraction of aluminium it must be purified. This usually involves digesting the bauxite with sodium hydroxide. This disolves the aluminium hydroxide, which is subsequently precipitated as pure alumina and leaves behind a residue of red mud. For every two tonnes of bauxite there is one tonne of residue.

This red mud is nearly always deposited in lagoons (Figure 9.27). It is highly alkaline from the sodium hydroxide, and consists of a coarse red sand and a finer silty red clay (or true red mud). Sea water is sometimes used to carry the red mud: the magnesium in the sea water reacts with the sodium hydroxide to form a magnesium hydroxide precipitate (which is innocuous) and sodium chloride: if fresh water is used, removal of the sodium hydroxide does not occur. So the dominant factor in red mud lagoons is the high level of sodium hydroxide, or sodium chloride, or both.

The red sand has very little ion exchange capacity and is very permeable. So if it is left for some time, the sodium chloride and hydroxide, which are soluble, will leach away. It then becomes possible to establish salt-tolerant

Figure 9.27. Red mud produced by the concentration of alumina from bauxite: very alkaline and high in sodium it is extremely difficult to revegetate unless covered with other material.

Bauxite

grasses such as rhodes grass (*Chloris gayana*) and pangola grass (*Digitaria decumbens*) if substantial fertiliser dressings (200 kg N/ha and 400 kg P/ha) are given. Plant establishment is easier in the salt water treated material. However, the texture of the sand is so poor that better growth is obtained if it can be mixed with some ameliorant such as fly ash.

The red clay is much more difficult to deal with because it is less permeable and has a higher ion exchange capacity. Leaching is therefore very slow. Although it may be possible to establish vegetation on it if sufficient time is allowed, it is not clear at the moment whether this will ever be practicable, especially on material deposited using fresh water. One solution is to deposit the red sand on top of the clay when the lagoon is filled. But long-distance transport of red sand is difficult and other coverings must be found. The soil can be removed from the lagoon site and stockpiled to use as a covering later. Red mud is a serious problem which the industry must deal with if it is not to make problem areas in the future.

9.5   CHINA CLAY

9.5.1   A major disturbance

Mining for china clay, kaolin, is not as old an industry as mining for the rougher clays used for bricks and pottery. In Britain, the industry only began about 1770 when William Cookworthy demonstrated china clay in Cornwall could be used for making chinaware as fine as any made in China itself.

To begin with it was a fairly small-scale industry serving only the needs of making porcelain. But in the nineteenth century it became clear that china clay had many other uses, notably in the manufacture of paper. Deposits of the mineral kaolinite are not uncommon, but commercially valuable china clay is produced in comparatively few places in the world. The deposits in south-west England are especially rich and are a prime export, 2·4 million tonnes in 1973 at a value of £34·4 million.

The deposits were produced by hydrothermal degradation of granite from below as it was formed. As a result, the deposits extend to considerable depths. In the formative process the feldspars were broken down to kaolinite: the quartz and the mica were relatively unchanged. So the deposits are worked in open pits (Figure 9.28). The quartz, as coarse sand, is taken out and deposited in large heaps, the mica is settled and pumped into lagoons, and the kaolin precipitated: in most pits there is also some undecomposed rock (stent). These materials are in the ratio kaolin 1: mica 1: stent 1: quartz sand 6—a large amount of waste material in comparison with product. It would be possible to put the stent and the sand back into the pit, but

Figure 9.28. China clay deposits in England are worked in open pits by high pressure water: most of the material extracted is waste but since the deposits are bottomless cannot be put back into the pits.

the deposits are effectively bottomless and are continuously being worked to greater depths. The sand, stent and any overburden are dumped on surrounding land: the mica is put into lagoons in convenient valleys. Since the land has been acquired relatively cheaply and costs must be kept to a minimum, no attempt is made to remove the soil before the waste is dumped. The result is a devastation on a vast scale, a complex of heaps, pits and lagoons with disused land in between (Figure 9.29). About 35 square miles has been affected in Cornwall and Devon, a phenomenal destruction of countryside.

If all the sand wastes were put in one place for the next 50 years, assuming the present rate of production, it would form a heap 1000 ft high and 5 miles across at the base. The sand is produced too far away and in too large quantities to be used for constructional purposes although some is made into bricks. The volume of mica is smaller but it is deposited less deeply and so the lagoons are large. The two wastes must therefore be dealt with *in situ*, bearing in mind that the major land-use of the surrounding area is dairy farming. The most reasonable solution would be to establish a grass cover, although on areas that cannot be grazed, scrub or woodland would also be in keeping with the surrounding countryside.

The sand is structurally and nutritionally very poor: there is a gross deficiency of silt and clay-sized particles

189 *China Clay*

Figure 9.29. Part of the china clay region of Cornwall north of St. Stephen in 1965: despoilation is due more to the waste heaps than to the extraction pits.

(Table 9.13). This leads to poor water-holding capacity, about one-third of that of a normal soil. However, the rainfall is high and evenly distributed, and potential evaporation is low (Figure 9.30) so that severe drying-out does not occur except after a long drought, and then only in the surface layers (Figure 5.4, page 64). The mica is finer and retains water very well.

Table 9.13. China clay sand waste has a texture completely unlike normal soil but mica is better: particle size distribution of china clay wastes in Cornwall

fraction	size limits (diameter in mm)	composition by weight (%)	
		sand	mica
gravel	>2	56	0
coarse sand	2–0·02	30	5
fine sand	0·2–0·02	11	44
silt	0·02–0·002	2	47
clay	<0·002	1	4

When deposited, the sand is loose and can blow in the wind: in heavy rain there can be surface erosion. But any natural vegetation that develops soon stabilises the surface.

There are considerable deficiencies in N P K Mg and Ca (Table 9.14), which are only to be expected from the origin

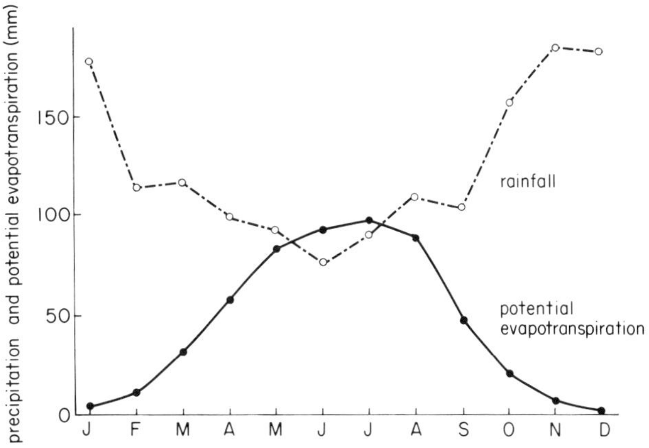

Figure 9.30. Precipitation and evaporation in Cornwall: on average, evaporation only exceeds precipitation during June so that grass can be established during most of the year: but damaging dry periods can occur.

of the material. But they are intensified by the soil texture and a low ion exchange capacity which allows rapid leaching. The lack of calcium means that the material is rather acid. But since the cation exchange capacity is very low (about 15 meq/kg) there is not a high lime requirement. The mica is similar.

Table 9.14. The wastes are extremely low in plant nutrients: a comparison of china clay wastes and neighbouring pastures

| site | material | available nutrients (ppm) | | | | total | pH[3] |
		K[1]	Mg[1]	Ca[1]	P[2]	N	
Maggie Pie	sand	10	16	85	2·0	9	4·5
	mica	13	20	115	2·8	18	4·0
Lee Moor	sand	8	14	90	4·6	11	4·5
	mica	12	28	110	5·6	24	3·9
Whitmore	ryegrass ley	176	130	990	46	1560	4·7
	old pasture	370	170	1700	70	1283	4·8
Bodmin Moor	old pasture	110	71	880	42	1275	4·2

[1] extracted with 1N ammonium acetate
[2] extracted with sodium bicarbonate
[3] measured in 0·01M $CaCl_2$

The sparse vegetation that slowly colonises the heaps is what might be expected on a nutrient-poor acid soil. There is a slow invasion of calcifuge grasses and shrubs and eventually a full cover is built up, except where physical factors intervene (Figure 9.31). In the more exposed situations, the succession goes no further than heathland. But on the more protected heaps, the leguminous species, gorse and tree lupin, invade and are followed by goat willow and rhododendron. The climax of the succession is an acid oak woodland (Figure 9.32).

The gross shortage of major plant nutrients, especially nitrogen, must retard the succession, so the appearance of legumes which can tolerate the acid nutrient-poor conditions is a critical step in the development of a vegetation cover. These are able to fix 30–50 kg N/ha/yr. Fully developed plant communities in a wide variety of sites appear to contain about 1000 kg N/ha. Before the legumes

China Clay

appear, nitrogen accumulation is very slow, but after they have invaded, a well-established stand of leguminous shrubs will take 20 years to accumulate enough nitrogen to form a fully active soil/plant ecosystem capable of supporting a large biomass.

Vegetation establishment on the mica waste is not very different, although the greater ability to retain water and nutrients means that the succession is faster and a wider range of species are involved.

Figure 9.31. A 30-year-old sand waste heap in Cornwall: natural colonisation is slow and limited to shrubs and grasses tolerant of acidity and lack of nutrients.

Figure 9.32. Eventually, old china clay workings become colonised by leguminous species and then by trees, to make an attractive wilderness: but this can take over 100 years.

9.5.2 A self-sustaining vegetation cover

For engineering reasons, the heaps are left with steep sides, at the natural angle of rest. If a grass cover is to be established on such slopes, hydroseeding is the only one possible method. It works well, using peat or wood pulp as a mulch and no stabiliser. Stabilisers do not adhere well to the sand, and they increase run-off and erosion and inhibit germination. The method is sensitive to periods when there could be surface drought after sowing and should only be used when the ground surface has recently been saturated. On flatter surfaces agricultural methods are feasible. But consolidation from the use of heavy machinery must be remedied or there can be substantial surface erosion.

To be in keeping with the surroundings and with the ecological problems of the wastes, a grass mixture containing red fescue (*Festuca rubra*) and bent grass (*Agrostis tenuis*) and other species is appropriate (Table 9.15). However, none of these species is a very rapid grower, so rye grass (*Lolium perenne*) is therefore included. At present, high seeding rates are used (>100 kg/ha): it would be satisfactory if this could be brought down to 60–70 kg/ha by improvements in the hydroseeding technique.

Table 9.15. The species sown must be tolerant of difficult conditions: a seeds mixture for grazing purposes for hydroseeding on china clay wastes in England

species		% wt
ryegrass	*Lolium perenne*	35
red fescue	*Festuca rubra*	25
sheep's fescue	*Festuca ovina*	10
bent grass	*Agrostis tenuis*	5
smooth-stalked meadow grass	*Poa pratensis*	5
white clover	*Trifolium repens*	10
red clover	*Trifolium pratense*	5
bird's foot trefoil	*Lotus corniculatus*	5

varieties should be those tolerant of grazed, low nutrient conditions

A heavy dressing of 600 kg/ha of a complete fertiliser (about 100 kg N, 60 kg P, 70 kg K) will give good growth. The lime requirement can be met with 1000 kg/ha of lime. However, with this treatment grass growth ceases within a season, and the sward becomes brown and moribund. Aftercare experiments show that growth is restored by nitrogen (Figure 5.9, page 71 and Figure 7.10, page 121). Regular dressings of a high-nitrogen fertiliser will therefore ensure good growth. But these dressings are expensive, and as soon as they are discontinued, growth ceases because of insufficient mineralisation and recycling of the nitrogen accumulated.

For this reason, legumes should be used. Legumes, clovers in particular, given adequate lime and phosphate treatments and properly inoculated, can accumulate over 100 kg N/ha/yr in a sward (Table 9.16). With this accumula-

193   *China Clay*

tion of nitrogen they could soon get eliminated by competition from the grass, but this can be prevented by grazing.

200 kg N/ha can easily be accumulated by means of either fertiliser or clover in 2–4 years. However, studies of nitrogen release by mineralisation, using an incubation technique, show that the nitrogen accumulated under fertilised grass swards is not mineralised readily, whereas that accumulated under clover-rich swards is mineralised remarkably easily (Figure 9.33). This explains why fertilised grass swards stop growing immediately fertiliser treatment is stopped. It is an important argument for the use of clover, quite apart from the fact that legumes provide the nitrogen at no cost.

Table 9.16. Legumes accumulate nitrogen very rapidly on china clay wastes: nitrogen accumulation by different legumes in the first two seasons after sowing

species	sand		mica	
	1972	1973	1972	1973
		(kg N/ha)		
Trifolium repens S184 (white clover)	89	181	74	200
Trifolium repens S100	59	199	45	258
Trifolium pratense S123 (red clover)	76	205	205	333
Trifolium pratense Early	65	236	100	463
Trifolium pratense Altaswede	85	152	124	80
Trifolium hybridum (alsike)	79	143	80	273
Trifolium dubium (yellow trefoil)	31	99	44	136
Medicago sativa (lucerne)	61	168	65	214
Medicago lupulina (black medick)	48	216	88	234
Lotus corniculatus (bird's foot trefoil)	67	166	100	319
Lupinus angustifolius (lupin)	32	–	108	–
Vicia sativa (common vetch)	14	–	51	–

With hydroseeding, legume establishment is very poor. But the problem can be obviated if no more than 100 kg/ha of mineral fertiliser is used in the hydroseeding and the rest is applied when the clover has germinated. Then excellent clover-rich swards can be obtained (Figure 9.34). However, these will only persist if a reasonable aftercare programme is maintained, as would occur in normal farming practice, with particular attention being paid to lime and phosphorus levels to maintain the clover (Figure 9.35). Given good management, it is possible to have swards which can carry at least 20 sheep/ha through the summer period.

However, on the steeper heaps, made up of very coarse quartz sand, the normal legumes such as clover do not persist readily because of surface drought and nutrient leaching. Yet the legumes tolerant of acid low-nutrient conditions, especially tree lupin (*Lupinus arboreus*) and gorse (*Ulex europaeus*), grow extremely well. The steep slopes are often not able to be grazed, so a scrub vegetation is appropriate, particularly if accompanied by small trees, such as the sallows (*Salix cinerea* and *S. aurita*) which are native to the area. In earlier days, there is no doubt that the pit captains spread tree lupin, which they recognised as a valuable plant, by scattering the seed.

Chapter 9: Strip Mines

Scrub, especially if it contains gorse, is a fire risk. For this reason, perhaps the best end point is a tree cover, hydroseeded or hand-planted. Tree lupins can be an excellent accompanying plant to provide protection and nitrogen fixation: in New Zealand, tree lupins have been shown to fix as much as 160 kg N/ha/yr in a poor sandy soil.

Many people would argue that the steep-sided heaps are wrong from a landscaping point of view and give unnecessary problems: more naturalistic contours should be attained. Reshaping is certainly not necessarily difficult, and in the process, overburden can be spread over the heaps to provide material with a better ion exchange capacity and potential fertility. Where this approach has been adopted, the results have been excellent.

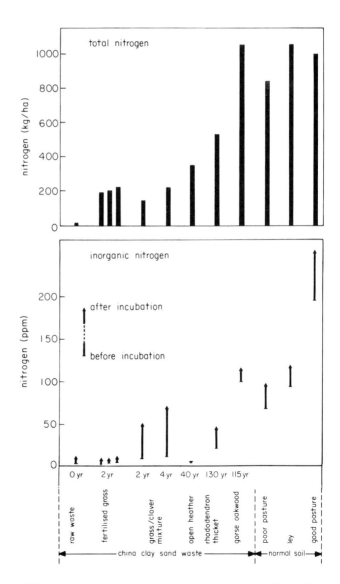

Figure 9.33. The key to reclamation of china clay wastes is in accumulation of nitrogen: this can be achieved by either fertilisers or legumes: however, the nitrogen released by mineralisation occurs most readily under legumes.

China Clay

Figure 9.34. A well-balanced grass/clover sward established on china clay waste at Hawkstor, Cornwall: up to 20 sheep graze per hectare.

Figure 9.35. Maintenance of legumes depends on proper aftercare: growth of white clover in a four-year-old sward on sand waste is improved by addition of both lime and phosphorus.

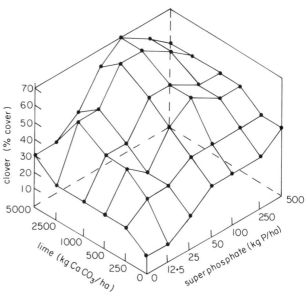

Figure 9.36. Mica waste has a very even texture and good retention of nutrients: when properly fertilised, it is excellent for vegetables such as potatoes.

The mica ponds are large and flat. Some of them are rather damp, but with proper drainage the mica wastes are not waterlogged even after heavy rain. Mica has twice the ion exchange capacity of sand and there is excellent nutrient retention after fertilisation. The material is free of pathogens and weeds.

As a result, a wide range of horticultural crops can be grown directly on the waste (Figure 9.36). The material will obviously be improved by the incorporation of organic matter, but crop yields in the first year are within the normal range, especially for potatoes and other root crops which are suited to the even-textured material. Mica ponds

196 *Chapter 9: Strip Mines*

are a remarkable example of industrial waste areas which can be utilised for productive purposes immediately. It is disappointing that this has not been done in the past.

9.5.3   Strip-mining in Georgia

Mining for china clay in the U S A began in Georgia in 1880, in a completely different type of deposit. It was deposited as alluvial sediments in the Cretaceous period from the weathering of crystalline igneous rocks, and occurs as beds of fairly pure kaolinite between sands and gravels. Originally the beds outcropped, but those now being worked are under sand and clay overburden up to 50 m deep. The overburden is stripped and replaced in a mixed state (Figure 9.37).

Figure 9.37. China clay mining in Georgia, U S A: the overburden is stripped, the clay removed, and the overburden replaced, planted with grass or trees.

About 3000 hectares have been strip-mined in Georgia alone since 1969, of which only one-sixth has been reclaimed. The land was previously used for timber and arable crops, although recently the emphasis has moved to improved pasture. The objective is therefore to return the land to productive pasture or timber.

The overburden is a mixture of sands and clays very low in nutrients and lacking in organic matter. Because of the presence of the clays, there is good retention of water, but low rates of infiltration of rain. There are devastating rains in the spring followed by excessive periods of drought in the summer. This leads to violent sheet erosion. Soil analysis shows an acute lack of nutrients, especially N, P and K but also Ca and Mg, but with considerable variability from one stratum to another. There may also be acidity problems due to the presence of pyritic material, taking the pH down to 1·8. So there is little establishment of vegetation.

Since the overburden is left in a very contorted state,

197   *China Clay*

with many slopes more than 15°, the first step is to level the heaps as far as possible. These must then be ripped to assist infiltration. Herbaceous vegetation can then be established without difficulty, sown by standard means, drilled into the soil and packed with a cultipacker. Because of the possibility of torrential rain, a mulch must often be added: this can be chopped straw, wood pulp or shredded bark. It is necessary to tack the mulch down with a bitumen binder on steep slopes.

The species used are a compromise between rapid germination and permanence, analogous to the mixture used on the English sand heaps (Table 9.17). Cereal rye (*Secale cereale*), which is only an annual, grows rapidly but dies in the autumn, leaving its dead remains to protect the ground. Since nutrient levels are extremely low, these must be added at the time of sowing, using about 100 kg N, 60 kg P and 80 kg K/ha.

Table 9.17. In South-east USA a simple combination of a legume with one or two grasses is usually satisfactory: species for sowing on china clay strip-mining overburden in Georgia

cereal rye	*Secale cereale*
tall fescue	*Festuca arundinacea*
bahiagrass	*Paspalum notatum*
bermuda grass	*Cynodon dactylon*
weeping lovegrass	*Eragrostis curvula*
sericea lespedeza	*Lespedeza cuneata*
kobe lespedeza	*Lespedeza striata*
white clover	*Trifolium repens*

Lime has to be applied, the amount dependent on the lime requirement. Since nitrogen is critical, a legume must be included. *Lespedeza* sp. are particularly successful and may mean that further nitrogen fertiliser is not necessary. But some aftercare fertilisation will usually be essential. In this way, a vigorous vegetation can be obtained which not only provides a robust ground cover, but also contributes

Figure 9.38. Trees can grow extremely well on china clay overburden in Georgia if properly fertilised: this is a plantation of Loblolly pine.

Chapter 9: Strip Mines

substantial amounts of organic matter to the soil and improves its structural qualities.

The material is equally satisfactory for tree planting. The absence of an initial vegetation cover means that there is no competing vegetation in the early stages, and that seedling transplants can establish quickly (Figure 9.38). However, fertiliser must be added. The species found to be successful, *Pinus elliottii*, *P. taeda*, *P. virginiana*, *Platanus occidentalis*, *Quercus acutissima* and *Alnus glutinosa* appear to require about 100 g of a 20:10:15 fertiliser per tree for optimum growth. This must be repeated in the third year. There are problems of soil erosion, but these can be controlled by the use of a wood fibre mulch, which lasts until the trees become properly established.

In these more complex sites in South Eastern USA, there are higher amounts of the finer soil fractions and a more favourable climate than in South West England. As a result, restoration of a vegetation cover is easier and subsequent growth more rapid.

FURTHER READING

Coal

Beyer L.E. & Hutnik R.J. 1969. *Acid and Aluminium Toxicity as Related to Strip-Mine Spoil Banks in Western Pennsylvania.* Pennsylvania: Coal Research Board.

Coaldrake J.E. & Russell M.J. 1978. Rehabilitation with pasture after open-cast mining at three sites in the Bowen Coal Basin of Queensland. *Reclamation Review*, **1**, 1–8.

Davis I.V. & Arguile R.T. 1975. Opencast coal mining: working, restoration and reclamation. In: *Minerals and the Environment*, ed. M.T. Jones. London: Institute of Mining and Metallurgy, 313–31.

Grim E.C. & Hill R.D. 1974. *Environmental Protection in Surface Mining of Coal.* Cincinatti, Ohio: Environmental Protection Agency.

Haynes R.J. & Klimstra W.D. 1975. *Illinois Lands Surface Mined for Coal.* Carbondale, Illinois: Cooperative Wildlife Research Laboratory, South Illinois University.

Industrial Environmental Research Laboratory. 1976. *Extensive Overburden Potentials for Soil and Water Quality.* Cincinnati, Ohio: US Environmental Protection Agency.

Jones W.G. 1970. *The New Forest.* Pennsylvania: Boalsburg.

Karr J.R. 1968. Habitat and avian diversity on strip-mined land in East-central Illinois. *Condor*, **70**, 348–57.

Kohnke H. 1950. The reclamation of coal mine spoils. *Adv. Agron.* **2**, 318–49.

Packer P.E. & Aldon E.F. 1978. Revegetation techniques for dry regions. In: *Reclamation of Drastically Disturbed Lands*, ed. F.W. Schaller and P. Sutton, 425–50. Madison: Amer. Soc. Agron.

Oil shale

Harbert H.P. & Berg W. 1978. *Vegetative Stabilisation of Spent Oil Shale.* Cincinatti, Ohio: Environmental Protection Agency.

Schmehl W.R. & McCaslin B.D. 1973. Some properties of spent oil-shale significant to plant growth. In: *Ecology and Reclamation of Devastated Land*, eds. R.J. Hutnik & G. Davis. New York: Gordon and Breach.

Anon. 1971. *Water Pollution Potential of Spent Oil Shale Residues*. Washington: Environmental Protection Agency.

Davis G. 1978. Oil shale. In: *Reclamation of Drastically Disturbed Lands*, ed. F.W. Schaller and P. Sutton, 609–18. Madison: Amer. Soc. Agron.

Iron ore

Backhouse G. & Nimmo M. 1956. Afforestation of ironstone workings in Northamptonshire. *J. Forestry Comm.* **25**, 125–30.

Blood J.W., Jackson H. & Ormrod J.F. 1961. Restoration to agriculture of land worked for ironstone and levelled without the addition of topsoil. *Expl. Husb.* **6**, 90–9.

Bridges E.M. 1961. Aspect and time in soil formation. *Agriculture, Lond.* **68**, 358–63.

Cowan R.J. & Dean R. 1975. Rehabilitation of ironstone workings. *Chartered Surveyor* **3**, 27–30.

Dickenson S.K. & Younghman D.G. 1971. Taconite tailing basin reclamation—a phase of multiple resource management. *Proceedings 32nd Annual Mining Symp.* 137–42.

Leisman G.A. 1957. A vegetation and soil chronosequence on the Mesabi Iron Range spoil banks, Minnesota. *Ecol. Monogr.* **27**, 221–45.

Manthey T.J. 1971. Mine land environment in Minnesota—a progress report. *Proceedings 32nd Annual Mining Symp.* 143–9.

Martinik W-G. 1977. Iron ore mining in the Pilbara: rehabilitation—a joint approach. In: 1977 Environmental Workshop. Canberra: Australian Mining Industry Research Council.

Smith R.M., Tryon E.H. & Tyner E.H. 1971. *Soil Development on Mine Spoil*. West Virginia: Univ. Agric. Exp. Sta. Bull. 604 T.

Whyte R.O. & Sisam J.W.E. 1949. *The Establishment of Vegetation on Industrial Waste Land*. Commonwealth Agric. Bur. Publ. 14. Aberystwyth: Commonwealth Bureau of Pastures and Field Crops.

Bauxite

Bevege D.I. 1974. Revegetating surface-mined areas and spoils in northern Australia, particularly bauxite at Weipa. *Proceedings of Regional Symposium on Mine Rehabilitation in Northern Australia*, 33–54. Weipa: Commonwealth Aluminium Corporation.

Howard R.A. & Proctor G.R. 1957. Vegetation of bauxite soils in Jamaica I, II. *Journ. Arnold Arbor.* **38**, 1–41, 151–69.

Leggate J. 1974. Weipa regeneration practice and policies. *Proceedings of Regional Symposium on Mine Rehabilitation in Northern Australia.* 12–32. Weipa: Commonwealth Aluminium Corporation.

Meecham J.R. & Bell L.C. 1971. Amelioration procedures for the establishment of vegetation on alumina refinery wastes. *Environmental Engineering Conference*, Canberra.

Morgan G.W. 1971. Rehabilitation of bauxite mine areas in Jamaica. *Jamaican Geographical Society*. May 1971

Morgan G.W. 1971. Reclamation and restoration research on bauxite-mined lands in Jamaica. *J. Geol. Soc. Jamaica, Bauxite/Alumina Symp.*, 73–8.

Morgan G.W. 1974. Crop productivity as affected by depths of topsoil spread for reclaiming bauxite-mined lands in Jamaica. *Trop. Agric. (Trinidad)* **51**, 332–46.

Younge O.R. & Moomaw J.C. 1960. Revegetation of strip-mined bauxite lands in Hawaii. *Econ. Bot.* **14**, 316–30.

China clay

Barton R.M. 1966. *A History of the Cornish China Clay Industry*. Truro, England: Bradford Barton.

Bradshaw A.D., Dancer W.S., Handley J.F. & Sheldon J.C. 1975. The biology of land revegetation and the reclamation of the china clay wastes of Cornwall. In: *The Ecology of Resource Degradation and Renewal*, ed. M.J. Chadwick and G.T. Goodman. Symp. Brit. Ecol. Soc. **15**, 363–84. Oxford: Blackwell Scientific Publications.

Dancer W.S., Handley J.F. & Bradshaw A.D. 1977. Nitrogen accumulation in kaolin mining wastes in Cornwall. I. Natural communities. *Plant and Soil*. **48**, 153–67.

Dancer W.S., Handley J.F. & Bradshaw A.D. 1977. Nitrogen accumulation in kaolin mining wastes in Cornwall. II. Forage legumes. *Plant and Soil*. **48**, 303–14.

May J.T. 1975. Renewal of china clay strip mining spoil in southeastern United States. In: *The Ecology of Resource Degradation and Renewal*, ed. M.J. Chadwick and G.T. Goodman. Symp. Brit. Ecol. Soc. **15**, 351–62. Oxford: Blackwell Scientific Publications.

May J.T. 1978. China (Kaolin) clays: mining and reclamation. In: *Environmental Management of Mineral Wastes*, ed. G.T. Goodman and M.J. Chadwick, 167–207. Netherlands: Sijthoff and Nordhoff.

Sheldon J.C. & Bradshaw A.D. 1977. The development of a hydraulic seeding technique for unstable sand slopes. I. Effects of fertilisers, mulches and stabilisers. *J. Appl. Ecol.* **14**, 905–18.

'We abuse the land because we regard it as a commodity belonging to us. When we see the land as a community to which we belong, we may begin to use it with love and respect.'

ALDO LEOPOLD.

A Sand County Almanac. 1949.

10   Quarries

Quarrying for rock and stone is as old as civilisation. Originally, before industrialisation and cheap transport made bricks, tiles and concrete universally available, hard rocks were quarried locally for building the houses we lived in, as well as for most other constructions, such as bridges and farm buildings. Many of the fine buildings of Europe are made of limestone. In the areas where hard rocks abound, in Britain especially in the north and west, the countryside is peppered with small quarries which served local needs. Most of these are now disused and have become incorporated in towns and built over, or colonised naturally, and so are not environmental problems.

But the development of cement and concrete, invented by the Romans, has changed the pattern of demand. Firstly, there is the need for limestone and clay, the raw materials for cement, and secondly, there is a need for aggregates for concrete, as well as ballast for roads and other foundations. All this involves crushing and processing rock and so tends to be concentrated in fewer larger sites where the machinery is permanently installed. The new uses are growing: modern quarries can be very large, as much as 1 km across and more than 50 m deep (Figure 10.1), in contrast to the older quarries which are

Figure 10.1. Modern quarries are immense and there is great need to find ways of making them an attractive part of the landscape: this limestone quarry in Derbyshire is surrounded by a National Park.

only often a deserted hollow at the end of a lonely road.

Alternatively, for ballast and aggregates sand and gravel can be used, quarried or dredged from open pits. Because transport costs are a large percentage of the total costs of the product, an over-riding factor in the choice of material is proximity to the point of use. So the winning of aggregates is an activity that is scattered over the countryside; gravel pits and quarries are widespread wherever the geological formations are appropriate. Conversely, where excesses occur of a waste product that could be used as an aggregate, such as slate and china clay waste, but in a region far from the point of demand, they are not used, and produce their own particular reclamation problems.

In a modern quarry there is usually very little waste since all the rock can be utilised. However, the overburden must be removed and dumped. Often this can be used in land-scaped banks to hide the main quarry operations: it can easily be revegetated. The main environmental problem is set by the quarry itself, by the bare rock face and quarry floor, or the pit flooded with water.

At first sight, the reclamation of modern quarries poses many problems. But they have a great deal of potential if the work is done wisely.

10.1 ACID ROCKS

10.1.1 A difficult problem

Acid rocks are those that have a high percentage of silica and naturally give rise to soils of low pH. They consist of sedimentary materials such as mudstones, slates and schists, as well as igneous materials such as granites and quartzites. Most of them are hard and can be used for many different purposes, so disused quarries are commonplace in all hard acid rock regions.

In certain situations, a large amount of waste rock is produced which can have considerable environmental impact. When slate is quarried, 95 per cent of the rock excavated is rejected, forming the sepulchral heaps so familiar in N. Wales and elsewhere. There are about 500×10^6 tonnes of slate waste in North Wales, all lying around the quarries (Figure 10.2). The slate industry has declined, but the waste remains as a gloomy reminder of past activity.

Hydroelectricity schemes are usually to be found in areas of hard acid rocks. Their construction involves the excava-tion of long tunnels, and subterranean halls for power plant, which produces quantities of waste rock, which for economic reasons must usually be dumped as near to its source as possible, possibly high up on a mountain side visible for long distances. In countries such as Norway, the impact of such schemes can therefore be considerable (Figure 10.3) and a lot of ingenuity has been employed by NVE, the Norwegian Authority, to find a solution.

Figure 10.2. The environmental impact of a slate quarry: a large pit surrounded by piles of coarse rock waste which is visible from all the surrounding unspoilt North Wales countryside.

Figure 10.3. A sharp geometrical gash in a wooded countryside: rock waste produced by the excavation of hydro-electricity tunnels in Norway.

Table 10.1. Hard rocks have important differences in the total amount of plant nutrients they contain: average chemical composition of different rock types

component	rhyolites	granites	diorites	basalts
SiO$_2$	72·80	70·18	58·90	49·06
TiO$_2$	0·33	0·39	0·76	1·36
Al$_2$O$_3$	13·49	14·47	16·47	15·70
Fe$_2$O$_3$	1·45	1·57	2·89	5·38
FeO	0·88	1·78	4·04	6·37
MnO	0·08	0·12	0·12	0·31
MgO	0·38	0·88	3·57	6·17
CaO	1·20	1·99	6·14	8·95
Na$_2$O	3·38	3·48	3·46	3·11
K$_2$O	4·46	4·11	2·11	1·52
H$_2$O	1·47	0·84	1·27	1·62
P$_2$O$_5$	0·08	0·19	0·27	0·45
CO$_2$	·	·	·	·
SO$_3$	·	·	·	·
BaO	·	·	·	·
C	·	·	·	·

(where data is not given analyses have not been made, usually because levels are low)

Chapter 10: Quarries

The waste rock is a miserable environment for plants. Acidic rocks are usually hard, so the fragments are large and there is no fine material. Water drains through the material very quickly and little is retained. Fine fragments tend to be washed down from the surface to the lower layers of the tip. Plants must be able to withstand complete desiccation, like the hair moss (*Rhacomitrium lanuginosum*) in cooler situations, or produce long roots which can penetrate into the lower layers where there is moisture, like the sessile oak (*Quercus petraea*) and birch (*Betula pubescens*).

Acidic rocks contain large quantities of silica and are very low in plant nutrients (Table 10.1). Since they are hard, they weather very slowly and release very little of the plant nutrients they contain. The major nutrient supply is through rain and is very restricted: the extreme conditions prevent nitrogen fixation by plants and the breakdown of organic matter. The only exception to this is where the rock is richer in bases, such as diorite or basalt.

The range of plants to be found colonising acidic rock waste or rock faces is therefore very restricted (Table 10.2). The range found on recently deposited rock wastes often consists only of a single moss, *Rhacomitrium lanuginosum*, and a single tree species, *Betula pubescens* (Figure 10.4). However, if the rock is softer and richer in nutrients, a wider range of species can be found, and natural rock crevices may shelter uncommon mountain species, such as rose root (*Rhodiola rosea*) and the globe flower (*Trollius europaeus*). But it is very unusual to find these species in disused quarries because their powers of migration are limited.

Quarry floors usually accumulate finer material and therefore are not so inhospitable. Scrub and woodland can develop naturally, consisting of species capable of tolerating low nutrient conditions such as wood sage (*Teucrium scorodonia*) and bramble (*Rubus fruticosus*) as well as trees,

dolerites	shales	sandstones	limestones
50·48	58·10	78·33	5·19
1·45	0·65	0·25	0·06
15·34	15·40	4·77	0·81
3·84	4·02	1·07	0·54
7·78	2·45	0·30	·
0·20	·	·	
5·79	2·44	1·16	7·89
8·94	3·11	5·50	42·57
3·07	1·30	0·45	0·05
0·97	3·24	1·31	0·33
1·89	5·00	1·63	0·77
0·25	0·17	0·08	0·04
·	2·63	5·03	41·54
·	0·64	0·07	0·05
·	0·05	0·05	·
·	0·80	·	·

Table 10.2. Plants can withstand the environment of acid rock: species to be found on acid mountain scree slopes and rock faces

such as rowan, birch and oak. If grazing occurs, an acid grassland will develop, dominated by bent grass (*Agrostis tenuis*) and sheep's fescue (*Festuca ovina*) or similar species which tolerate poor conditions.

on extremely poor hard rocks			
Agrostis canina	(bent grass)	*Galium saxatile*	(heath bedstraw)
Andraea petrophila	(rockmoss)	*Lycopodium selago*	(fir club moss)
Calluna vulgaris	(heather)	*Rhacomitrium lanuginosum*	(woolly hair moss)
Deschampsia flexuosa	(wavy hair-grass)	*Vaccinum myrtillus*	(bilberry)
Empetrum nigrum	(crowberry)	*V. vitis-idaea*	(cowberry)

on slightly richer rocks			
Agrostis tenuis	(bent grass)	*Cystopteris fragilis*	(brittle bladder-fern)
Alchemilla alpina	(alpine lady's-mantle)	*Deschampsia caespitosa*	(tufted hair-grass)
Anthoxanthum odoratum	(sweet vernal-grass)	*Dryopteris abbreviata*	(mountain fern)
Athyrium alpestre	(mountain lady-fern)	*Rumex acetosa*	(sorrel)
Cryptogramme crispa	(parsley fern)	*Salix herbacea*	(least willow)

Figure 10.4. Coarse slate waste in North Wales naturally colonised by trees: once the trees have overcome the problem of establishment they find sufficient water and nutrients by their deep roots.

10.1.2   Vegetation establishment is not easy
With such severe conditions, there may seem to be no solution without resorting to a substantial soil cover. Yet the existence of occasional plants growing well, suggests that the problems are not insuperable.

The lack of fine material at the surface of rock waste can be overcome if the heap is reshaped and the coarse material removed to uncover the finer material below: the passage of heavy machinery will also create fine particles. In some situations, the operations also generate fine material: the Norwegian Water Resources and Electricity Board (NVE) spread the final cleanings of newly constructed tunnels on to the surface of coarse waste. They may even modify the blasting technique to generate fine material. Sometimes overburden is available.

In the fine material, a wide variety of species can be planted. The choice can depend on landscape requirements, but the ecological limitations of a raw, nutrient-poor acid material remain. Fertilisers and some lime must be applied, and will need to be re-applied in subsequent years to maintain growth (Figure 10.5). Since the material will always be poor and acid, species must be chosen which are tolerant of these conditions, in temperate regions, grasses like *Agrostis tenuis* and *Festuca ovina* and *F. rubra*. A broad range of species may be a good insurance: this may be achieved by using hay barn sweepings. Legumes will be valuable to provide nitrogen in the first few years, but the lime and phosphorus will have to be maintained correctly, as in all acid upland areas (Chapter 5). With proper treatment, excellent grazing land has been produced in Norway, better than any existing previously.

Figure 10.5. Grass and trees can be grown directly on rock waste if properly fertilised: this heap in Norway was seeded and fertilised but a stream prevented the contractor from returning to give more fertiliser to the further area.

Providing fine material is available, broadcast seeding onto rocky surfaces is very successful and low seeding rates can be used. In Norway, 1 seed per cm^2 is suggested (about 40 kg/ha). The seeds fall into crevices and pockets where they find moisture and protection. But these crevices must not be more than a few centimetres deep or the seedling will not establish properly.

Trees can also be planted. This has been done very successfully by NVE (Figure 10.6). In a drier climate, considerable success has been obtained in the Stonyfell Quarry outside Adelaide, S. Australia (Figure 10.7). But it is essential that the material is fertilised in the second and subsequent years after planting.

In areas where there is no fine material, trees are the only plants that can be used, for they have the capacity to root downwards into moist layers. But to establish, they must be provided with a pocket of water-absorbent material of sufficient size (about 5 litres) to provide enough moisture during drought periods, and containing an adequate supply of slow-release fertiliser. The best material is moss peat

Acid Rocks

derived from *Sphagnum*. It can be pumped on the sites as slurry. This technique has been shown to work remarkably well in North Wales on coarse slate waste (Figure 10.8). The trees root out of the pocket and become independent of it in about two seasons.

Figure 10.6. A rock waste heap in Norway being treated by standard NVE methods: *left* planting in pockets with soil mixture; *right* 5 years later after additions of fertiliser—now ready to be left alone.

Figure 10.7. Trees established directly into acid rock waste from a stone quarry in a Mediterranean climate where only fertiliser has been provided: Stoneyfell Quarry, Adelaide, S. Australia.

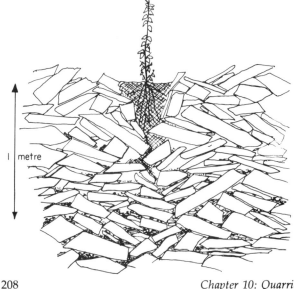

Figure 10.8. In coarse slate waste trees can be established on a pocket of moisture- and nutrient-retaining material: an organic compost can be pumped into position as a slurry.

1 metre

Chapter 10: Quarries

The species of tree used on acid rock waste must be those that are tolerant of poor conditions. In Europe, these include alder (*Alnus incana*), sallows (*Salix caprea* and *S. aurita*), birch (*Betula pubescens*), Scots pine (*Pinus sylvestris*) and oak (*Quercus petraea*). In other countries, the more resilient of the species listed in Chapter 6 can be used. Natural colonisation of native species may occur: these will be better than introduced material because they will be of the local adapted ecotype. Grazing must be excluded.

The rock faces are more difficult, but plant growth on natural faces shows that it is not impossible. Norwegian experience suggests that it is sufficiently difficult to induce colonisation that bare rock faces should always be avoided, if necessary, by covering them with waste rock. The ambitious plans for the Kerr Quarry, Victoria, Australia, include reshaping, cracking the underlying rock, as well as covering with overburden. It should always be possible to blast the final face and seed it, using a slurry system similar to that outlined for limestone quarries.

10.2   CALCAREOUS ROCKS

10.2.1   Problems but possibilities
Limestone and chalk are common rocks that consist almost entirely of calcium carbonate (Table 10.1) deposited as shells of small animals in clear seas usually without mud or other contaminants. They differ mainly in hardness.

Originally used mainly for building, because of their special composition they now have a very wide range of uses. Cement is made from a combination of calcium carbonate with clay. The chemical and manufacturing industries use them as a primary raw material for chemical processes, glass and steel. Limestones, particularly the older deposits such as of the Carboniferous period, can be very hard and yet can be crushed: these are extensively used for aggregates. And chalk, and limestone after burning, have for centuries played an important role in agriculture for liming farm land and reducing its acidity.

As a result, chalk and limestone are probably more heavily exploited than any other type of deposit, particularly in the more highly developed countries. Large quarries and fleets of trucks carrying lime products are now, alas, a characteristic feature of most limestone and chalk areas. The small older quarries were small and scattered and are now mostly disused. With the passage of time, they have become colonised with plants.

The newer quarries are large, making enormous scars on the countryside. Since limestone rocks are usually associated with an attractive topography and countryside, such as the Peak District of England, limestone quarries can be particular problems. They must be assimilated back into the landscape by the restoration of the original vegetation or the provision of an alternative vegetation cover.

Because chalk and limestone are almost pure calcium carbonate, they seem at first sight to be rather odd, extreme materials on which it might be difficult to get plants to grow. But, although from the point of view of plant nutrition they are very unbalanced, calcium carbonate itself is not a toxic or difficult material for plants.

Since chalk and limestone are so pure, a great depth of soil does not usually develop, and what does is dominated by the underlying rock. The soils are nearly always deficient in phosphorus, nitrogen and potassium (Table 10.3).

Table 10.3. Calcareous rocks are deficient in plant nutrients: raw limestone and chalk materials compared with well developed calcareous grassland soils overlying them

material	pH	CaCO$_3$ (%)	organic matter (%)	N (total %)	Mg	K	P
					(available ppm)		
Chalk (Cretaceous, Chatham, Kent)							
material	8·6	97·0	–	0·02	20	25	11
grassland	7·8	70·0	–	0·34	45	61	10
Limestone (Carboniferous, Buxton, Derbyshire)							
material	8·4	97·5	0·1	0·01	72	11	7·9
grassland	7·6	52·6	17·9	0·76	185	172	16·9

At the same time, although their pH is not extreme (less than pH 8) it causes some nutrients, especially iron and phosphorus, to be unavailable except to plants which are specially adapted. Such plants, calcicoles, are able to cope well with the calcareous conditions. By contrast, acid-loving plants, calcifuges, such as rhodendrons and heathers, develop a marked yellowing and die due to upset in their iron and magnesium metabolism. Most plants of neutral soils can be made to grow on calcareous soils, providing they are supplied with extra phosphorus and potassium.

But in a limestone or chalk quarry, the material in which plants can root will be the raw rock which is hard and contains very little plant nutrients other than calcium (Table 10.3). Only if overburden or soil become incorporated will physical conditions be adequate and there be any reasonable quantities of plant nutrients available to plants. On quarry floors, these materials are often extremely consolidated. As a result, colonisation even by specialised calcicole plants is very slow; on the English chalk, colonisation and the formation of a closed community may take as long as 50 years. There will always be open, uncolonised areas and little or no competition from vigorous plants.

These conditions provide ideal habitats for specialised species which are excluded from older, more fertile habitats. The result is that old limestone and chalk quarries, and even lime beds, can be important havens for rare and local plants such as the gentians (*Gentianella germanica* and *G. amarella*), and the bee, fly and musk orchids (*Ophrys apifera*, *O. muscifera* and *Herminium monorchis*), whose wind-blown, dust-like seeds allow them to be early colonists. The medieval Jurassic limestone quarries at Barnack Hills in Northants are an important site for the rare pasque flower (*Anemone pulsatilla*) and the man orchid (*Aceras anthropophorum*), also found in Kent (Figure 10.9a).

But there is a wide range of species characteristic of calcareous soils: examples are given in Table 10.4. These can form communities of considerable interest. In the absence of grazing, scrub and trees can invade and provide a complex wild vegetation (Figure 10.9b), hardly ever found now in the heavily settled and well-used parts of the world, where every acre is regimented for productive use. As a result, disused calcareous quarries in Britain are important refuges for wild life (Chapter 2).

Figure 10.9a. Here only because of quarrying: the man orchid in its only site in Kent in a chalk pit.

Figure 10.9b. Disused limestone and chalk quarries ultimately become colonised by a wide range of plants: after sixty years this chalk pit at Grays in Kent is a remarkable wilderness.

Calcareous Rocks

Table 10.4. The nature conservation potential of limestone quarries: some of the species already found in limestone quarries in the Peak District

species already found in Miller's Dale quarry (total 81)		other species found on limestone in the Peak District which are local or rare
common species (examples only given)	local or rare species	
Carex flacca	Aira praecox	Asplenium viride
Chrysanthemum leucanthemum	Botrychium lunaria	Carex digitata
Corylus avellana	Dactylorhiza fuchsii	C. ornithopoda
Crataegus monogyna	Daphne mezereum	Cirsium acaulon
Festuca rubra	Galium sterneri	C. heterophyllum
Fragaria vesca	Listera ovata	Cynoglossum officinale
Fraxinus excelsior	Ophioglossum vulgatum	Dianthus deltoides
Geranium robertianum	Ophrys apifera	Epipactis atrorubens
Hieracium pilosella	Orchis macula	Gagea lutea
Leontodon hispidus	Parnassia palustris	Helleborus viridis
Linum catharticum	Primula veris	Hornungia petraea
Origanum vulgare	Prunus padus	Orobanche purpurea
Prunella vulgaris	Saxifraga tridactylites	Potentilla tabernaemontani
Salix caprea	Thalictrum minus	P. crantzii
Teucrium scorodonia	Viburnum opulus	Silene nutans
Thymus praecox		Thelypteris robertiana
Trisetum flavescens		

10.2.3 The solutions are challenging

The first step must be to overcome the physical problems. This is not so difficult as it seems at first. Hard or consolidated surfaces can often be broken down by surface cultivation using heavy harrows. Very hard surfaces can be covered with fine material, either overburden clays, etc., or even fine limestone (Figure 10.10). Hard rock often has many clay-filled fissures which in nature are well-colonised: where these do not occur, they can be produced by judicious blasting. Blasting is also an important way in which rock faces can be shaped to give more naturalistic land forms (Figure 10.11). On suitable sites, such as the Nesher quarry, Israel, terraces can be formed with the aid of wire netting.

All quarry materials are likely to be lacking in organic matter and therefore poor in moisture retention. This may not matter on flat ground or in damp conditions. But on coarse materials and on high quarry faces, especially in dry climates, it can be very restrictive, particularly in the early stages of plant growth. It can often be overcome by seeding or planting in the wet season, as would happen in nature. But a very effective way is to cover the rock and waste surfaces with a mulch of a moisture-retaining organic material.

The mulching materials include wastes such as sewage sludge and composted household refuse, or other organic materials. They can be spread dry or mixed with water to form a thick slurry and poured from a normal tanker down rock faces and over waste heaps. The slurry runs into cracks and crevices and forms ideal microhabitats connected with deeper, damper regions into which plants can root. Seed of trees, shrubs and herbs can be incorporated in the mulch and will be carried into the crevices where germination will be optimal. This technique not only overcomes problems of physical factors and methods of sowing but also provides an excellent slow-release supply of nutrients (Table 10.5).

Figure 10.10. Plants can be established on quarry floors if a thin mulch of soil or organic matter is used as a seed bed: experiments in a limestone quarry in New York State, with different materials.

Figure 10.11. Large quarry faces need to be shaped to give naturalistic land forms: a 30 m high face has been blasted to give terraces and a rock slope at the foot.

On softer materials, direct seeding without a mulch is feasible (see Chapter 5). However, in the absence of nutrients from organic materials, they must be added in the form of mineral fertilisers. The growth on fine limestone waste in response to nitrogen and phosphorus is excellent (Figure 10.12). A similar response is obtained on chemical lime beds and lime wastes. However, these materials may

213   *Calcareous Rocks*

species	seed number sown (per m²)	cover (%)		
		sewage sludge	soil	mushroom compost
total vegetation		55	40	70
bryophytes		15	50	–
grasses				
Festuca rubra (red fescue) ⎱	2800	10	5	5
F. ovina (sheep's fescue) ⎰				
Lolium perenne (rye grass)	300	20	15	60
Dactylis glomerata (cocksfoot)	1150	20	5	10
Poa pratensis (meadow grass)	50	+	+	
Agrostis tenuis (bent grass)	250			+
Phleum pratense (timothy)	50		+	+
Cynosurus cristatus (crested dogstail)	50		+	+
legumes				
Trifolium pratense (red clover)	100	1	5	(+)
T. repens (white clover)	150	1	10	+
Medicago sativa (lucerne)	50	+	+	
Vicia sativa (vetch)	50	(+)	(+)	(+)
Onobrychis viciifolia (sainfoin)	50	+	+	
Lotus corniculatus (bird's foot trefoil)	100		+	
shrubs and trees				
Quercus robur (english oak)	1	(+)	(+)	
Rosa canina (dog rose)	40	+	+	(+)
Fraxinus excelsior (ash)	19	+	+	+
Crataegus monogyna (hawthorn)	6	+	+	
Acer campestre (field maple)	19	+	+	+
Viburnum opulus (guelder rose)	14			
Sorbus aucuparia (rowan)	1			

+ present in small numbers   (+) present in first summer but not subsequently

Table 10.5. Vegetation can be established on quarry faces by mulching: establishment of species on a limestone quarry face after treatment with different seed-containing mulches one year previously

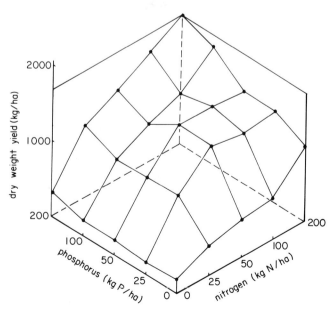

Figure 10.12. Plants will grow on fine calcareous materials if adequate nutrients are given: growth of red fescue on limestone waste requires both nitrogen and phosphorus.

be strongly alkaline (pH>9) due to the presence of calcium hydroxide: in this case it is best to cover the material with a thick layer of organic matter or soil.

Agricultural species can be used. But the development of a vigorous effective vegetative cover without the excessive use of fertilisers will be aided by the wise choice of species. Legumes adapted to grow in calcareous soils should be included, such as alfalfa (*Medicago sativa*), sainfoin (*Onobrychis viciifolia*), kidney vetch (*Anthyllis vulneraria*) and crimson clover (*Trifolium incarnatum*), all commercially available. They will, however, require phosphorus. Grass species should include those adapted to poor calcareous dry conditions such as red fescue (*Festuca rubra*) and cat's tail (*Phleum bertolonii*). On a world scale, the choice is far wider.

The wild herbaceous species of calcareous soils are many and various. They will sometimes be available commercially; if not, limited quantities can be collected by hand and used as an inoculum in the seeds mixture.

In abandoned quarries, the most appropriate species may be trees and shrubs, such as ash (*Fraxinus excelsior*) and hawthorn (*Crataegus monogyna*), or salt bush (*Atriplex* spp) and sage bush (*Salvia* sp.) in drier climates. Establishment by seed can be very effective when combined with a mulch, particularly in areas inaccessible to normal planting. If normal transplants are used, these must be placed in pockets of moisture-retaining material, as on acid rocks: with this, excellent survival can be obtained in temperate climates even in a dry season. Nevertheless, in arid climates, irrigation may be necessary.

The endpoint in hard rock quarries can be the 'hanging gardens' suggested by Danziger (Figure 10.13), or a more truly wild community. If the attractive missing wild species are given an opportunity to invade, by having their seed scattered over the area, calcareous rock quarries can be

Figure 10.13. 'Hanging' gardens on a steep slope in a Mediterranean climate being watered over the establishment phase: the reclamation of the Nesher limestone quarry in Israel.

Calcareous Rocks

Figure 10.14. The landscaping possibilities in quarries are immense: here near Buxton, Derbyshire, a face has been mulched and seeded, and the rock slope planted with trees established in pockets (compare with Figure 10.11—3 years earlier).

transformed into areas of immense nature conservation interest. Some suggestion of species are given in Table 10.4. The endpoint on reasonable gradients of softer materials can be agricultural grasslands or even arable as productive as that discussed in Chapter 5.

Phosphorus in very calcareous soils becomes locked up in the form of apatites, and will then be unavailable to most plants. So aftercare treatments of phosphorus will be important. If legumes are not included, then there is need, as in other coarse wastes, for aftercare to build up an adequate capital of nitrogen. While at the initial planning stage, this may seem reasonable, in practice it will be difficult to ensure that enough nitrogen is applied. When nitrogen is applied, there is a short burst of growth when the sward goes green followed by a browning off later because the nitrogen becomes unavailable. By contrast, if clover is included, growth is less extreme and continuous, and colour is maintained, because the nitrogen formed is readily mineralised (Table 6.6, page 95).

In many parts of the world, attractive calcareous areas are under great pressure from tourism and industry. Quarries are often on the outskirts of large conurbations such as those for the cement industry around London and the chemical industry in the north of New York State, or in very prominent sites, such as the side of the Rhone Valley near Vallance. Properly designed programmes of rehabilitation to provide wilderness or public open space, as well as agricultural land, could turn large areas now degraded into immense assets (Figure 10.14).

10.3   SAND AND GRAVEL

10.3.1   Natural colonisation is considerable

Sand and gravel extraction is now an enormous, insatiable industry. In Great Britain about 1000 ha of land are used every year to produce 100 million tonnes of sand and gravel. In the United States 800 million tonnes are produced annually from a total of about 7000 different operations. The demand for building aggregates is, of course, not met by sand and gravel alone, because crushed rock is an alternative. But rock crushing is expensive and where sand and gravel are available they are nearly always used.

Sand and gravel pits can be dry, when the deposits being worked are above the water table, or wet, when the deposits are below the water table. Wet pits are common since many deposits are in river valleys. When they are finished, they are nearly always allowed to flood to become artificial lakes, and are therefore very different from dry pits. They can become immensely attractive additions to the countryside.

The material at the bottom of a sand and gravel pit

usually has a higher clay or silt fraction than in the material removed, and washery wastes, consisting of clay or silt, are often put back into the pit. As a result, the material left behind usually has a texture which is satisfactory for plant growth. Because of this, and because most sands and gravels are alluvial in origin, the nutrient levels, although lower than in normal soil, may be much better than the levels, for instance, in china clay sand waste. The pits are also excavated in strata that are usually permeable and low-lying and so will usually be well-supplied with water even when they are not flooded. This water brings with it further nutrients and maintains a neutral pH.

The result is that even dry, disused sand and gravel pits are more satisfactory for plant growth than other types of degraded land. Perhaps the only limiting factor, besides nitrogen which is always in short supply, is a lack of phosphorus, since most sand deposits have low phosphate levels and it has low solubility in water. But this is not enough to stop rapid invasion by a wide variety of plants. On the top of Hampstead Heath in London is a delightful wilderness area which Londoners made into the first public park bought by public subscription. It was once the source of sand for the development of Georgian London (Figure 10.15). Where the deposits are deep, acidic and nutrient deficient, as in the Lower Greensand deposits in S. England, there may be more constraints on plant growth and the plants may be those more characteristic of heathland.

Figure 10.15. Once providing sand and gravel for Georgian London, this pit has now developed naturally into a delightful wilderness area within a city: part of Hampstead Heath, London.

Wet pits have two extra facets in their environment provided by the water—the waterlogged shoreline and the open water itself. Each of them is a distinct habitat with interesting and beautiful plants: reed mace (*Typha angustifolia*), yellow iris (*Iris pseudacorus*), codlins and cream (*Epilobium hirsutum*), water mint (*Mentha aquatica*) on the margins; bur-reed (*Sparganium ramosum*), pond weed (*Potamogeton pectinatus*), and starwort (*Callitriche stagnalis*)

217   *Sand and Gravel*

in the water (Figure 10.16). But trees also, such as alder (*Alnus glutinosa*), willow (*Salix alba*), sallow (*Salix atrocinerea*), find the margins an ideal environment and make rapid growth.

There are habitats for duck, such as mallard (*Anas platyrhynchos*), gadwall (*Anas strepera*), pochard (*Aythya ferina*) and tufted duck (*Aythya fuligula*), feeding on the water plants: and waders such as snipe (*Gallinago gallinago*), green sand piper (*Tringa ochropus*) and redshank (*Tringa totanus*) feeding on the insect larvae and other animals in the mud. Inevitably moorhen (*Gallinula chloropus*) and coot (*Fulica atra*) also appear, as well as many migrants and rarer birds (Figure 10.17). The total effect of the sand and gravel industry has been remarkable. In 1900 the delightful great crested grebe (*Podiceps cristatus*) was an unusual bird to find in the south of England: now it is very common, breeding on innumerable pits. The little ringed plover (*Charadrius dubius*) had never bred in Britain before 1938; now it breeds as far north as Durham almost entirely on gravel pits.

Below the water surface, a myriad of species will rapidly colonise. Populations of fish such as perch (*Perca fluviatilis*)

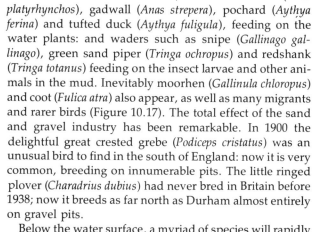

Figure 10.16. Fishing in a sand pit: codlins-and-cream, club rush, yellow flag, gipsywort and white willow provide concealment.

Chapter 10: Quarries

and roach (*Rutilus rutilus*) quickly develop once they get in. So a whole viable ecosystem quickly develops. It is an ecosystem of immense attraction to people that can be enjoyed for aquatic pursuits of all sorts, the wild life providing an attractive and peaceful background.

10.3.2 The improvement of dry pits

Alluvial soils are often first-class farming land, grade 2 at least on the British agricultural land classification system. Here it is obviously wrong to lose the old top soil, and rely on the slow processes of soil formation for the re-creation of a productive agricultural soil, which could take over fifty years. In these areas, therefore, the top soil and subsoil must be replaced, in order that a high-quality working soil about 1 m deep is restored after extraction.

Proper drainage of the working must be ensured, and if necessary the floor graded and ripped to assist natural drainage. Top soil and subsoil must be handled with the care and attention which has been discussed in Chapter 6. The materials must only be moved when they are reasonably dry and friable, particularly if they contain an appreci-

Figure 10.17. Greylag geese naturalised in Sevenoaks Reserve: one of the most admired of the birds living on the reserve.

Sand and Gravel

able clay fraction: they should never be moved during rain (Figure 10.18).

In many situations, pits provide valuable sites for the dumping of power station ash and rubbish of all sorts. Providing the rubbish is inert, this is satisfactory, but if possible the better quality materials should be reserved for the upper layers of fill. If the land is being restored to agriculture or if the local water supplies could be affected, toxic materials must be excluded or tipped only with care.

Figure 10.18. Sand and gravel pits can be returned to productive agriculture: at Longtown, part of this site near Carlisle was deepened to form a lake while the rest was filled and soiled for agriculture. Before and after.

Even if subsoil and top soil are replaced, the new vegetation will need larger amounts of nutrients than usual, particularly nitrogen. The nutrients will cause the vegetation to grow vigorously and help restore the soil organic matter and structure.

In the absence of top soil, the establishment of a vegetation cover is still very feasible, although it will usually have to be a grass sward. The lime and nutrient deficiencies must be assessed and treated, and the cultivations carried out thoroughly. The seeds mixture must include a legume because nitrogen will be in short supply. It may be preferable to plant trees using normal planting techniques. Species such as Corsican pine (*Pinus nigra*) or Eucalypts which are tolerant of poor soils should be chosen.

10.3.3   The improvement of wet pits

A wet pit is more than just an area of open water. It can become a complex area of wild life, or at the other extreme, be devoted entirely to water sports. So before a pit is flooded, it must be graded to provide a final shape appropriate to the intended use. If the area is to be for wild life, banks must be shaped to give shallow water in which water plants can root, islands to provide refuge for birds, and secluded bays and loafing spots to provide protected areas for young wild fowl. Often the islands and the hollows can be made in one operation: islands and promontories can be made of material from elsewhere, and pools by explosives. The object will be to provide a variety of different habitats, such as in the Sevenoaks Gravel Pit Reserve (Figure 10.19).

Figure 10.19. A gravel pit
shaped to give islands and a
protected shore line to
encourage wild fowl. *top*
before planting; *below* three
years later: nesting tufted
duck, crested grebe and coot
are concealed in the bushes.

221   *Sand and Gravel*

The area must then be planted because the natural invasion by a full variety of wild species would take a long time. All that is necessary is to copy faithfully the vegetation of natural lakes and ponds in the vicinity. Nearly all the native water plants are perennials and can be established by transplanting pieces of vegetative material in the spring (Figure 10.20); the water containing nutrients makes establishment easy and obviates the need for aftercare. It may be possible to introduce aquatic plants in dredgings brought from adjacent waters. Species must be chosen carefully: it will be wrong to plant tall plants such as reed (*Phragmites australis*) and reed mace (*Typha angustifolia*) everywhere, because they will eliminate other plants: but reed beds in suitable places will be of considerable beauty and important habitats for birds such as reed warblers (*Acrocephalus scirpaceus*).

Figure 10.20. If gravel pits are inoculated with the correct plant material, a good vegetation cover can be quickly established: a boat full of rushes for planting.

If wild-fowl and other birds are to be encouraged, attention must be paid to the plant species which are their favoured foods. This has been done with great success at the Sevenoaks Reserve: a list of the herbaceous plants used is given in Table 10.6. The only alien plant used was sea spike rush (*Scirpus maritimus*), the seeds of which are a popular food for dabbling duck. The results of such a positive manipulation can be seen in the records for the numbers of breeding birds (Figure 10.21).

Trees are an obvious part of any planting programme, for their contribution to the developing landscape, and the protection they can afford to wild life. The choice of species can again be determined by those that grow locally in damp places. Many willows can be readily planted by hammering in stakes of young wood in the spring.

Where an area is being used for water sports the constraints are different and it may be important to exclude certain water plants and restrict planting of banks to normal grass/clover mixtures. Nevertheless, tree planting may be important for amenity purposes, restricted to

222

Table 10.6. In wet pits species can be planted specifically to encourage bird life: the herbaceous planting programme at Sevenoaks Gravel Pit Reserve 1960–74

Atriplex patula (orache)	55
Carex pendula (pendulous sedge)	6
Carex riparia (pond sedge)	743
Ceratophyllum demersum (hornwort)	16
Chara sp. (stonewort)	23
Eleocharis palustris (spike rush)	34
Glyceria maxima (reed-grass)	1797
Hippurus vulgaris (mare's tail)	55
Hottonia palustris (water violet)	6
Iris pseudocorus (yellow iris)	48
Juncus articulatus (jointed rush)	14
Juncus inflexus (hard rush)	746
Lupinus arboreus (tree lupin)	172
Mentha aquatica (water mint)	3
Phragmites australis (norfolk reed)	149
Polygonum amphibium (amphibious bistort)	75
Polygonum hydropiper (water pepper)	57
Polygonum persicaria (redleg)	22
Potamogeton crispus (curled pondweed)	24
Potamogeton pectinatus (fennel-leaved pondweed)	16
Rorippa nasturtium-aquaticum (water cress)	101
Rumex hydrolapathum (giant water dock)	66
Scirpus maritimus (sea club rush)	607
Scirpus tabernaemontani (glaucous club rush)	138
Sparganium sp. (bur-reed)	2088
Typha latifolia (lesser reed mace)	20
Veronica anagallis-aquatica (water speedwell)	18
total	6194

Figure 10.21. Careful design and planting can create a favourable environment for a wide variety of species: development of the breeding bird population at Sevenoaks Gravel Pit Reserve over ten years.

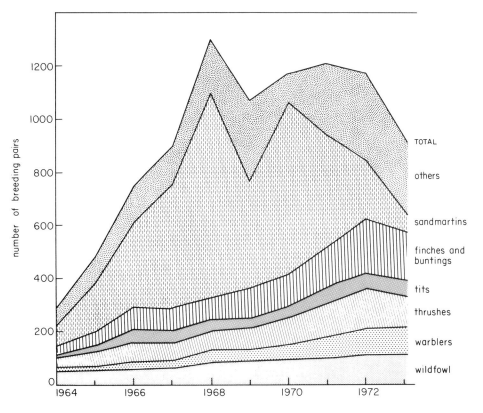

Figure 10.22. An extensive area of gravel pits becoming a major recreation and wild life area from the combined efforts of local authorities, industry and nature conservation bodies: part of the Cotswold Water Park, Gloucestershire.

species such as willows (*Salix alba* and *S. fragilis*) and alder (*Alnus glutinosa*) which do not spread rapidly.

In a large area of workings, individual pits can be developed for different purposes, creating a complex which provides a wide range of amenities. An excellent British example of such forward planning is the Cotswold Water Park near South Cerney, Gloucestershire, which is providing a much needed addition to recreation amenities in the west of England although the layout is not particularly imaginative (Figure 10.22).

In the United States, the main emphasis has been on the development of extracted areas for real estate purposes, and so major reconstruction and building work has usually been carried out. But when allied with good restoration of vegetation and wild life, the results can be outstanding and very profitable. At Port Jefferson, Ohio, 700 acres bought in 1961 for $150/acre, was mined for sand and gravel, developed as a lake park, and sold for $325/acre.

Chapter 10: Quarries

FURTHER READING

Acid rocks

Clarke F.W. 1924. *The Data of Geochemistry* (5th ed.) Bulletin 770, Washington: United States Geological Survey.

Elliott R.J. 1976. The Kerr Quarry project. In: *Landscaping and Land Use Planning as related to Mining Operations*. The Australasian Institute of Mining and Metallurgy, Victoria, Australia, 177–228.

Gutt W., Nixon P.J., Smith M.A., Harrison W.H & Russell A.D. 1974. A survey of the locations, disposal and prospective uses of the major industrial by-products and waste materials. *Building Research Establishment Current Paper* 19/74.

Hillestad K.D. 1973. *Sprengstein Tipp og Landskap*. Kraft Og Miljø 2. Oslo: Norges vassdrags—og elektrisitetsvesen.

Raven J. & Walters M. 1956. *Mountain Flowers*. London: Collins.

Sheldon J.C. & Bradshaw A.D. 1975. The reclamation of slate waste tips by tree planting. *Landscape Design, J. Inst. Landsc. Arch.* **113**, 31–3.

Tansley A.G. 1939. *The British Islands and their Vegetation.* Cambridge: Cambridge University Press.

Calcareous rocks

Associated Portland Cement Manufacturers. 1970. *Dunbar Works—a Study in Conservation*. London: Blue Circle Group.

Bradshaw A.D. 1977. Conservation problems of the future. *Proc. Roy. Soc. Lond.* B.197, 77–96.

Bradshaw A.D., Humphries R.N., Johnson M.S. & Roberts R.D. 1977. The restoration of vegetation on derelict land produced by industrial activity. In: *The Rehabilitation of Severely Damaged Lund and Freshwater Ecosystems in Temperate Zones*, ed. M.W. Holdgate and M.J. Woodman, 249–78, NATO.

Danziger K. 1971. *The Rehabilitation of the Nesher Quarry*. Nesher, Israel: Israel Portland Cement Works.

Davis B.N.K. 1976. Wildlife, urbanisation and industry. *Biol. Conserv.* **10**, 249–91.

Grime J.P. & Curtis A.V. 1976. The interaction of drought and mineral nutrient stress in calcareous grassland. *J. Ecol.* **64**, 975–88.

Haywood S.M. 1974. *Quarries and the Landscape*. London: British Quarrying and Slag Federation.

Humphries R.N. 1977. The development of vegetation in limestone quarries. Transactions Institute of Quarrying: Quarry Management and Products. 4, 43–7.

Ratcliffe D. 1974. Ecological effects of mineral exploitation in the United Kingdom and their significance to nature conservation. *Proc. Roy. Soc. Lond.* A339, 355–72.

Tansley A.G. & Adamson R.S. 1925. Studies of the vegetation of the English Chalk III. The chalk grasslands of the Hampshire—Sussex border. *J. Ecol.* **13**, 177–223.

Sand and gravel

Catchpole C.K. & Tydeman C.F. 1975. Gravel pits as new wetland habitats for the conservation of breeding bird communities. *Biol. Conserv.* **8**, 47–60.

Cotswold Water Park Joint Committee, 1969. *Cotswold Water Park—Draft Report*. Gloucester: Gloucestershire County Council.

Godwin H. 1923. Dispersal of pond floras. *J. Ecol.* **11**, 160–4.

Goodland N.L. 1959. Reclaiming gravel lands. *World Crops.* **11**, 431–3.

Harrison J. 1974. *The Sevenoaks Gravel Pit Reserve*. Chester: WAGBI.

Further Reading

Ministry of Agriculture, Fisheries & Food. 1966. *Agricultural Land Classification*. Agricultural land service, Techn. Report 11, London: Ministry of Agriculture, Fisheries & Food.

Ministry of Agriculture, Fisheries & Food. 1971. *The Restoration of Sand and Gravel Pits*. London: Ministry of Agriculture, Fisheries & Food.

Morley J. 1962. Gravel pit reclamation in the You Yangs. *Forestry Commission Victoria, Forestry Technical Paper 8*.

'Whose rutty Bancke the which his River hemmes,
Was paynted all with variable flowers,
And all the meades adorned with daintie gemmes
Fit to decke maydens bowres.'
EDMUND SPENSER
Prothalamnion. *Circa* 1590.

11 Domestic and Industrial Wastes

In modern society, labour is becoming relatively more expensive than materials, so despite the present concern for recycling, we throw away more and more. In industrialised societies each individual produces about 350 kg of waste material (domestic and commercial) annually. In the United Kingdom this amounts to 18 million tonnes per annum (in the USA it is far more). But there are also 23 million tonnes of general industrial waste, 60 million tonnes from mining and 50, 12 and 3 million tonnes from quarrying power stations and building respectively.

The wastes from industrial processes are from making steel, chemicals and other important products. Some of these are quite innocuous; others are particularly toxic and require special disposal techniques. The power station ash presents substantial disposal problems often forgotten by proponents of other methods of power generation.

All these wastes have to be disposed of, usually on land, in ways that are neither hazardous to public health, nor destructive of the environment. They are all somebody's problem.

11.1   URBAN REFUSE

11.1.1   A very real problem

Over half of domestic refuse is composed of easily combustible material (mainly paper, paper products and plastics). The rest is glass, pottery, ferrous and non-ferrous metals, coal- and wood-ash, rags, kitchen waste (mostly vegetable) and garden refuse (Figure 11.1). The composition is highly variable. Generally the material is composed of inert materials and biodegradable materials only, seldom is anything toxic present.

In many large urban conurbations disposal has become a problem of immense proportions. There no longer exists for many urban authorities areas of land on which domestic and commercial refuse can be disposed. So other disposal methods are being adopted. These include disposal at sea, incineration (including its use as fuel), microbial and chemical treatment, composting and the reduction of bulk by reclaiming products from the waste (paper, bottles, metals) for recycling. But disposal on land still remains the commonest method.

Figure 11.1. Urban refuse is a complex mixture of organic matter, solid objects and mineral materials: close-up of a city's domestic refuse.

It is very difficult to be specific about the composition of a refuse tip: so much depends on the origin of the material. But the mixture of vegetable and other organic material with a wide variety of inorganic mineral materials such as ashes and building wastes ensures a satisfactory medium for plant growth. This is often diluted by inert materials such as plastic and iron containers, and glass and pottery, but these will not prevent plants from rooting into the fine material. This is very apparent from the vegetation that establishes on disused refuse tips. The variety of species show that there are usually few limiting factors, and their vigour that there is a plentiful supply of nutrients (Figure 11.2). Colonisation takes a little time to occur but soon a well-defined flora develops. In Britain, the early colonisers are nitrogen-fixing blue-green algae (*Nostoc*, *Oscillatoria*), followed by lichens. Fungi colonise decaying organic matter and liverworts and mosses appear (*Lunularia cruciata* and *Bryum argenteum* are examples). Annuals are early colonisers such as annual meadow grass (*Poa annua*), shepherd's purse (*Capsella bursa-pastoris*), groundsel (*Senecio vulgaris*), fat hen (*Chenopodium album*) and many other demanding weedy species. The perennials which soon appear include many composites like spear thistle

(*Cirsium vulgare*), hawkbits (*Leontodon*) and hawkweeds (*Hieracium*). Legumes are particularly common and so are rhizomatous and stoloniferous species. The vegetation cover is often complete within two years, the proportion of annuals decreasing as more perennials become established.

Figure 11.2. Refuse as it decomposes is a good medium for plant growth: the vigour of the weeds on this refuse tip demonstrate its fertility.

These plants are accompanied by a rich soil fauna. Earthworms (*Allolobophora calliginosa*), the rose worm (*Eisenia rosea*) and also nematodes, enchytraeid worms and springtails occur. Flying insects (bees, wasps, flies and gnats) are also common and give rise to concern over the spread of disease. Gulls are a well-known feature of refuse-tip sites particularly in the winter (Figure 11.3). The enormous increase in gulls in Britain in urban and rural areas has been attributed to the food supply provided by increasing areas of refuse tips, little of which are covered rapidly enough to prevent gulls feeding.

Figure 11.3. Birds, particularly gull species, are frequent visitors to domestic refuse tipping areas: changes in the ratios of the five gull species visiting a tip in SE England outside the breeding season.

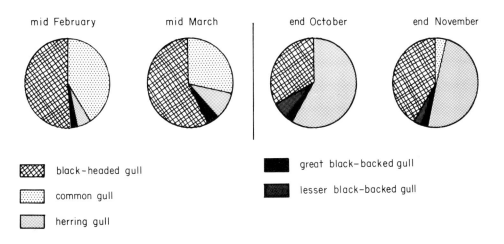

11.1.2 Potential for new land

The problems must be dealt with by the adoption of proper disposal plans on licensed and well-regulated sites. In Great Britain this duty has been placed on local authorities by the Control of Pollution Act 1974.

But there is a great shortage of sites. One way of reducing the area of land needed is to compost it after useful materials and bulky non-biodegradable materials have been removed. The raw refuse is shredded and crushed, aerated and warmed in fermentation chambers. A finely divided compost results which can be used as soil fertiliser despite its rather high carbon/nitrogen ratio. When composted, domestic refuse is added as a fertiliser to colliery spoil, it gives lower yields of grass than other nitrogen sources and the least recovery of the nitrogen applied, but the results are not unsatisfactory and show its potential for plant growth (Table 11.1).

Table 11.1. Composted domestic refuse is a reasonable source of nutrients: yield (kg/ha) of ryegrass on colliery spoil to which nitrogen has been added in the form of different materials

material		N applied (ppm)		
		50	100	200
composted domestic refuse	yield	1498	1291	1589
	% N recovered	9·5	4·8	3·2
digested sewage sludge	yield	1570	1821	3120
	% N recovered	9·6	6·9	4·6
ammonium sulphate	yield	1849	2089	1652
	% N recovered	15·0	9·2	5·3

initial N content (%):	composted domestic refuse	0·85
	digested sewage sludge	1·55
	ammonium sulphate	21·2

When disposal is into a refuse tip, the nature of the waste and the features of the site must be taken into account to avoid immediate nuisance and long-term problems. Ground or surface water pollution must not be allowed to occur and wells nearby may need continuous monitoring. The after-use of the site must be considered.

Sites must have adequate roads leading to them and water courses diverted or culverted. They will need a suitable fence (with screening hedges where possible) to retain light waste, like paper and polythene, blown by the wind. Moveable fences can be valuable.

The top soil and subsoil is removed from an area within the site and stored. The area prepared should not be greater than what is required for reasonable ease of working at any one time. If the subsoil at the bottom of the pit is clayey in texture and can be puddled to form an impermeable layer, this is ideal.

Waste is then deposited, usually by lorry. If the waste can be shredded there are a number of advantages: it is more easily controlled and manoeuvred, it is less of a fire risk, less attractive to insects and rodents and requires a shallower depth of subsequent covering than untreated waste. Alternatively, it can be compressed by an hydraulically operated machine into bales. This allows a large volume to be filled as if with huge building bricks. This method is being used successfully in schemes to rehabilitate areas degraded by other forms of waste (Figure 11.4). Problems of dispersal during transport and tipping are minimised and the risk of water pollution reduced.

If the waste is not baled, it needs to be compacted at regular intervals after tipping. It should certainly not be left to the end of each working day before this is done. The compacted layer should not exceed 2·5 m in depth, be level, with a slight slope away from the point of working and materials of different consistency and capacity for decay spread over one another in thin layers so that uneven subsidence does not occur later. After this, a blinding layer of subsoil, building waste or some other inert material should be used to give an adequate covering before a new compacted layer is formed. Finally, the British specification requires that at least one metre of top soil must be replaced so that subsequent land-use is not too restricted. In comparison with other sorts of land restoration this seems excessive in view of the shortage of top soil. One metre of

Figure 11.4. Derelict land reclamation schemes can incorporate refuse disposal: a West Yorkshire colliery spoil reclamation site at Middleton Broom where a huge amphitheatre has been formed to take high-density bales of refuse.

Urban Refuse

subsoil covered with 20 cm of top soil would be adequate for agriculture: for public open space, 10 cm of top soil over the last blinding layer would be quite sufficient.

It has to be admitted that operations often do not proceed in this ideal way. Less than adequate compaction occurs and the cover given is too little and too late. Paper and other material is blown from the site and fires start accidentally. Land filled with domestic refuse, covered with soil, can give rise to considerable gas production: first nitrogen and oxygen, then carbon dioxide, hydrogen and finally, relatively high concentrations of methane and hydrogen sulphide. Where the gases seep to the surface they can cause death of natural and planted vegetation. The problem is worst where there is insufficient inert material included.

Nevertheless, some remarkable areas of land have been produced from refuse disposal sites, so good that most people would never have an idea of what made up the land they enjoyed. One outstanding example is Otterspool Promenade beside the River Mersey at Liverpool, four miles of playground, ornamental shrubberies and playing fields with a view across a busy river to the mountains of North Wales (Figure 2.8, page 23). But there are many other dirty hollows and old gravel pits which have been filled with refuse and are now good agricultural land.

11.2   PULVERISED FUEL ASH

11.2.1   A by-product of electricity generation
Well over half of the electricity generated in the United Kingdom uses coal as its primary fuel and the same is true elsewhere: in the USA it is nearly half and the percentage is rising annually. Modern, coal-fired electricity generating stations use coal that has been ground to the consistency of face-powder (75 per cent is less than 75 μm in diameter). The pulverised fuel is suspended in an air stream and blown into the furnace. All but a small proportion of the carbon is burnt off and the ash melts to produce pulverised fuel ash (PFA).

This ash is separated from fuel gases by cyclonic and electrostatic precipitators and then must be disposed of. One method is to mix the ash with one and a half times its own weight of water and transport the slurry through pipes to a lagoon. The ash settles and the water evaporates or can be drained away and re-cycled. Alternatively, a much smaller proportion of water is added to suppress dust (about 15 per cent) and the ash transported in lorries or wagons for disposal in tips or pits.

PFA can be used for fill: very large quantities in England have gone to fill in old brick pits around Peterborough. But its pozzolanic properties (ability to react with lime and form 'cement') enable it to be used for building blocks and as a kind of concrete. This, however, only uses a proportion of the ash (about 50 per cent in the United Kingdom) and as rates of production increase, the disposal of huge amounts of PFA will become a serious problem. The production of ash from Drax 'A' and 'B' power stations in Yorkshire in the next 30 years will be about 32 million tonnes: at a height of 52 m it would cover an area nearly 2·5 km long and 800 m wide. A modern 200 mW capacity generating station produces 2 tonnes of ash each minute.

PFA is mainly made up of colourless, glassy spherical particles. Some of the spheres are solid, others contain a few or many bubbles which can float.

Usually over 95 per cent of PFA is in the fine-sand and silt size range. Although as little as 1 per cent of particles are clay sized, the water-holding properties of the material are reasonable. The texture approximates to a fine silty soil. However, when dry, light particles, particularly the floaters, are liable to wind erosion. As organic matter is absent, larger stable aggregates do not occur. But the capping that occurs after heavy rain, when cementation has commenced, reduces the tendency for erosion.

Cement-like layers form in ash lagoons because of pozzolanic activity. These reduce permeability and cause impeded drainage. Air is excluded and root penetration reduced: the likelihood of drought conditions increases. Where ash is tipped, this cementation and compaction only occurs at the surface.

Obviously the chemical composition of ash will depend upon the composition of the coal from which it originates. This, in turn, depends upon the original plant composition: traces of most naturally occurring elements are present.

When the level of available elements in PFA are compared with normal soil (Table 11.2) it appears that only nitrogen is deficient. In practice, however, phosphorus is also found to be so, possibly because high levels of soluble aluminium fix the phosphorus in a form unavailable to plants. About 2–5 per cent of the ash is water soluble,

Table 11.2. Pulverised fuel ash has high levels of soluble componds: levels of available elements in PFA and a typical soil (ppm)

element	in PFA	in soil
P	94	63
K	348	224
Na	550	200
Ca	900	800
Mg	1500	240
Fe	570	130
S	3900	600
N (total)	nil	1800
Mn	99	4·8
B	43	2·5
Zn	2	2·5
Cr	25	2·5
Mo	5	0·2

Pulverised Fuel Ash

giving very alkaline saline conditions (pH values of 11–12, with electrical conductivity values up to 13 mmhos/cm). Lagooned ash is about pH 9·0. The early natural colonisers of PFA are therefore salt-tolerant, halophytic, species (Table 11.3).

Table 11.3. Only certain species can cope with the toxicities and nutrient deficiencies found in pulverised fuel ash: natural colonisers of PFA in the United Kingdom

Stage I	*Funaria hygrometrica* (hair moss)	
Stage II	*Atriplex hastata* (orache)	
Stage III	*Tussilago farfara* (colt's foot)	*Rumex obtusifolius* (dock)
	Chenopodium album (fat hen)	*R. acetosella* (sheep's sorrel)
	Sysimbrium altissimum (rocket)	*Artemisia vulgaris* (mugwort)
	Lotus corniculatus (bird's foot trefoil)	*Trifolium pratense* (red clover)
	Medicago lupulina (black medick)	*T. repens* (white clover)
	Agrostis stolonifera (creeping bent)	*Poa pratensis* (smooth stalked meadow grass)
		P. annua (annual meadow grass)
Stage IV	*Betula pendula* (birch)	*Ulex europaeus* (gorse)
	Salix spp. (sallow)	

When plants are grown on fresh ash of a relatively low salinity, even when nitrogen and phosphorus are added, growth problems are still evident, particularly in plants that are sensitive to high levels of boron (barley, peas and beans). The high available boron concentrations appear to be a major problem (Table 11.4). Values as high as 250 ppm B have been recorded.

Table 11.4. Boron is an important problem: toxicity of boron in pulverised fuel ash

available B (ppm)	degree of toxicity
<4	non toxic
4–10	slightly toxic
11–20	moderately toxic
21–30	toxic
>30	highly toxic

normal soil levels are usually less than 3 ppm B.

Once PFA is dumped, weathering takes place. pH values fall gradually to about 8 and electrical conductivity values to below 4 mmhos/cm during lagooning or after 2–3 years in the field: the available boron level is also reduced. But levels of nitrogen and phosphorus do not build up naturally very quickly, particularly as ash retains nutrients poorly, and weathering does not improve the physical conditions of the ash unless colonisation takes place.

11.2.2 Good land can be produced

Attention to the physical condition of PFA can give amelioration of other problems. The physical problems arise through lack of fine clay particles and organic matter and the effect this has on crumb structure. Many methods of improving PFA structure have been tried. 5–10 cm of organic or fine material worked into the surface improves the structural stability. Clay, sewage sludge, river silt, soil, ground straw, bituminous emulsions, peat and sawdust are all useful. As well as improving surface conditions, some of the additives have the effect of reducing cementation and also immobilising boron or at least diluting it. On the other hand, additions of clay can increase problems of permeability.

Probably the most successful method of dealing with the whole gamut of physical problems is to cover the ash with a silty soil and then cultivate to a depth which mixes the soil and ash. This will overcome capping problems, cementation and in some cases enable hard pans to be broken up. Grass yield is very good with only 8 cm of soil, both when mixed with ash by deep cultivation and when unmixed. Wheat yields are best with greater depths but quite satisfactory yields are also obtained with 8 cm of soil (Figures 11.5 and 11.6).

Other materials can be substituted for soil, indeed some have a greater ameliorating affect. Acid peat reduces the pH of PFA and the boron content of plants grown on it. Acid colliery spoil and peat, mixed with ash, produce good yields of barley and oats and again reduce the boron content of the plants. Where trees are planted, soil also improves survival and growth, but then the soil is not spread over the whole PFA area. Instead, pits (30 cm diameter and 40 cm deep) are excavated and filled with soil (Figure 11.7).

Various attempts have been made to counter the boron toxicity. The available boron is greatest in fresh ash and less

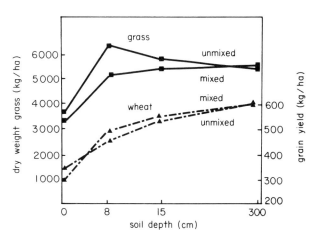

Figure 11.5. Good yields of herbage and wheat can be obtained on PFA with only a small covering of soil: the effect of soil depth and mixing on yields of grass and wheat.

235

in lagooned PFA; the lagooning process can reduce available boron by 50 per cent. One method of reducing the boron content of PFA is to leave it to leach out in situ by normal weathering process (Figure 11.8). Attempts to speed this process by chemical methods have been found to be uneconomic on a large scale. The problem is therefore met by using soil coverings and mixtures or dilutions of the ash with bulky organic materials (Table 11.5).

Concern has been expressed over the potential toxicity of crop crops grown on PFA, both for humans and stock. Some analyses are given in Table 11.6. Arsenic levels in pasture growing on ash may be somewhat high, but on a fresh weight basis, the concentration would be greatly reduced. Boron levels appear high only in kale. Cobalt levels are depressed (optimum 0·1 ppm Co for sheep), but chromium, copper and fluorine all are well within safe

Figure 11.6. A good crop of wheat on PFA: trials to investigate the value of soil additions.

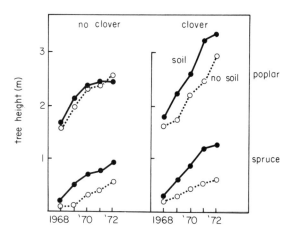

Figure 11.7. Tree growth on PFA can be improved by planting in soil pockets and under-sowing with a legume: growth of poplar and sitka spruce on PFA.

Chapter 11: Domestic and Industrial Wastes

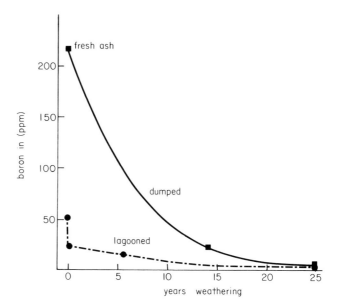

Figure 11.8. Boron levels in PFA are reduced by the lagooning process and also slowly by weathering in non-lagooned samples: reduction in ash boron content with time.

Table 11.5. Toxicities of PFA begin to disappear with weathering: boron content of oats and barley when unweathered and weathered PFA are diluted by 50 percent (volume) with various ameliorants

	boron content (ppm)	
ameliorant & pH	unweathered PFA	weathered PFA
sand (5·7)	957	278
loam (6·3)	553	105
acid colliery spoil (2·8)	441	71
peat (3·8)	175	55
sewage sludge (5·5)	657	206
peat + acid colliery spoil	266	88
pure loam (no PFA)	28	29

Table 11.6. Crops grown on PFA do not appear to be a hazard: trace element content (ppm) of dry weight in some selected crops grown on PFA and soil

crop	As	B	Co	Cr	Cu	F	Mn	Mo	Pb	Zn
barley grain on ash	0·68	20·7	0·03	0·18	3·7	1·4	8·3	1·8	0·9	56
barley grain on soil	0·46	2·4	0·05	0·22	2·3	0·86	11·0	0·87	1·0	35
pasture on ash	2·3	16·2	0·15	nd	9·0	3·2	83	5·14	nd	65
pasture on soiled ash	0·87	27·9	0·20	nd	9·7	3·5	62	1·53	nd	37
kale on ash	nd	122	0·52	1·5	5·6	nd	nd	5·0	11·0	72
potato tuber on ash	0·07	11	nd	2	nd	nd	9	nd	1	
sugar beet root on ash	0·30	13·3	0·08	1·3	4·6	0·5	12·1	0·22	2·2	28·8
sugar beet root on soil	0·28	16·6	0·06	nd	4·8	0·5	17·8	0·12	0·4	13·6

Pulverised Fuel Ash

limits. The high levels of molybdenum could be offset by dosing with copper. Manganese, lead and zinc levels appear within normal ranges. It can be concluded that there is no serious bar to the use of weathered PFA for herbage production or the growth of arable crops.

Pasture and arable crops, and tree species, all vary in their sensitivity to boron toxicity (Table 11.7 and 11.8).

Table 11.7. Care in selection of crops for growth on PFA is advisable: tolerance to PFA by agricultural and horticultural crops

tolerant:			
beet	*Beta vulgaris*	sweet clover	*Melilotus alba*
chicory	*Chichorium intybus*		

semi tolerant:			
bent grass	*Agrostis tenuis*	perennial ryegrass	*Lolium perenne*
swede	*Brassica napus*	lucerne	*Medicago sativa*
mustard	*B. nigra*	sainfoin	*Onobrychis sativa*
kale/cabbage	*B. oleracea*	radish	*Raphanus sativus*
turnip	*B. rapa*	rye	*Secale cereale*
cocksfoot	*Dactylis glomerata*	alsike clover	*Trifolium hybridum*
carrot	*Daucus carota*	red clover	*T. pratense*
red fescue	*Festuca rubra*	white clover	*T. repens*
		maize	*Zea mays*

sensitive:			
oats	*Avena sativa*	runner bean	*Phaseolus vulgaris*
Brussels sprouts	*Brassica oleracea*	timothy	*Phleum pratense*
meadow fescue	*Festuca pratensis*	pea	*Pisum sativum*
barley	*Hordeum vulgare*	potato	*Solanum tuberosum*
lettuce	*Lactuca sativa*	wheat	*Triticum aestivum*
lupin	*Lupinus luteus*	broad bean	*Vicia faba*

Table 11.8. There are considerable differences in the tolerances of trees: tolerance to PFA of certain trees and shrubs

tolerant:	
Alnus glutinosa	*Hippophae rhamnoides*
Artemisia arboratum	*Picea sitchensis*
Atriplex halimus	*Populus alba*
Berberis thunbergii	*P. nigra italica*
Colutea arborescens	*Ribes aureum*
Elaeagnus angustifolia	*Salix britzensis*
Erica carnea	*Spartium junceum*
Forsythia ovata	*Tamaria gallica-indica*
Gleditschia triacanthos	*Tsuga canadensis*

semi-tolerant:	
Acer pseudoplatanus	*Hypericum calycinum*
Ailanthus glandulosa	*Picea amorika*
Berberis linearifolia	*Ribes sanguinea*
Betula pendula	*Robinia pseudoacacia*
Ceanothus azoreus	*Ulex europaeus*
Clematis vitalba	*Veronica buxifolia*

sensitive:	
Amorpha fruticosa	*Fagus sylvatica*
Chamaecyparis lawsoniana	*Elaeagnus umbellata*
Cytisus scoparius	*Fraxinus excelsior*
C. nigricans	*Veronica angustifolia*

Until boron levels have been reduced, it is important that tolerant species are used. This is illustrated by the two seeds mixtures which are now standard recommendations for PFA in Britain (Table 11.9).

Table 11.9. Pastures must be established from tolerant species: seeds mixtures for the establishment of a grass cover on PFA in Britain

mixture 1 suitable for toxic PFA containing 25–35 ppm boron		kg/ha
Italian ryegrass	*Lolium multiflorum*	22·5
white sweet clover	*Melilotus alba*	11·5
		34·0
mixture 2 suitable for PFA containing < 25 ppm boron		
Italian ryegrass	*Lolium multiflorum*	4·5
perennial ryegrass (S23)	*Lolium perenne*	4·5
perennial ryegrass (S24)	*Lolium perenne*	11·0
rough-stalked meadow grass	*Poa trivialis*	4·5
red clover (S123)	*Trifolium pratense*	3·0
red clover (late flowering)	*Trifolium pratense*	4·0
white clover (S100)	*Trifolium repens*	2·5
		34·0

the legumes must be inoculated with the appropriate *Rhizobium* in all cases

The addition of nitrogen fertiliser or the accumulation by means of legumes is essential for normal plant growth. Conveniently, common vigorous legumes are tolerant of boron and can be established easily. Most species also respond to phosphorus, but potassium has little effect in enhancing growth and may even depress it. If nitrogen fertilisers are used, their form is important, as high pH values mean that ammonium fertilisers suffer from loss of gaseous ammonia and the lack of nitrifying bacteria gives rise to only very slow rates of conversion to nitrate. Organic nitrogenous fertilisers suffer similar drawbacks.

Tree species respond to application of nitrogen fertilisers or the presence of nitrogen-fixing plants such as clover (*Trifolium repens*) (Figure 11.7). For the same reason, stands of *Pica sitchensis* mixed with one of three nitrogen-fixing species (*Elaeagnus angustifolia*, *Alnus glutinosa* or *Robinia pseudoacacia*) have given increased growth in height of the conifer over that attained in a pure stand.

Fertiliser rates used in successful plant establishment schemes on PFA have been high: up to 500 kg/ha N, 250 P and 150 K. This obviously is expensive and methods of maintaining levels of fertility have to be devised. The use of legumes, or other nitrogen-fixing species represents one way of encouraging successful reclamation at relatively low cost. In the case of trees, the legume element would be introduced after establishment. If crops are taken annually

Pulverised Fuel Ash

Figure 11.9. PFA is valuable as land fill for excavations: these brick pits in Northamptonshire which were once a disastrous mess are now good agricultural land.

nutrients will be removed; as a result it will be necessary to replace nitrogen and phosphorus at levels at least as high as those used on arable soils.

As a result of all this intensive research, the disposal of PFA does not really now present technical problems. We can use it for land fill (Figure 11.9) and can contemplate enormous deposition sites such as that at Gale Common in Yorkshire which is built over an area where subsidence is occurring due to deep mining for coal. The site could ultimately be an attractive and productive addition to the landscape (Figure 11.10). However, this sort of scheme has still to justify itself in practice.

Figure 11.10. Disposal of PFA in the future: the Gale Common scheme serving three power stations in Yorkshire as it will look when it is finished in twenty years' time.

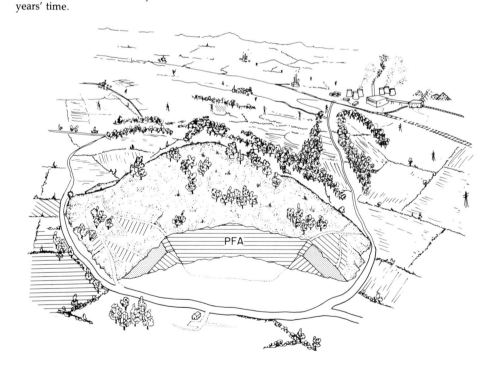

11.3 CHEMICAL WASTES

11.3.1 Individual problems

As a result of manufacturing and chemical processes, appreciable quantities of chemical wastes have to be disposed of. In Britain approximately 23 million tonnes of general industrial waste are produced every year. The problem with these wastes is that they differ greatly in composition, from relatively benign materials such as lime wastes from the Solvay ammonia process to extremely toxic materials such as chromate wastes: they can include materials which are physically difficult such as steels smelter slag, or others that are relatively satisfactory.

As a result, it is impossible to generalise about them. The alkali wastes from the Leblanc soda ash process are naturally very alkaline because of calcium hydroxide and the hydrolysis of calcium sulphide. However, in time they weather to give carbonate-dominated surface layers, with pH < 8, on which plants can grow. Their low-nutrient status with alkalinity limit plant growth, but allow colonisation, because of the lack of competition, by a range of attractive and rare species (Table 11.10): these can be a great surprise to find in old industrial areas such as south-west Lancashire. Old lime beds can also be excellent for common and unusual birds: on the Solvay lime beds in Cheshire grey phalarope (*Phalaropus fulicarius*), dunlin (*Calidris alpina*), caspian tern (*Hydroprogne tschegrava*) and red-breasted merganser (*Mergus serrator*) have all been seen.

Table 11.10. Old chemical wastes can be a refuge for rare and interesting plants: species found on 80-year-old lime waste in Lancashire rare or absent from neighbouring areas

Carlina vulgaris (carline thistle)	*Euphrasia nemorosa var. calcarea* (eyebright)
Centaurium erythraea (centaury)	*Gymnadenia conopsea* (fragrant orchid)
Dactylorhiza fuchsii (common spotted orchid)	*Linum catharticum* (wild flax)
Dactylorhiza incarnata (early marsh orchid)	*Orobanche minor* (broomrape)
Dactylorhiza purpurella (northern marsh orchid)	*Sisyrinchium bermudiana* (blue eyed grass)
Erigeron acer (fleabane)	

But at the opposite extreme, sodium chromate production for the tanning industry, at Bolton in Lancashire for instance, has produced extremely alkaline wastes which are also very toxic due to the chromate left after processing: there has been no colonisation in fifty years except in places where less innocuous wastes have been included. They have remained an astonishing carcinogenic hazard for people and a source of serious river pollution. The heaps have released sodium chromate into the River Croal at the rate of about 5 tonnes of Cr^{6+}/yr for the last thirty years at least.

When gas is produced from heating coal to a high temperature it must be cleansed of sulphur and other compounds by being passed through ferric oxide. When the oxide is saturated it has to be disposed of and replaced by new material. As a result, piles of spent oxide waste are produced. Because of iron sulphide they develop an intense acidity on exposure to air, with pH < 2: they also contain ferrocyanide. So this is another example of a waste which does not get colonised by plants and remains a permanent eyesore. In the UK it is now a waste whose existence must be notified to the Department of the Environment.

11.3.2   Individual solutions

In many ways the treatment of chemical wastes follows the same principle as the treatment of metalliferous wastes (Chapter 8). Benign materials can be improved by direct treatment, or left as nature reserves to develop into wilderness. Since the extreme alkalinity of many hydroxide lime wastes disappears on exposure to air, it is often sufficient on an old waste to provide only nitrogen, phosphorus and potassium together with an appropriate grass/legume mixture to get a good sward established. But whether this is possible will depend on the origin and detailed characteristics of the material: if hydroxide lime wastes are disturbed, fresh horizons will be exposed which cannot be so treated. The lime by-product of the ammonia soda Solvay process contains considerable quantities of sodium chloride, which may limit plant growth until leaching has occurred. But since the material itself is mainly calcium carbonate, establishment of vegetation is ultimately very easy: only complete fertiliser is necessary.

Lime waste produced as a by-product of lime burning to obtain calcium oxide and hydroxide consists only of calcium hydroxide and undecomposed limestone. It does not carbonate quickly and retains a pH of > 12 due to the calcium hydroxide for long periods, which prevents plant colonisation. A very effective solution is to cover it with a layer of organic matter: in Derbyshire, spent mushroom compost has been available. A 10 cm layer provides an

Figure 11.11. Organic amendments can sometimes be used to treat benign chemical wastes: the effect of 10 cm of mushroom compost on hydroxide lime waste in Derbyshire: *left* before; *right* after.

Chapter 11: Domestic and Industrial Wastes

excellent growth medium for plants, and increases the rate of carbonation of the underlying lime waste so that plants root into it. Excellent agricultural land can be produced (Figure 11.11).

Toxic materials, such as spent oxide or chromate waste, will require complete physical isolation by a covering of inert material: very toxic materials can require a layer as much as 1 m deep: this need not be soil, but can be subsoil, brick rubble or another inert material (Table 6.1, page 81), covered with not more than 10 cm of top soil. In many cases special combinations of treatments reduce the amount of covering needed. The chromate waste in Lancashire was treated by a combination of subsoil cover, ferrous sulphate and organic matter: this reduced the depth of subsoil required and obviated the need for top soil (Table 11.11) cutting costs considerably.

Table 11.11. If treatments are planned carefully the depth of covering needed to isolate a waste can be reduced: summary of method for establishing vegetation on chromate smelter waste

Amendments (in order of addition)	Rate	Method	Effect
porous subsoil	25–30 cm depth for grass 200 cm for trees	spread on surface of waste after completion of levelling and grading	provides rooting medium and restricts mobility of chromate
ferrous sulphate ($FeSO_47H_2O$)	up to 40t/ha	spread on surface and incorporated by discing and harrowing	chemical reduction of chromate and neutralisation of alkalinity
period of exposure allowed for natural leaching of ferrous sulphate into substratum prior to organic matter and amelioration and planting			
organic matter (peat or sewage sludge)	100t/ha or more	spread on surface and incorporated by discing and harrowing	lowers concentrations of chromate and other toxic salts. Provides nutrients and humus

Figure 11.12. New land, new golfer: toxic chemical waste in Cheshire reclaimed by covering with 50 cm of subsoil and 10 cm of top soil

In the end chemical waste disposal areas can, like other sorts of derelict land, be reclaimed for a variety of useful purposes. Since they very often occur in older urban areas they can be very important sources of land for amenity purposes (Figure 11.12). But each site must be properly assessed before reclamation to ensure that the appropriate reclamation technique is chosen and long-term toxicity and potential pollution hazards are taken care of.

FURTHER READING

Urban refuse

Department of the Environment *Refuse Disposal: Report of the Working Party*. London: HMSO.

Chemical Wastes

Anon. 1976. *Reclamation, Treatment and Disposal of Wastes*. DOE Waste Management Paper No. 1. London: HMSO.

Anon. 1976. *Guideline for the Preparation of a Waste Disposal Plan*. DOE Waste Management Paper No. 3. London: HMSO.

Anon. 1976. *The Licensing of Waste Disposal Sites*. DOE Waste Management Paper No. 4. London: HMSO.

Darlington A. 1969. *Ecology of Refuse Tips*. London: Heinemann.

Pulverised fuel ash

Barber E.G. 1975. *Win Back the Acres*. London: Central Electricity Generating Board.

Capp J.P. 1978. Power plant fly ash utilization for land reclamation in the eastern United States. In: *Reclamation of Drastically Disturbed Lands*, ed. F.W. Schaller & P. Sutton, 339–53. Madison: Amer. Soc. Agron.

Hodgson D.R. & Buckley G.P. 1975. A practical approach towards the establishment of trees and shrubs on pulverized fuel ash. In: *The Ecology of Resource Degradation and Renewal*, ed. M.J. Chadwick & G.T. Goodman. Symp. Brit. Ecol. Soc. **15,** 305–29. Oxford: Blackwell Scientific Publications.

Hodgson D.R. & Townsend W.N. 1973. The amelioration and revegetation of pulverized fuel ash. In: *Ecology and Reclamation of Devastated Land*, ed. R.J. Hutnik & G. Davis. New York: Gordon and Breach.

Townsend W.N. & Gillham E.W.F. 1975. Pulverized fuel ash as a medium for plant growth. In: *The Ecology of Resource Degradation and Renewal*, ed. M.J. Chadwick & G.T. Goodman. Symp. Brit. Ecol. Soc. **15,** 287–304. Oxford: Blackwell Scientific Publications.

Townsend W. & Hodgson D.R. 1973. Edaphological problems associated with deposits of pulverized fuel ash. In: *Ecology and Reclamation of Devastated Land*, ed. R.J. Hutnik & G. Davis. New York: Gordon and Breach.

Chemical wastes

Gemmell R.P. 1973, 1974. Revegetation of derelict land polluted by a chromate smelter. *Environ Poll*. **5,** 181–97: **6,** 31–7.

Gemmell R.P. 1975. Establishment of grass on waste from iron smelting. *Environ. Poll*. **8,** 35–44.

Greenwood E.F. & Gemmell R.P. 1978. Derelict industrial land as a habitat for rare plants in S. Lancs and W. Lancs, *Watsonia* **12,** 33–40.

Kelcey J.G. 1975. Industrial development and wildlife conservation, *Environ. Conserv*. **2,** 99–108.

'We need authority that shall be jealous of the land, intolerant of its waste and defilement. All the world over there seems to be little public conscience of this duty that man owes to the land, that he shall hand it on at least unimpaired to his successors.'

SIR DANIEL HALL
1941

12   Coast Lands

Coast lands have always had an attraction to man. Where sea and land meet, they have been an avenue for migration, and a major source of food. As seas have receded because of sedimentation and the rise of land masses, they have provided new land quickly available for agriculture. Now in times of affluence they are being overwhelmed by recreation, and even mining.

Each of these waves of use has left its mark. Migration and the search for food have left prehistoric and present-day settlements, with major, but localised impact. Reclaimed new land has provided us with important new areas for agriculture once properly treated. Pressure from recreation and mining has produced a new and major threat to the sandy areas of our coasts. It is the last two problems we must consider.

12.1   LAND FROM THE SEA

12.1.1   Salt and drainage

In many coastal regions the action of waves causes erosion and the wearing away of the land. In other regions deposition of sand, silt and clay, carried by the sea results in shallow coastal waters, often with scattered off-shore islands. For centuries, efforts have been made to wrest parts of these coastal areas from the sea and turn them into productive land.

Land was being reclaimed in the Low Countries as early as the Middle Ages: a quarter of the total land area of the Netherlands has originated in this way. An earth embankment or dike was built to enclose a shallow area of the sea. Windpumps took the water from the surface, and also from drainage channels to maintain a lower water table in the soil. The land created was often below sea level and so the pumping was crucial.

The world-famous Zuiderzee project in the Netherlands began in the 1920s. A dam was started in 1927 to enclose the Wieringermeer Polder (of over 20 000 ha); at the same time the construction commenced of a 32 km barrier dam across the mouth of the Zuiderzee itself, to form a great lake into which the Yssel river drained (Figure 12.1). This allowed control of tidal movements and made the building of further polders easier. The barrier was completed in 1932 and it now encloses fresh water (Lake Yssel) and 165 000 ha of reclaimed polders.

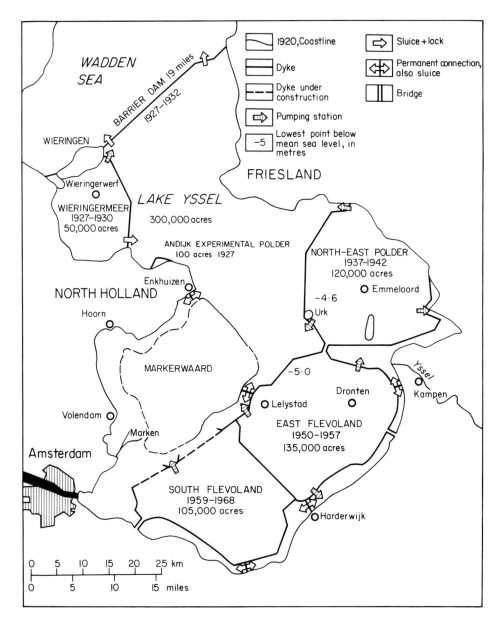

Figure 12.1. The Zuiderzee regions of the Netherlands in 1920 was a large marine estuary: after enclosing the mouth of the Yssel river, areas were reclaimed sequentially so it now consists of intensively farmed polders and a fresh water lake.

The dikes or dams are constructed of boulder clay (on the seaward side) as the core of the dike, and then made taller and broader with sand reinforced with willow branches matted together and weighted down with stones. These are faced with blocks of basalt (Figures 12.2 and 12.3).

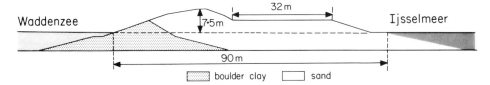

Waddenzee — 7·5m — 32 m — Ijsselmeer — 90 m — boulder clay — sand

Figure 12.2. Dikes must be constructed of a core of materials such as boulder clay with sand for support: a section across the barrier at the mouth of the old Zuiderzee.

Figure 12.3. Constructing a dike is a lengthy process and easier in protected waters: this dike is the beginning of a new polder within Lake Yssel.

In eastern England, particularly around the Wash, salt marsh areas fringing the sea have been reclaimed for many centuries. In these areas the sea and rivers deposit silty material around the shore. As the silt builds up, the frequency with which it is inundated by the tide decreases, allowing a salt marsh vegetation to develop. At high tides, the presence of rooted plants causes a decrease in the velocity of the water and more silt is deposited. When the

247   *Land from the Sea*

level has reached 3–4 m above sea level, a sea wall of local material is constructed to enclose the area of marsh, usually 3–4 m above the level of the marsh surface. This gives protection from the sea. A ditch is constructed inside the new wall, to allow drainage and to give protection against sea-water seepage. The drainage water is able to leave through a tidal sluice and, unlike Holland, no pumping takes place.

In fact the same system was practised in Holland. It was sometimes elaborated by the formation of a network of basins which encouraged the more rapid deposition of mud. Unlike the Zuiderzee project it is a slow process of land winning, yet practised for many centuries can have remarkable results. It is possible to recognise the extension sea-wards of land from towns and villages that are now inland but were once on the coast (Figure 12.4).

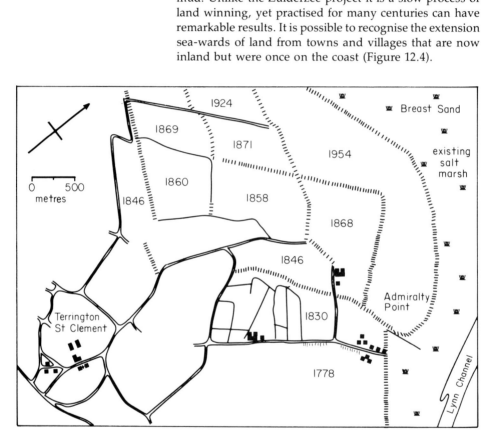

Figure 12.4. Villages, once on the coast, become 'stranded' by land reclamation: map of the region near Terrington St. Clement, Norfolk.

When areas of salt marsh are enclosed they are dominated by vegetation adapted to high salt contents in the soil. Often the area is grazed and is dominated by a few species, sea poa (*Puccinellia maritima*) and red fescue (*Festuca rubra*). Areas reclaimed from Lake Yssel, of course, have no vegetation initially and are less salty.

The enclosed area is left for 2 or 3 years and rain begins the process of leaching out the sodium and other soluble ions. Vigorous plants adapted to conditions of lower salinity invade, taking advantage of the soil fertility. As this occurs, a better structure develops and the soil that was

Chapter 12: Coast Lands

waterlogged due to tidal water has air replacing some of the water in the soil voids. But this means that compounds in the reduced form, such as ferrous sulphide, become oxidised; the resulting acidity causes a lowering of the soil pH.

In the polders this can become a considerable problem in reclaimed soils, resulting in acid sulphate soils (or cat clays). If the sediments are calcareous, from shell fragments, the acidity is neutralised, but in the Wieringermeer Polder in the Zuiderzee, over 50 per cent of the 20 000 ha showed acid strata in the soil, requiring up to 150 t/ha of lime.

12.1.1 Centuries of success

In eastern England, once a new sea wall has been built and the area left free from tidal influences for two or three years, the natural drainage channels of the salt marsh can be filled in. New drainage channels may be constructed. A grass ley, with legumes, is sown and may be used for grazing sheep or cattle for 10–15 years. During this time, soluble salts are leached from the surface horizons to lower levels, calcium gradually replaces sodium as the dominant ion in the soil exchange complex, organic matter accumulates and soil structure is greatly improved. The period under grass can be shortened to 3–5 years if gypsum ($CaSO_4$) is added when the grass is ploughed in, because this causes the sodium in the soil to be replaced by calcium.

This heralds the arable phase of reclamation. Generally wheat or barley is sown and crop production under fairly normal conditions ensues. The soil needs fertiliser applications, but often not particularly heavy ones: the soil shows good water-holding capacity. Saline conditions may still occur at depth and small patches may occasionally show crop failure due to salinity. Even in older reclaimed areas soil pH values are relatively high (pH > 8·0). But overall the changes with time are very satisfactory (Table 12.1).

Table 12.1. Salinity disappears with time: alteration of surface soil characteristics after reclamation in coastal areas in eastern England

| time since reclamation | exchangeable cations (%) | | | |
	Ca	Mg	Na	K
unreclaimed salt marsh	23	34	34	9
1954 reclamation	59	23	11	7
1924 reclamation	74	19	0·1	7
1870 reclamation	60	29	2	9
1830 reclamation	87	10	0·8	2

In the Dutch polders the soil has similar problems. However, a number of features are different. In particular, because the polder areas are usually at or below sea level, major drainage works are required.

Where acid sulphate soils are a problem, high water levels are sometimes maintained to minimise oxidation. With these conditions grassland farming must predominate. However, very often highly calcareous sediments lie under the shallow sulphidic layers and deeper ploughing allows much of the acidity to be neutralised. Otherwise, calcareous materials can be applied (Table 12.2).

Table 12.2. Acidity may develop in reclaimed soils once they have been drained: soil changes in the Wieringermeerpolder with the application of calcareous material to counteract acid sulphate effects

treatment	soil depth (cm)	pH before	pH after
nil	0–10	4·0	3·9
	10–30	3·2	3·4
	30–40	3·5	3·1
10 cm calcareous sediment	0–10	3·7	6·7
	10–30	3·1	6·5
	30–40	3·7	3·4
marl	0–10	4·0	6·7
	10–30	3·1	6·3
	30–40	3·4	3·3

Since estuarine and coastal deposits are usually high in silt particles and rarely have excess of either sand or clay, the soils ultimately produced are excellent for a wide variety of agricultural uses (Table 12.3). The modern face of the Zuiderzee is very impressive (Figure 12.5). Such is the competition for the land that would-be farmers must submit to a rigorous examination to be chosen.

Table 12.3. The final product can be very rich agricultural land: average yields (t/ha) in the IJsselmeerpolders and in the Netherlands as a whole, 1973

crop	Ijsselmeer-polders	Nether-lands	IJsselmeer-polders relative to Netherlands average = 100
sugar beet	57·0	47·5	120
potatoes: for food	50·2	38·5	130
: seed	31·0	25·0	124
onions	40·0	36·5	110
winter wheat	5·9	5·4	109
spring barley	4·3	4·2	110
oats	5·5	4·4	125

The success story of reclamation of land from the sea should be an inspiration to land restorers throughout the world. However, even success stories are subject to qualifications! Shallow coastal waters, receiving as they do, much drainage from the land, are extremely fertile parts of the sea. They provide breeding grounds for fish and protected habitats for their young. In the New World, land reclamation from the sea has not been such a feature of salt marsh areas and American ecologists feel that it has been wise to avoid this practice. In the Netherlands now, the balance of reclaiming land from the sea and preserving highly productive nursery grounds for fish has been

Figure 12.5. Areas reclaimed from the Zuiderzee become high-class agricultural land: a view of Medemblick in the North East Polder.

reached, and it is unlikely that large schemes, such as that suggested for the Wadden Zee inshore of the Friesian Islands, will be undertaken again.

12.2 COASTAL SANDS

12.2.1 Fragile ecosystems

We value coastal sands for their own sake, as wild open country with an interesting and unusual vegetation, but also as a support area for the beaches themselves. Recently there has been an enormous increase in pressure on them.

Sand dunes are made almost entirely of silica particles and are deficient in water, organic matter and nutrients. There is a characteristic vegetation which manages to cope with the difficulties of the environment (Figure 12.6). Sand dunes are naturally open and unstable and shifting due to the combined effects of wind and waves. The impact of people aggravates this, because the plants are not resistant to trampling or disturbance.

As a result, where sand dunes are heavily used, there is always an enormous increase in bare and shifting sand (Figure 12.7). Houses and roads can be engulfed by shifting sand and the dunes can cease to be an adequate defence against the sea. In England there are 39 000 ha of coastal sands of which a large proportion are damaged: large-scale

251   *Coastal Sands*

Figure 12.6. Undamaged sand dunes: although there is one natural blowout on the left, the main area of these dunes at Blakeney, Norfolk, is completely colonised by marram grass and other specialised species.

Figure 12.7. Trampling destroys the vegetation cover of sand dunes and devastating erosion can occur: in this dune system near Southport, Merseyside, the main access point is the road to the beach. The numbers on the beach are the average number of cars parked at the weekend.

sea flooding due to sand dune damage occurred on the East Coast as recently as 1963.

But destruction does not come only from recreation. In certain areas, particularly the east coast of Australia, the coastal sand contains the valuable minerals zircon, rutile and ilmenite. At the moment about 750 ha of coastal sands in Australia are mined every year, producing about 60 per cent of the world's rutile, mainly for white paint pigments. The natural vegetation is removed and the complete sand mass is processed in a treatment plant, which usually floats in a moving pond, to remove the heavy minerals. The sand is redeposited and reshaped as the excavation moves forward (Figure 12.8).

Figure 12.8. In mineral sand mining in Australia whole dunes are destroyed but almost all the material is redeposited after mining: legislation requires that the original natural vegetation is re-established.

There is total destruction of the original ecosystem, often in areas of natural beauty and great recreation value. As a result, some very exacting requirements for restoration have to be met by the mineral sand mining industry, entailing the total replacement of the natural vegetation. The restoration system is therefore one of the most careful of its kind in the world.

An analysis of young sand dune soils shows that they are very low in major plant nutrients, particularly nitrogen and phosphorus. If fertilisers are added to existing dune vegetation the change and growth of the vegetation are remarkable. The sand usually contains calcareous shell fragments which maintain the pH between 6 and 7·5. In older sand areas the calcareous material is often leached away and the pH may fall to 4–5. There are few ion exchange sites on the soil particles so other nutrients are also lost rapidly.

The areas immediately near to the sea may have quite

Coastal Sands

high sodium levels, but these are reduced by natural leaching. The most important factor apart from nutrient shortage is drought. The sand has a relatively uniform coarse particle size which, coupled with little organic matter, causes a poor water-holding capacity; in periods of drought the surface 20 cm may contain almost no moisture, certainly less than the permanent wilting point. Because of the lack of finer particles, the soil is very loose and easily eroded, particularly in the absence of a plant cover. Since the other environmental conditions restrict plant growth and the sand is usually exposed to coastal winds, the ecosystem is physically fragile.

In the frontal areas the major plants are marram grass (*Ammophila arenaria*) in Europe, beach grass (*A. breviligulata*) in America, and sand spinifex (*Spinifex hirsutus*) in warmer climates. They are deep rooting with considerable powers of vegetative spread. They tolerate drought, burial by sand, and low nutrients. They tend to be replaced in stable dunes by other species either because they need to be constantly buried with sand, or because they cannot tolerate low pH. They are accompanied by other rather similar species, or by a group of species which take advantage of the open nature of the habitat (Table 12.4): legumes are few, perhaps because of the lack of phosphorus.

In the more stable rear dune areas a greater number of other species appear such as creeping willow (*Salix repens*) and sand sedge (*Carex arenaria*) in Britain. The slacks or hollows left by blow-outs from the wind may be at the water table and support an interesting flora and other wild life.

Table 12.4. Sand dunes are colonised by a very characteristic set of plants: species common on coastal sand dunes in Britain

fore dunes	
Agropyron junceum (sea couch)	perennial, main builder
Cakile maritima (sea-kale)	annual
Honckenya peploides (sea sandwort)	perennial, forms small hummocks
Salsola kali (saltwort)	annual
main dunes	
Ammophila arenaria (marram grass)	perennial, main builder
Calystegia soldanella (sea bindweed)	perennial, surface creeping
Elymus arenarius (sea lyme grass)	perennial, less common builder
Eryngium maritimum (sea holly)	perennial, scattered
Euphorbia paralias (sea spurge)	perennial, scattered
Festuca rubra (sand fescue)	perennial, spreads in surface
Matricaria inodora (mayweed)	annual, scattered
Senecio vulgaris (groundsel)	annual, scattered
Sonchus asper (sow thistle)	annual, scattered

Soils in regions which have been stable for long periods of time lose their calcium, become acidic and nutrient-deficient podzols, and bear a heath or acidic woodland vegetation. In Australia, the heathland is very distinctive, with several members of the southern hemisphere family, the Proteaceae, such as *Banksia serrata* and *B. integrifolia* (Table 12.5), species adapted to very low calcium and low phosphorus levels.

Table 12.5. In Australian mineral sand mining the original vegetation must be faithfully restored: species typical of the Australian coastal heaths and woodland which are replaced

Acacia longifolia (coastal wattle)	*Cupaniopsis anacardioides* (tuckeroo)
Alphitonia excelsa (red ash)	
Angophora costata (red gum)	*Eucalyptus gummifera* (blood-wood)
Banksia integrifolia (coastal honeysuckle)	*Eucalyptus intermedia* (blood-wood)
Banksia serrata (sawtooth banksia)	*Eucalyptus pilularis* (blackbutt)
Casuarina equisetifolia (horsetail oak)	*Leptospermum laevigatum* (coastal tea tree)
	Tristania conferta (brush box)

12.2.2 Solutions for frontal dunes

When dune areas are being restored, the first step is to ensure adequate protection from sea erosion, by wave screens or groynes. To encourage dune building and sand accumulation, permeable fences of brushwood, wood stobs or palings can be used. Probably the best material now is plastic netting of a grade specially designed for sand stabilisation: it has the advantage that it can be re-used if it does get buried. At the same time, the dunes must be shaped to give smooth aerodynamic profiles to prevent local turbulence and erosion.

Obviously the original vegetation must be re-established where it has been destroyed. Sea lyme grass (*Elymus arenarius*) is valuable in building fore-dunes because it tolerates a high degree of salinity. Where there is active sand accumulation, marram grass (*Ammophila arenaria*) and beach grass (*A. breviligulata*) are important. These do not establish effectively from seed and vegetative pieces are planted by hand or machine, preferably in winter. The optimum transplant or sett consists of a group of three to six tillers attached to a portion of rhizome, planted 20 cm deep at approximately 40 cm spacing. The setts are best taken from vigorously growing material established and fertilised for the purpose. *Spinifex hirsutus*, used in warm climates, establishes excellently from seed. Since it spreads rapidly by stolons, it can be sown in rows 1 m or more apart.

A number of other species which are adapted to the extreme environment can be planted, such as sea couch (*Agropyron junceum*), or sown, such as red fescue (*Festuca rubra*) in cool areas, and sea oats (*Uniola paniculata*), beach bean (*Canavalia maritima*) in warmer ones.

After planting, the sand surface itself will often need stabilisation. A time-honoured method is to lay brushwood: it is sufficient if half the ground is covered. Where seed has been sown, mulches of chopped stout sorghum-

Coastal Sands

Figure 12.9. Restoration of frontal dunes on the east coast of Australia after total destruction by mineral sand mining: spinifex is resown and well fertilised and the surface stabilised (see Figure 6.13, page 89).

type straw laid on the surface, or of softer wheat-type straw disced into the ground are very effective. Successful restoration depends on a combination of these techniques (Figure 12.9).

Stabilisers of the bitumen or latex type are widely advocated for sand stabilisation and can be effective if applied properly. However, their stabilising effect is often so short lived, only two or three months, and they are so inhibitory of plant growth that they are not worth the expense. Cover crops of vigorous large-seeded annuals such as cereal rye (*Secale cereale*), sorghum (*Sorghum vulgare*) can be very valuable if sown at low density (< 7 kg/ha). Even if they grow for only a short time from their own seed reserves, they stabilise the sand surface effectively.

It is easy to think that once the plants have rooted the restoration is complete. Yet subsequent plant growth is so slow that the restoration deteriorates and by the second season there is little left because of gross nutrient deficiency of the sand. Substantial and repeated fertiliser dressings are imperative; their cost is justified by the speed and reliability of restoration and the reduced need to maintain other forms of protection. Experience from many different parts of the world indicates that in the first year 100 kg/ha N and 25 kg/ha P are essential, given in two or three applications: the plants can take advantage of it better once they are established, and newly planted material may be damaged by a single large application. These species are able to respond in a remarkable manner (Figure 12.10). The nitrogen and phosphorus applications should be repeated two or three times during the second season at the same rate if further vigorous growth is important. Slow-release fertilisers are valuable but are very expensive.

Moribund dunes, where there is still a scattered plant cover, can be improved considerably by applications of

Chapter 12: Coast Lands

nitrogen. In Australia, areas of *Spinifex hirsutus* have been transformed by aerial applications of 50 kg/ha N and 25 kg/ha P given at six-monthly intervals. A remarkable alternative, where it is available, is digested sewage sludge, sprayed or poured onto flat areas to form layers about 3 cm thick (Figure 12.11). It not only provides appreciable

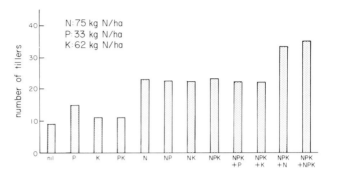

Figure 12.10. Sand dune plants respond well to the addition of nutrients: the growth of marram grass has been tripled by addition of nitrogen—other nutrients had little effect.

Figure 12.11. Sewage sludge poured into badly eroded hollows can be a powerful technique for dune restoration: on eroded dunes in N. Wales the sludge has stabilised the sand and provided an excellent seed bed for native plants; *top* before treatment, *below* 2 years later.

Coastal Sands

amounts of nitrogen in a slow-release form but also acts as a stabiliser. It tends to crack when it is dry, and may tend to blow away in exposed areas, but it can be held down by brushwood or scattered on new or existing plants, and then traps natural seed and acts as a seed bed.

Finally, people must be excluded by one means or another. In extreme cases, paling fences may be the only effective method, as at Camber, Sussex, which must be maintained carefully as long as they are necessary. Provision of properly surfaced paths may be sufficient. Then, if well-fertilised, the vegetation will be able to withstand the reduced amount of damage from trampling that continues.

12.2.3   Solutions for rear dunes

In the mineral sand mining areas of Australia more than half the workings are in heathland and forest areas and a faithful reinstatement of the original vegetation is required.

Before mining, a vegetation survey to record the frequencies of individual species is carried out to provide the yardstick by which the final restoration can be judged. Since the mining process is more or less continuous, restoration takes place behind the workings as they move forward: at any one time only a few hectares are exposed.

The bushes have to be removed. Since they are valuable for stabilisation and as sources of seed, they are often not burnt but are carried directly to where they are needed. The top soil 15–30 cm, is removed and either stored briefly or carried immediately to the areas being reinstated. The sand is mined and redeposited behind the workings in its original topography, and the top soil spread.

Since the top soil is never stored for more than a few months, it contains seed and vegetative portions of the native vegetation from which the herbaceous vegetation can establish. Unfortunately, the bushes such as the Banksias do not regenerate easily from vegetative material and have no dormant buried seed. However, the brush can be cut at the appropriate time of the year and laid on the top soil to shed its seed, or seed collected and spread by hand or used for raising seedlings in a central nursery (Figure 12.12).

The brush also acts as a stabiliser. But a cover crop is sown to protect the ground and the developing vegetation until the latter forms a good cover. The most effective is sorghum (*Sorghum vulgare*) sown at a very low density: in places molasses grass (*Melinus minutiflora*) has been used but it is too competitive for the native species.

Since top soil is being returned it could be argued that no fertilising would be needed. But significant amounts of nitrogen and phosphorus (up to 30 kg/ha of each) are lost by leaching during the whole process, and without any addition the growth of the cover crop and the native species is so slow that erosion may occur before the vegeta-

Figure 12.12. A nursery producing tubed seedlings of native trees and shrubs which will not re-establish easily by themselves: this mineral sand mining company in Australia produces 100 000 seedlings annually.

tion re-establishes. As a result, 40 kg/ha N, 20 P and 20 K are applied during the first year, and smaller quantities of N and P subsequently. Lime is not added since this would totally alter the nature of the habitat.

The first shrubs to grow are usually Acacias such as the coastal wattle (*Acacia sophorae*). This is short lived but provides shelter for the slower, more permanent, tree species such as *Banksia*, *Eucalyptus*, and *Angophora* (Figure 12.13). Difficult species are planted as young tubed seedlings in the second year of the restoration. After four years, the developing stands of vegetation are checked against the original records and if there are serious deficiencies, these are made good by planting.

A great deal of experimentation has gone into developing this technique. Its total cost is about $A2000–4500, but 90 per cent may be the cost of earth-moving and shaping including topsoiling. It demonstrates how fierce requirements for restoration can be met by careful research at both the fundamental, ecological and the applied, field, level.

Figure 12.13. Restoration of coastal heathland in Australia after ten years: in this case the main species, black oak, heath banksia and tea tree have re-established both from seed in the top soil and from planted seedlings.

Where it is not important to restore the native vegetation, attention is concentrated on shrubs, notably legumes such as *Lupinus arboreus* and *Cytisus scoparius*, which grow

Coastal Sands

rapidly and can act as a nurse for subsequent tree planting. Since *Lupinus arboreus* has been shown to contribute about 160 kg/ha/yr N ecosystem, it can play an important nutritional role. Tree species such as Monterey pine (*Pinus radiata*), Corsican pine (*P. nigra*) and lodgepole pine (*P. contorta*) can be used, depending on climatic and commercial considerations. Inevitably some fertilising will be necessary just as it is for herbaceous vegetation because of the poverty of the situation: it may have to continue for several years.

FURTHER READING

Land from the sea
Anon. 1975. *Zuyder Zee—Lake Ijssel Guide*. The Hague: Inf. and Documen. Centre for Geography of the Netherlands.
Dost H. (ed.) 1973. *Acid Sulphate Soils (Vols. I & II)*. Wageningen: Int. Inst. for Land Reclam. and Improvement.
de Glopper R.K. & Smits H. Reclamation of land from the sea and lakes in the Netherlands. *Outlook on Agriculture* **8**, 148–55.

Coastal sands
Barr D.A. & Golinski K.D. 1969. Marram grass, mulch and bitumen—a successful trial. *J. Soil Conserv. Serv. N.S.W.* **25**, 251–7.
Brooks D.R. 1976. Rehabilitation following mineral sand mining on North Stradbrooke Island, Queensland. In: *Landscaping and Land Use Planning as Related to Mining Operations*, Australian Inst. Min. Metall. 93–104. Adelaide: Australasian Inst. Min. Metall.
Brown R.L. & Hafenrichter A.L. 1948. Factors influencing the production and use of beach grass and dune grass clones for erosion control. 3. Influence of kinds and amounts of fertiliser on production. *Agron. J.* **40**, 677–84.
Coaldrake J.E. 1973. Conservation problems of coastal sand and open-cast mining. In: *Nature conservation in the Pacific* (ed.) A.B. Costin & R.H. Groves. 299–314. Canberra: Australian National Univ. Press.
Edlin H.L. 1978. The Culbin Sands. In: *Reclamation* (ed.) J. Lenihan and W.W. Fletcher. 1–31. Glasgow: Blackie.
Lewis J.W. 1976. Regeneration of coastal ecosystems after mineral sand mining. *Australian Mining*, July 1976, 1–3.
Gadgil R.L. 1971. The nutritional role of *Lupinus arboreus* in coastal sand dune forestry. 3. Nitrogen distribution in the ecosystem before tree planting. *Pl. Soil 35*, 113–26.
Pizzey J. 1975. Assessment of dune stabilisation at Camber, Sussex, using air photographs. *Biol. Cons.* **7**, 275–88.
Zak J.M. 1965. Sand dune erosion control at Provincetown, Massachusetts. *J. Soil. Wat. Conserv.* **20**, 188–9.

'In so much as that in a place commonly called Tilney Smeth there feed much about 30 000 sheepe: but so subject to the beating, and overflowing of the roaring maine sea, which very often meaketh, teareth and troubleth it so grievously, that hardly it can be holden off with chargeable wals and workes.'
WILLIAM CAMDEN Britannia. 1673.

13   Roads, Reservoirs and Renewal

This book has been a catalogue of assaults on our environment. Whatever we do seems to cause a mess and gives us a less attractive environment than we should have, but perhaps one we deserve. For if we do not take the trouble to care for our environment we must put up with the consequences.

Nowhere is this more obvious than with roadsides. It is perfectly possible to have attractive, very beautiful roads. Many old roads are full of plants and animals and some new roads are object lessons in man-created beauty. But roads in general represent one of the most savage assaults on our environment at the present time, yet need not be.

Reservoirs have an intrinsic beauty from the interplay of land and water. Yet they can be spoilt in detail by their margins, particularly the draw-down zone which is inevitable because of water-use. Nature shows us what can be done, but there is no need to wait patiently for her.

The final problem is perhaps the greatest affront to society of any of the problems we have considered, because it is part of the every-day lives of millions of city dwellers. This is the meaningless mess left when buildings are torn down and nothing is put up in their place for several years. The official term is 'interim lands': a better term would be urban deserts. At first sight they are unpromising material. But of all the problems in this book this is, surprisingly, one of the easiest to solve.

These last three problems appear somewhat unrelated. And yet, they have one thing in common—that the guidance for what should be done is provided by nature herself.

13.1   ROADSIDES

13.1.1   An assault on the environment

The new Interstate Highway system in the USA has added 400 000 ha to an existing 1 000 000 ha of roadverge area: the metalled road surface is only a quarter more. In Britain there are 200 000 ha of central reservation and roadside verge.

The vegetation that covers road verges, embankments and cuttings has important amenity functions. A well-designed and planted roadside can make a great difference to the pleasure of a journey. Roadside vegetation is also crucial for erosion control. In Europe, roadsides have always been covered with vegetation; but in the first rush of highway construction in America in the 1920s, little was done about vegetation cover, and highway engineers soon became alarmed at the amount of erosion, which could become serious enough to threaten the highways themselves.

But roadsides also have a more general function. As agriculture becomes more intensive and even the smallest corner is cultivated, they are becoming an important habitat for many small plants and animals, some of which no longer exist elsewhere. They are also a very large area under public ownership which can be used for large-scale landscape purposes. In particular, by planting trees, the tendency of the countryside to become increasingly bleak and open can be resisted.

There are as many different sorts of roadsides as there are natural environments. Since roads are constructed all over the world, there is no common set of characteristics, except that in modern highways, which are designed to give very low gradients to avoid speed reductions by heavy vehicles, the road will often be in a cutting or on an embankment. As a result, roadside vegetation commonly has to grow on cut or fill slopes of 3:1 or steeper and one of the most critical environmental considerations is soil erosion. However, this erosion is only a problem in the establishment phase before the vegetation has formed a complete cover.

The soil characteristics of roadsides depend firstly on whether or not top soil has been used to cover them. There is a divergence of practice between different countries over this, particularly between the Old World and the New. Perhaps this is because the ethic of conservation is more developed in the Old World where resources are shorter than in the New where labour is expensive and areas needing treatment are large. Whether this is true or not, in the former (particularly Britain) top soil is regularly used and in the latter less often.

At first sight it would seem better if top soil were used whenever possible. But roadsides are a place where the normal need to restore a productive soil/plant ecosystem does not apply. Since the only uses of roadside vegetation are erosion control, visual amenity, and wild life habitats, the soil must be good enough to allow vegetation to satisfy these requirements: but a vigorous vegetation will be a liability, since it requires frequent mowing, or if not mown becomes a source of weeds for agricultural land or a fire hazard.

The use of top soil with a vigorous seeds mixture results in a productive sward from which most other species will tend to be excluded by competition. If the surrounding environment is fertile permanent pasture, this treatment produces roadsides which are in keeping with their surroundings. The relationship breaks down, however, if mowing is not maintained. There are a few species which can stand the competition of the grass, such as the docks *Rumex obtusifolius* and *R. crispus* and the thistles *Cirsium vulgare* and *C. arvense*, which are not at all beautiful and are serious agricultural weeds (Figure 13.1).

Figure 13.1. An uninspiring newly-established roadside verge: the weeds (docks and thistles) and long grass are the unfortunate outcome of a policy of using top soil and no mowing in Britain.

Where top soil is not used, the situation is different. The material exposed will be subsoil and underlying rocks, deficient in nitrogen and phosphorus. The rocks will have their own particular chemical and physical characteristics. Left to their own devices, they will become colonised by their own attractive collections of plant species, a point made very forcibly by the late Nan Fairbrother (Figure 13.2). Indeed, road cuts which have been in existence for a long time have accumulated important floras. In Britain, at least 27 very rare species have their main occurrences on roadsides. These are nearly all old sites where top soil will not have been used, allowing colonisation by species intolerant of competition (Table 13.1).

But the problem with road cuts, like other types of disturbed land, is that the species adapted to the particular characteristics of the environment may not occur naturally in sites near enough to be able to invade easily. This is particularly the case where a cut is made through an agricultural area. So the natural invasion of appropriate higher plants has usually been slow, often not perceptible over decades, even where road cuts have been through very characteristic rocks.

Areas of fill on the sides of embankments are usually of less interest, partly because they are less visible to road users, but also because fill materials are usually an amalgam of different rocks and subsoils and are not so extreme. Nevertheless, where one rock type has been used, a characteristic flora can develop.

Figure 13.2. The late Nan Fairbrother made a plea for more natural roadsides: the beauty of the vegetation on an old-established roadside in Wales.

Animals colonise roadside vegetation rapidly. The undisturbed rough herbage is a haven for small mammals such as mice, voles and shrews. Substantial populations can develop, which in their turn attract predators: kestrels (*Falco tinnunculus*) hovering overhead are a characteristic feature of British motorways.

Roadsides have not escaped pollution: they are subject particularly to lead from car exhausts and salt used for ice removal. But although lead gets into soils and vegetation on roadsides (about 500 ppm in soil is common now) the levels are not toxic to vegetation. Nevertheless, unless the use of lead is stopped, toxicity is bound to develop. Indeed, metal-tolerant plants are beginning to be found on roadsides.

Salt is a much more serious problem. Over twenty years the amount of salt used in the USA has gone up by a factor of 12 and is now over 6 million tonnes/yr. In Britain, in a cold year, over 1 million tonnes are used at about a rate of 6 tonnes/km of road. Sodium levels in the soils of roadside verges can reach over 1000 ppm, with the same concentration in plant tissues: normal concentrations in plants are about 50 ppm. These are levels approaching those found in coastal salt marshes.

Table 13.1. Roadsides are an important habitat for wild life: very rare plants occurring on roadside verges in Britain

Allium babingtonii (wild leek)	**Linum anglicum* (perennial flax)
Aristolochia clematitis (birthwort)	**Melampyrum arvense* (field cow-wheat)
Artemisia compestris (field southernwood)	**Muscari atlanticum* (grape hyacinth)
Asarum europaeum (asarabacca)	**Orobanche caryophyllacea* (clove-scented broom rape)
*Beta trigyna (wildbeat)	*Phleum phleoides* (Bohmers cat's-tail)
**Bupleurum falcatum (hare's ear)	**Phyteuma spicatum* (rampion)
Carex filiformis (downy sedge)	**Pyrus cordata* (shrubby pear)
Carex montana (mountain sedge)	*Salvia pratensis* (meadow clary)
Cynoglossum germanicum (green hound's-tongue)	*Scrophularia scorodonia* (balm-leaved figwort)
Epipogium aphyllum (ghost orchid)	*Silene otites* (spanish catchfly)
Erica ciliaris (Dorset heath)	*Stachys germanica* (downy woundwort)
Herniaria glabra (glabrous rupture-wort)	*Tetragonolobus maritimus* (trefoil)
Himantoglossum hircinum (lizard orchid)	*Verbascum pulverulentum* (hoary mullein)
Hypochaeris maculata (spotted cat's ear)	

* species only found on roadsides
** now extinct due to road widening

These levels fall off rapidly away from the roadway but salt toxicity is now common close to salted roads, and may lead to death of the vegetation. Some grass species such as red fescue (*Festuca rubra*) are more tolerant to salt than others and may persist; if the vegetation dies, salt-tolerant annuals such as orache (*Atriplex hastata*) and mayweed (*Tripleurospermum maritimum*) invade. Trees root deeper and usually escape the effects of salt in the soil, but they can suffer leaf damage due to spray drift. Sugar maple (*Acer saccharum*) widely planted in the USA as a roadside tree is particularly sensitive and trees within 10 m of heavily salted roads can be killed.

13.1.2 Ecological ingenuity

The first decision must be whether to use top soil. This should not be based just on whether it is available at low cost or not, but what final type of vegetation cover is required. The inherent fertility of top soil will be important if a vigorous grass sward is wanted. It will also be important for planted trees and shrubs. The British standard treatment for roadside verges requires 15 cm of top soil spread uniformly. With it is associated a seed mixture in which perennial ryegrass and red fescue predominate (Table 13.2). This gives rise to a dense turf which, although fairly low-growing because the varieties chosen are prostrate, is productive and is most satisfactory only when mown regularly. Clover is included to provide a source of nitrogen, but is usually suppressed by the grass growth; nevertheless, it is an insurance where the top soil has inadequate nitrogen and grass growth is reduced. To ensure satisfactory growth in the early stages 500 kg/ha of a 10:10:20 is recommended. It would seem more appropriate to use a 10:20:10 mixture giving about 50 kg/ha of N, P and K because potassium is rarely very deficient. Lime must be added to correct acidity.

Table 13.2. There are several possible seeds mixtures: standard and modified seeds mixture for British roadside verges

British standard mixture		%
perennial ryegrass (S23)	*Lolium perenne*	45
red fescue (S59)	*Festuca rubra*	15
smooth-stalked meadow grass	*Poa pratensis*	15
crested dog's tail	*Cynosurus cristatus*	15
white clover (S100)	*Trifolium repens*	10

A less aggressive mixture for use on neutral soils		%
creeping red fescue (dwarf var. e.g., Dawson)	*Festuca rubra* v *rubra*	15
chewings fescue	*Festuca rubra* v *commutata*	35
creeping bent	*Agrostis stolonifera*	10
common bent	*Agrostis tenuis*	10
smooth-stalked meadow grass	*Poa pratensis*	10
white clover (dwarf var. e.g., Kent)	*Trifolium repens*	15
bird's foot trefoil	*Lotus corniculatus*	5

A less aggressive mixture used on acid soils (will need nitrogen aftercare)		%
smooth stalked meadow grass	*Poa pratensis*	10
common bent	*Agrostis tenuis*	5
red fescue	*Festuca rubra*	50
sheep's fescue	*Festuca ovina*	20
brown bent	*Agrostis canina* v *montana*	10
wavy hairgrass	*Deschampsia flexuosa*	5

When top soil is applied, the underlying material must not remain consolidated by the heavy machinery spreading the top soil, and should be cultivated so that there is about 25 cm of tilled material including the top soil.

In North America and elsewhere, top soil is often not used. It is particularly expensive to spread on slopes. In France, because of the considerable economies in cost, it is sensibly recommended that top soil should be omitted except where the soil is an extreme sand or clay. But experiments have shown that, apart from the expense, topsoiled slopes are more liable to erosion because heavy rain caps the surface, and seed establishment is best in rough subsoil (Table 13.3). The soil fertility will have to be built up to ensure a rapid growth of grass in the early stages. Commonly 1000 kg/ha of a 10:20:10 fertiliser is used, giving roughly 100 kg/ha of N, P and K, together with lime up to the lime requirement (to raise the pH to 6·0).

Table 13.3. Vegetation can easily be established without top soil: the effect of top soiling, smooth and rough surfaces and incorporation of lime and fertiliser on the establishment of legumes (white clover and crownvetch) on a roadside in Virginia

treatment	plants established (plants/m²)		
	smooth		rough
	lime and fertiliser on surface		lime and fertiliser incorporated
topsoil	31·2	138·8	243·2
subsoil only	17·2	92·5	250·7

Preparation of the seed bed is again very important to minimise erosion. It may be necessary to chisel plough the material to break it up sufficiently. Where heavy rainstorms are expected, slopes should be stair-step graded with vertical walls not exceeding 50 cm, or deeply grooved, 10–20 cm deep, across the slope. It is essential that the surface is left rough.

The seeds mixture needs to be chosen with care. Firstly, the species needs to be tolerant of poorer conditions (Table 13.2); secondly, legumes become more important; thirdly, it may be valuable to include a nurse species. A perennial legume such as crown vetch (*Coronilla varia*) (Figure 13.3) or lespedeza (*Lespedeza sericea*)can be very successful sown only with a single grass species, such as tall fescue (*Festuca arundinacea*), as a nurse crop, a technique widely used in N. America. Recommendations for some different climatic regions are given in Table 13.4 but they can only be illustrative of what is possible.

If salt damage is expected then species must be salt-tolerant (Table 13.5). Amongst these it may be possible to find varieties which are particularly tolerant. If lead becomes toxic in roadside situations the only method which will combat it in the long-term is the use of the metal-tolerant material (Chapter 8).

Any normal seeding technique can be used. On steep

Figure 13.3. Where a maintenance-free dense vegetation cover is required on slopes without top soil, legumes such as crown vetch are invaluable: a roadside in W. Virginia.

Table 13.4. The different regions of a large country require very different seeds mixtures: recommendations for roadsides in different regions of the United States (rates in kg/ha)

species		non mown areas	mown areas
North East			
perennial ryegrass	*Lolium perenne*	45	
or red fescue	*Festuca rubra*	40	50
Kentucky bluegrass	*Poa pratensis*		20
red top	*Agrostis gigantea*		5
crown vetch	*Coronilla varia*	30	
North Central			
buffalo grass	*Buchloe dactyloides*	2	20
intermediate wheatgrass	*Agropyron intermedium*	15	
slender wheatgrass	*Agropyron trachycaulum*	2	1
crested wheatgrass	*Agropyron desertorum*	10	3
alfalfa	*Medicago sativa*	5	7
smooth brome	*Bromus inermis*	5	
Central			
tall fescue	*Festuca arundinacea*	40	
Kentucky bluegrass	*Poa pratensis*		30
red top	*Agrostis gigantea*	10	10
red fescue	*Festuca rubra*	12	20
white clover	*Trifolium repens*	5	5
South West			
weeping lovegrass	*Eragrostis curvula*	6	1
yellow bluestem	*Andropogon ischaemum*	2	2
blue grama	*Bouteloua gracilis*	2	2
Bermuda grass	*Cyndon dactylon*	5	5
South East			
tall fescue	*Festuca arundinacea*	40	
Kentucky bluegrass	*Poa pratensis*		40
annual lespedeza	*Lespedeza striata*	20	
or sericea	*Lespedeza cuneata*	30	
or crown vetch	*Coronilla varia*	5	
white clover	*Trifolium repens*		3

Chapter 13: Roads, Reservoirs and Renewal

slopes, hand seeding by a fiddle or a portable cyclone seeder is often the most economic method. If the seed bed is rough there is no need for subsequent cultivations. On slopes where access is difficult, hydraulic seeding is valuable: it is made easier by the presence of the roadway. But fertiliser rates must be reduced if legumes are to establish. In regions where there is heavy rainfall mulching is essential. Hay, straw or wood bark tacked down with wood fibre or asphalt is a particularly effective combination: chemical stabilisers have rarely been found to be useful.

Trees and shrubs can be seeded at the same time. The disadvantages are the variable germination and variable population densities achieved, but the method offers great economies. Where trees are planted growth will be better if top soil is provided either as an overall cover or in planting pits. A ground cover must be provided. Usually this is the same seeds mixture as for the rest of the area, but it may be

Table 13.5. Salt is becoming a serious problem on roadsides: salt tolerant plants suitable for use in salt-affected roadside environments

grasses and legumes
Agrostis stolonifera (creeping bent)
Dactylis glomerata (cocksfoot)
Festuca rubra (red fescue)
Holcus lanatus (Yorkshire fog)
Lolium perenne (rye grass)
Poa pratensis (smooth-stalked meadow grass)
Lotus corniculatus (bird's foot trefoil)
Trifolium repens (white clover)

shrubs
Atriplex halimus (salt bush)
Cornus alba sibirica (Siberian dogwood)
Crataegus monogyna (haw thorn)
Cytisus scoparius (broom)
Euonymus europaeus (spindle tree)
Hippophaë rhamnoides (sea buckthorn)
Ligustrum spp. (privet)
Myrica pennsylvanica (northern bayberry)
Prunus spinosa (blackthorn)
Symphoricarpos rivularis (snowberry)
Tamarix spp. (tamarisk)

trees
Pinus nigra (Austrian pine)
Populus alba (white poplar)
P. canescens (grey poplar)
P. tremula (aspen)
Prunus avium (wild cherry)
P. serotina (black cherry)
Quercus robur (English oak)
Q. rubra (northern red oak)
Q. petraea (durmast oak)
Robinia pseudoacacia (false acacia)
Salix alba (white willow)
S. babylonica (weeping willow)
Thuja spp. (arborvitae)
Ulmus carpinifolia (smooth elm)
U. procera (English elm)

better to use a prostrate legume such as white clover (*Trifolium repens*) which will provide nitrogen for the trees and at the same time not be too competitive (Figure 13.4).

Figure 13.4. Legume provide an excellent ground cover and contribute about 100 kg N/ha/yr to the soil and trees: trees at Runcorn, Cheshire, underplanted with clover.

Trees and shrubs are a most important element in modern highway design to provide variety of landscape. Dense plantings of shrubs such as hawthorn (*Crataegus* sp.) can provide an attractive cover which is maintenance-free (Figure 13.5). But they must be chosen and sited with care to relate to the surrounding landscape and native trees of the region. In the preparation of any highway planting plan a careful ecological survey of the terrain is essential so that the appropriate species are chosen. Horticultural cover plants such as ivy (*Hedera* sp.) and *Cotoneaster* sp. can be very effective but generally properly chosen grass/legume mixtures or native shrubs are easier to establish and more reliable in the long term.

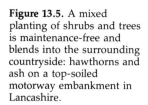

Figure 13.5. A mixed planting of shrubs and trees is maintenance-free and blends into the surrounding countryside: hawthorns and ash on a top-soiled motorway embankment in Lancashire.

In many situations it would be best if wild species invaded. However, the aggressive behaviour of species such as crown vetch may not permit this. Although it is a very effective cover plant it would hardly be satisfactory if the highways were covered endlessly with it: yet this is happening in parts of the USA. The ryegrass/fescue mixture so standard in Britain is similarly unattractive.

This is a strong argument for less aggressive seeds mixtures and no top soil, so that natural invasion by attractive species will occur (Figure 13.6). However, colonisation by local species may have to be encouraged by sowing seed specially collected from wild species, by transplanting individuals to act as starters of colonisation, or by scattering soil containing dormant seed or vegetative fragments (see Chapter 6). The range of attractive species which would be worth introducing is immense (Table 13.6): lists like this can be made for countries throughout the world. It may be sensible to include legumes because of inevitable problems of nitrogen deficiency, and a nurse species with a short life span.

Figure 13.6. Scrub can develop naturally if seed parents are nearby, top soil is not used and a non-competitive seeds mixture sown: attractive scrub invading naturally near Bala, N. Wales.

In the most favourable climatic regions of the world, such as the tropics, natural colonisation is usually so rapid that it is not necessary to seed at all or only in the simplest possible manner to provide some stabilisation. Then all that is required is one or two applications of fertiliser, to encourage stabilisation and colonisation (Figure 13.7).

13.1.3 Aftercare
Management of the vegetation will determine what is finally developed. Close mowing will maintain a grass sward. However, the amount of mowing required has been shown to be much less than that usually practised. One or two instead of the four cuts a year common in Britain gives economies, maintains a grass sward and allows meadow species to remain in or to invade the sward. In the complete absence of cutting, trees and shrubs will invade sooner or later depending on the nearness of seed parents.

The need for fertilising will depend on the situation. Where top soil has been used there will usually be little need, nor should there be where legumes have been employed. The only cases where fertilising is likely to be necessary is where top soil has not been used and legumes have not been established. Under these conditions treatment of 200 kg/ha of a high-nitrogen complete fertiliser for one or two years will be necessary if the vegetation is not to degenerate.

Roadsides are a situation where well-established formulas exist for vegetation establishment. Yet in different countries quite different methods are adopted. At the same time, opportunities are being lost to improve the diversity and amenity value of an environment which is becoming a significant part of our lives. Recently, much more imagination has begun to be used in the treatment of roadsides (Figure 13.8), but not enough. There is still scope for biological expertise to improve the end product.

Table 13.6. Wild species could be introduced: attractive wild species likely to be adapted to roadside habitats in Europe

---

herbs

	Ranunculus acris (buttercup)		*Chaerophyllum temulentum* (chervil)
	Chelidonium majus (greater celandine)		*Anthriscus sylvestris* (cow parsley
C	*Reseda lutea* (mignonette)		*Heracleum sphondylium* (hogweed)
C	*Viola lutea* (pansy)	C	*Primula veris* (cowslip)
A	*Hypericum perforatum* (St. John's Wort)		*Primula vulgaris* (primrose)
	Silene dioica (red campion)		*Linaria vulgaris* (toad flax)
	Silene vulgaris (bladder campion)		*Rhinanthus minor* (yellow rattle)
W	*Lychnis floscuculi* (ragged robin)	C	*Origanum vulgare* (marjoram)
	Stellaria holostea (stitchwort)		*Prunella vulgaris* (self heal)
	Malva sylvestris (mallow)		*Betonica officinalis* (betony)
	Geranium pratense (meadow crane's bill)	A	*Teucrium scorodonia* (wood sage)
C	*Ononis repens* (rest harrow)		*Campanula latifolia* (bell flower)
	Trifolium fragiferum (strawberry clover)	A	*Campanula rotundifolia* (harebell)
	Trifolium pratense (red clover)		*Valeriana officinalis* (valerian)
C	*Anthyllis vulneraria* (kidney vetch)		*Dipsacus fullonum* (teasel)
	Lotus corniculatus (bird's foot trefoil)		*Knautia arvensis* (field scabious)
	Lotus uliginosus (trefoil)	A	*Solidago virgaurea* (golden rod)
	Vicia sepium (vetch)		*Achillea millefolium* (yarrow)
	Lathyrus pratensis (meadow vetchling)		*Chrysanthemum leucanthemum* (ox-eye daisy)
	Lathyrus sylvestris (everlasting pea)	C	*Centaurea scabiosa* (knapweed)
W	*Filipendula ulmaria* (meadow sweet)		*Cichorium intybus* (chicory)
A	*Potentilla erecta* (tormentil)		*Endymion nonscriptus* (bluebell)
	Potentilla reptans (cinquefoil)		*Narcissus pseudonarcissus* (wild daffodil)
	Geum urbanum (wood avens)		*Orchis mascula* (early purple orchid)
W	*Lythrum salicaria* (purple loosestrife)		

---

shrubs

	Clematis vitalba (traveller's joy)		*Sorbus aucuparia* (rowan)
C	*Helianthemum nummularium* (rockrose)	C	*Sorbus aria* (white beam)
C	*Acer campestre* (field maple)	C	*Cornus sanguinea* (dogwood)
	Euonymus europaeus (spindle)		*Corylus avellana* (hazel)
A	*Genista anglica* (petty whin)		*Salix cinerea* (sallow)
	Ulex europaeus (gorse)	A	*Calluna vulgaris* (heather)
A	*Ulex gallii* (dwarf gorse)	A	*Erica cinerea* (bell heather)
	Cytisus scoparius (broom)	A	*Vaccinium myrtillus* (bilberry)
	Rubus fruticosus (bramble)	C	*Viburnum lantana* (guelder rose)
	Rosa sp. (wild rose)		*Viburnum opulus* (wayfaring tree)
	Prunus spinosa (black thorn)		*Lonicera periclymenum* (honeysuckle)
	Crataegus monogyna (hawthorn)		

A   acidic soils
C   calcareous soils
W   wet soils

Figure 13.7. In the tropics growth is rapid: this road cut on Bougainville was lightly sown with molasses grass, siratro and *Desmodium* and fertilised: after six years native species such as *Casuarina* and *Miscanthus* have taken over.

Figure 13.8. A well-landscaped road can be a considerable contribution to the countryside: a bad one is a disaster.

Roadsides

13.2   RESERVOIRS

13.2.1   An ecological challenge

Reservoirs, although produced for a quite different purpose, are very similar to wet gravel pits from a reclamation point of view. In the past, for reasons of water purity, people have been excluded from reservoirs, which were treated as water tanks rather than as additions to the countryside. Now, because of public pressure, multiple use has been accepted by water authorities, so there is now a need to make them into attractive areas which people can use and enjoy.

But there is a problem of fluctuating water levels. At times of water draw-down, a large expanse of bare mud and stone is inevitably exposed, not a very attractive sight (Figure 13.9). This is made worse by the tendency to keep the margins clear of all vegetation for reasons of water quality. Yet in older reservoirs, nature has done its best and found plants to colonise the margins. In the most protected areas herbaceous species will grow, but where there is some exposure the main colonists are shrubs, such as *Salix caprea* and *S. cinerea* in Europe, and *Salix lutea* in North America, all of which can tolerate flooding of their roots for long periods. These provide the key to a successful technique for they certainly soften the harsh outlines of the draw-down zone (Figure 13.10). Although in the past vegetation was removed from reservoir margins because of its possible adverse effect on water quality there is little evidence for this.

The draw-down zone is marked by alternating periods of flooding and emergence. During the periods of flooding it can suffer erosion from wave action. On the most exposed areas this will preclude the establishment of any vegetation. But in protected areas planting is possible, particularly of trees, since these can stand some wave action and are large enough to make a positive contribution to the landscape.

There are many tree species which are tolerant of flooding (Table 13.7). How far down this zone they will grow depends on the draw-down regime. Plants can stand flooding best when they are not growing rapidly, in the winter. Storage reservoirs which have their water levels highest during the winter can therefore be more extensively planted than regulatory reservoirs which tend to have their water levels highest in the summer.

In the protected parts of reservoirs, herbaceous plants can be introduced, particularly species such as reed (*Phragmites communis*) and reed grass (*Phalaris arundinacea*), which can tolerate a fluctuating water regime and are large enough to make an effective landscape contribution.

Figure 13.9. A reservoir with the water drawn-down is not attractive: planting treatment is required to soften the harsh and dismal appearance.

Figure 13.10. The sort of development that should be encouraged on new reservoirs: attractive natural colonisation on the fifty-year-old reservoir, Lake Vyrnwy, in Wales.

Table 13.7. Tree species in temperate regions tolerant of flooding

very tolerant	tolerant
Alnus glutinosa (common alder)	*Betula pendula* (silver birch)
Alnus incana (grey alder)	*Chamaecyparis thyoides* (white cedar)
Cephalanthus occidentalis (buttonball)	*Fraxinus americana* (white ash)
Cornus stolonifera (red osier dogwood)	*Fraxinus excelsior* (common ash)
Forestiera acuminata (swamp privet)	*Fraxinus pennsylvanica* (green ash)
Nyssa aquatica (water tupelo)	*Liquidamber styraciflua* (sweet gum)
Planera aquatica (swamp iron wood)	*Populus alba* (white poplar)
Populus x *euramericana* (hybrid black poplar)	*Populus balsamifera* (tacamahac)
Populus nigra (black poplar)	*Populus deltoides* (cotton wood)
Quercus lyrata (overcup oak)	*Quercus palustris* (pin oak)
Salix cinerea (common sallow)	*Quercus phellos* (willow oak)
Salix caprea (goat willow)	*Salix alba* (white willow)
Salix lutea (yellow willow)	*Salix fragilis* (crack willow)
Salix nigra (black willow)	*Salix phylicifolia* (tea-leaved willow)
Salix pentandra (bay willow)	*Salix purpurea* (purple osier)
Salix viminalis (common osier)	*Salix triandra)* (almond
Taxodium distichum (swamp cypress)	willow)

Reservoirs

13.3 URBAN CLEARANCE AREAS

13.3.1 An affront on society

Too many inner city areas in Britain and America have fallen derelict and have had to be cleared. Unfortunately, rebuilding has not always followed and we have been left with bleak open areas of building waste, covered with weeds, stones and odd bricks, in just the areas which are visible to people (Figure 13.11). Such sites attract rubbish and illegal tipping of other waste. Of all the forms of derelict and degraded land, they are one of the most obvious and inexcusable. Yet in one city alone, London, there are 6500 ha of these interim lands at the moment, and in the whole of Gt. Britain there is as much as 100 000 ha.

It is obviously not necessary to make great improvements, since these are areas which will eventually be redeveloped. But if they remain derelict for five years (and many of them are derelict for a decade) this is the complete pre-school life time of the children who live nearby. So some simple treatment is essential.

The usual constituents are bricks, mortar (sand and lime) and garden soil, sometimes with subsoil, ashes or other rubbish. The pH is well over 7, the calcium levels are high and what is likely to be missing is, like so many materials, nitrogen and sometimes phosphorus (Table 13.8). But the surface is often heavily consolidated and difficult for plant establishment.

Figure 13.11. It is remarkable that we suffer this sort of environmental horror in the middle of our cities: there are over 500 hectares in this English city, mostly owned by the City Council.

Chapter 13: Roads, Reservoirs and Renewal

This is borne out by the species to be found, such as annual meadow grass (*Poa annua*), creeping bent grass (*Agrostis stolonifera*) and white clover (*Trifolium repens*), plants excellent at colonising consolidated neutral or calcareous open ground. The excellent growth of clover and equivalent legumes once they have colonised suggests again that the only real problem is nitrogen.

Table 13.8. Clearance sites are badly deficient only in nitrogen: nutrient levels in some typical urban clearance areas in Liverpool

| site | pH | N (total %) | P | K | Ca |
			(available ppm)		
Grove Street	7·2	·05	36	220	3830
Tennyson Street	6·7	·08	65	450	1070
Brunswick Road	7·0	·05	19	290	8830
garden soil	6·3	·14	61	140	1030

It is obviously possible to use top soil on the building waste of urban clearance areas just as on refuse disposal sites. However, the areas are usually temporary, and rarely have serious problems of glass, etc., in the surface layers. Since the cost of 10 cm of top soil in urban areas is now as much as £2000/ha it is sensible to establish a plant cover without it. This is not at all difficult.

If urban clearance sites can be caught immediately on clearance the material will be relatively soft and easy to deal with if it has been flattened by a bulldozer with ribbed tracks which leave the ground surface broken but flat (Figure 13.12). Otherwise the ground will need a light cultivation to a depth of 5 cm. Any simple resilient seeds mixture should be sown at 60 kg/ha, containing ryegrass if wear is expected, and clover to provide nitrogen in the long term. Complete fertiliser at approximately 400 kg/ha should accompany the seed. If dry weather is expected a light cultivation to bury the seed will be valuable, otherwise it will be naturally covered by the effects of rain. The whole area should then be stone picked. Of all the operations this may be the most expensive, perhaps £100/ha, but compared with the alternative of top soil, it is negligible.

A grass sward will establish quickly. A second fertiliser dressing will be necessary either towards the end of the first growing season or at the beginning of the second. After that, nitrogen will be provided by the clover which is favoured by such conditions. Mowing can be restricted to one, or at the most, two cuts per year, using a flail mower in case of stones.

Swards which have been established in this manner can be as good as, or better then, those established on top soil, in cover and resistance to wear (Figure 13.13). If they have to be left for many years because of lack of redevelopment, they will not degenerate but will in fact improve continuously. Because of the underlying hardcore, they are versatile, and can even be used as temporary car parks.

Figure 13.12. A good seed bed can be established directly on bricks, rubble and mortar if a little care is taken: a well-prepared urban clearance site.

277

Figure 13.13. Which is better, this or Figure 13.11?: urban clearance areas can grow good grass without top soil if properly fertilised.

Better areas can be turned into allotments for vegetable growing (Figure 13.14). But it is essential that any nutrient deficiencies are identified and remedied or the results will be disappointing. It will be well worthwhile digging in organic matter to improve moisture and nutrient retention. Even unrotted leaves will be excellent provided that they are backed up by generous use of fertilisers (Table 13.9).

Figure 13.14. Vegetables are a real possibility for the better urban land: this 3/4 hectare in Redbridge, London, supplies vegetables for ten families.

Tree planting is perfectly possible. Growth is better if trees are planted into pits filled with good-quality soil. Where small transplants are being used in extensive planting schemes, soil pits are not necessary and normal forestry practice can be followed. In heavily used areas, damage to trees by children must be expected. It is often called vandalism, but it is usually an unthinking use of the trees for some other purpose. Good posts and ties must be provided and often treeguards.

Aftercare is as essential as anywhere else. The first need is to ensure that the restoration has been completely finished; many restored sites are ruined by some unfinished margin or pile of forgotten rubbish. Then there will be occasional mowing, and some sites may need fertiliser, particularly high phosphorus to encourage legumes.

Trees must be cared for otherwise there is no point in planting them in the first place. Children respect trees which are obviously cared for. If they can be involved so much the better. A tree which is not loved and cared for will seem fair material for them to exploit for other purposes.

Table 13.9. A use for urban wasteland: a simple programme for cultivating vegetables successfully on any poor piece of ground, whether old building site, railway embankment, or waste land

1. Buy a potato fork (a fork with flat prongs), 56 lbs of ordinary garden fertiliser (7% N, 7% P_2O_5, 7% K_2O), 56 lbs of lime; borrow a wheelbarrow.
2. Collect as much organic matter (garden rubbish, leaves, vegetable waste) as you can: ask the man who sweeps the road to dump his autumn sweepings, or get the local Council to bring them by lorry.
3. If you think the ground is acid (get someone to test it) lime the whole patch you want to cultivate at 8 oz/yd².
4. Dig out trench 9 ins deep at end of the patch and take material to the other end.
5. Put at least 4 ins of organic matter in trench.
6. Sprinkle this with 2 oz/yd² of fertiliser.
7. Dig next trench alongside first by filling in the first, and then fill it with organic matter as before.
8. Use the fork to dig with and as you turn the soil into the trench separate out any stones, bricks or weeds into the wheelbarrow.
9. Go on until you finish the patch, and fill in the last trench with the material from the first trench.
10. Leave until planting time.
11. When you plant scatter 2 oz/yd² fertiliser and lightly fork it into the surface.
12. Scatter another 1 oz/yd² on three separate occasions while the crop is growing.
13. If the ground is very weedy grow potatoes in the first year to smother the weeds: otherwise choose any robust crop.

The fertiliser provides the nutrients: the organic matter holds water and the nutrients, and as it breaks down will improve the soil texture: since the organic matter is rough material with a high carbon/nitrogen ratio it will not provide much in the way of nutrients: this is why the fertiliser is essential and must be continued throughout the season.

The scope in urban areas is unlimited, play areas, parks, allotments, even nature reserves (Figures 13.15 and 13.16). But they require imagination in their establishment and care afterwards. Anyone finding themselves in New York should visit the corner of Third Street and La Guardia Place to see what care and imagination can achieve. Our underprivileged urban populations should have the chance to enjoy attractive, well cared for surroundings like anybody else. Otherwise the present trouble and unhappiness in cities will continue to grow.

Figure 13.15. Over three acres of waste land now providing for activities from bike scrambling to rock climbing: Meanwhile Gardens in Paddington, London.

Figure 13.16. Wilderness for wild life being created from derelict land in the heart of a city: the William Curtis Ecological Park in London.

FURTHER READING

Roadsides

Arnal G. 1977. Planches experimentales d'engazonnement sur talus routiers: premier bilan. *Bull. Liaison Labo*. P. et Ch. **88**, 45–60.

Carpenter P.L., Walker T.D. & Lanphear F.O. 1975. *Plants in the Landscape*. San Francisco: Freeman.

Henensal P. & Spake A. 1974. *Engazonnement de l'emprise routiere*. Service d'Etudes Techniques des Routes et Autoroutes Paris: Ministere de l'Equipement.

Hottenstein W.L. 1969. Highway roadsides. In: *Turfgrass Science*, ed. A.A. Hanson and F.V. Juska, 603–37. Madison: Amer. Soc. Agron.

Nebauer N.R. & Good R.B. 1971. Techniques employed in road stabilization. *Journ. Soil Cons. Service of N.S. Wales*. **27**, 14–24.

Ranwell D.S., Winn J.M. & Allen S.E. 1973. *Road salting effects on soil and plants*. London: Natural Environment Research Council.

Way J.M. (ed.) 1969. *Road Verges: their Function and Management*. Monk's Wood Experimental Station Symp. London: Natural Environment Research Council.

Way J.M. 1976. *Grasses and Planted Areas by Motorways*. Monk's Wood Experimental Station, Occ. Rep. 3. London: Natural Environment Research Council.

Williams-Ellis C. 1955. *Roads in The Landscape*. Ministry of Transport London: HMSO.

Wright D.L., Perry H.D. & Blaser R.E. 1978. Persistent low maintenance vegetation for erosion control and aesthetics in highway corridors. In: *Reclamation of Drastically Disturbed Lands*, ed. F.W. Schaller and P. Sutton, 553–83. Madison: Amer. Soc. Agron.

Zak J.M. & Bredakis E.J. 1967. *Establishment and management of roadside vegetative cover in Massachusetts—final report*. Bull. 562. Mass. Agric. Exp. Sta., Univ. Massachusetts.

Reservoirs

Gill C.J. 1977. Some aspects of the design and management of reservoir margins for multiple use. *Appl. Biol.* **2**, 129–82.

Gill C.J. & Bradshaw A.D. 1971. The landscaping of reservoir margins. *Landscape Design* **95**, 31–4.

Urban clearance areas

Bradshaw A.D. & Handley J.F. 1972. Low cost grassing of sites awaiting redevelopment. *Landscape Design* **99**.

Cantell T. 1977. *Urban Wasteland*. London: Civic Trust.

Fairbrother N. 1970. *New Lives, New Landscapes*. London: Architectural Press.

Royal Horticultural Society 1972. *The Vegetable Garden Displayed*. London: Royal Horticultural Society.

'The din of the dusty world and the locked-in-ness of human habitations are what human nature abhors; while on the contrary, haze, mist, and the haunting spirits of the mountains are what human nature seeks, and yet can rarely find.'

KUO HSI

An essay on landscape painting. C11.

14 Prospect

Inevitably the pressure we exert on our environment will continue to increase. Despite the arguments of some people that we should return to simpler styles of living, it would be a bold person who would prophesy that this will happen. A very large part of the world puts up with incomes one-tenth of the size that the richest nations enjoy: they are unlikely to be persuaded.

Table 14.1. Gross national product per individual of various countries in US dollars in 1975

USA	6640	Germany	5890	China	300
Canada	6080	Denmark	5820	Nigeria	240
Argentina	1900	UK	3360	Tanzania	140
Mexico	1000	Poland	2450	India	130
Brazil	900	USSR	2300	Burma	90
Chile	820	Spain	1960	Ethiopia	90

But even if standards of living are slow to increase, the world's population will increase, whether we like it or not. The importance of population control, and the inevitability of trouble if control is not achieved, are beginning to be realised. But the best estimate that can be made at the moment is that the world's population is increasing at 2 per cent per year, which means that it will double in the next 35 years.

Against this background the need to maintain our basic resource of land is only too obvious. In the history of the world there have been a number of very successful civilisations in which the concept of careful husbandry of resources was an integral part of their outlook. Greek stoic philosophy believed that life should be in accord with 'φύσις' which we can poorly translate as 'nature'. The Chinese have demonstrated in practice over two thousand years how a balanced way of life can be achieved, guided by the Confucian concept of virtue and self-control. In Islam, respect for order is a fundamental concept.

Yet the recent position over care for the land in many, particularly Western, countries suggests that the message has often not been heard and certainly has not regularly been acted upon. The wasteful acquisitive behaviour of Western civilisation as it spread through the world has become legendary: it is still much the same today. We still believe we can move on from one resource to another as each is used up: and we are prepared even, as in many mining operations, to destroy one resource—the land—in order to get another—the buried minerals.

282

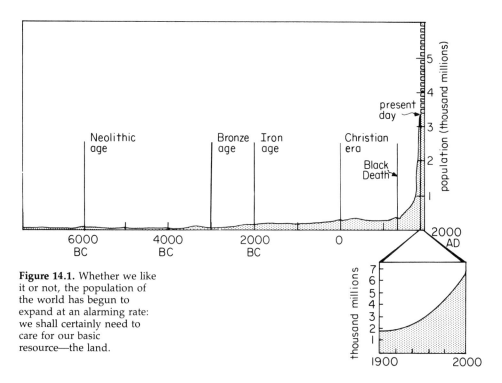

Figure 14.1. Whether we like it or not, the population of the world has begun to expand at an alarming rate: we shall certainly need to care for our basic resource—the land.

If the halcyon days are over, then our response has been to rediscover the principle of conservation and the recycling of land. We are beginning to require proper management and restoration as an integral part of resource exploitation, which is excellent. But there are many exploiters who still cry 'impossible' or 'too expensive'! They are frightened that the restoration process will put too great demands on them and will make it difficult for them to continue their activities. If this is really true, that the cost to society of exploiting a resource is more than the benefit gained by exploiting it, then it should not be exploited. But it is no use expecting that mineral and other resources can never be used: we have to live and we will want to live comfortably, in which case exploitation will be necessary.

If there is any message from this book it is that exploitation of mineral resources is possible and the cost of land restoration afterwards is not necessarily expensive. We can hope and expect to use our land resources for a succession of different purposes without it ever lying derelict, so long as we insist that restoration is carried out. It is obviously best if restoration is planned to be included in the exploiting operation from the very beginning: then the operation can be arranged so that restoration costs are minimised.

Even when the exploitation has been carried out in the past and we inherit land long derelict, the problems are not insurmountable. Indeed, the restoration may often be very

Prospect

Figure 14.2. A land used for a thousand years but still in good heart: view over Church Stretton in Shropshire looking north-east to the Long Mynd.

simple. The key is the identification and correction of the individual problems which cause the land to remain dere-lict. The correction may take a little time, in the same way that natural soil development takes time. But materials and methods now available mean that we can hasten the pro-cess considerably.

Whatever the methods used, they must be based on an understanding of natural processes, because the end point is some kind of ecosystem, an integrated system of soil, plants and animals. This involves understanding soil pro-cesses and knowing how they can be encouraged. It also involves understanding the requirements of plants and the other organisms which interact with them.

In earth-moving and mining operations, it is clear that engineers are key people. In land restoration it should be clear that biologists and soil-scientists are key people, whether they operate as agriculturalists, ecologists or landscape architects. A mining operation would not use biologists to design and oversee its working faces: simi-larly, engineers (or metallurgists or chemists) should not be the people carrying out revegetation programmes, although they will obviously work with biologists to be responsible for earth-moving and other structural aspects. Success, which means economy, only comes when the proper skills are employed. Yet there are many restoration

284   *Chapter 14: Prospect*

operations in private industry and local government where engineers rather than biologists are in control and are creating ecosystems governed by processes they do not really understand.

Success will also only come when the will exists to carry out the work, from the beginning to its proper completion, including whatever aftercare is necessary. This will must be in the operating company, from the boardroom down to the employee, and in the public, from the planning office of the local authority down to the ordinary individual. A society only gets the sort of land treatment it desires. Without a will to achieve a proper end-product, the inevitable laziness of individuals and the pressures of economic circumstances mean that little restoration will occur.

In the past, the will to carry out restoration has been blunted by the worry that it would be difficult and expensive, and price the exploiting company out of international markets with consequent loss of jobs. Now that we understand how restoration can be achieved, this need no longer dominate our thoughts on the subject. It is very important that both exploiters and public realise this; the exploiters so that they can plan restoration into their operations from the beginning, the public so they can insist on restoration being done. Obviously restoration costs something: but the cost does not need to be outrageous. The critical point is that the style and costs of restoration can be adjusted to suit individual circumstances. Anyway, it is fair to ask for some cost and effort to be expended, if not for ourselves, at least for what we leave for succeeding generations.

Once restoration has been accepted as the norm of behaviour, this does not mean that any sort of restoration will do. There is perhaps a temptation for exploiters to try to pass off a superficial, temporary, cosmetic treatment as fully satisfying restoration requirements. A complete restoration of the land and landscape as it was may be

Figure 14.3. We can make derelict land into something for people to enjoy, now and in the future: part of the major reclamation area in Stoke-on-Trent, Staffordshire.

285

impossible, but full and viable restoration of a self-sustaining ecosystem must be obtained.

In this respect, the word restoration has disadvantages since it implies that exactly what was there previously must be replaced. This may be impossible, or, even if it were possible, not desirable. Disturbance of land by mining wipes the slate clean, so to speak. When the disturbance is over, new land-uses may be possible or even preferable. The disturbance itself will permit total reshaping of the landscape in new and exciting ways.

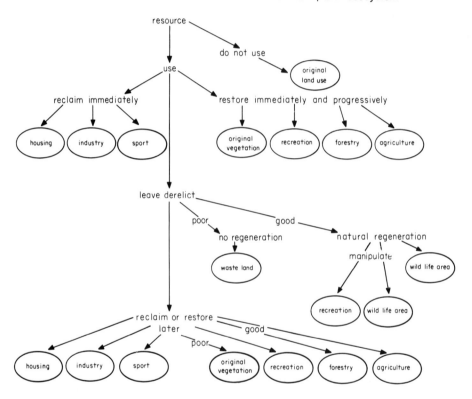

Figure 14.4. Disturbance of land is not a disaster: it is an opportunity and a challenge.

We have never previously had such opportunities to refashion our landscape. The great Chinese landscape tradition and the activities of the British landscape architects of the eighteenth century point to what should be possible. Although wilderness or agriculture are clear endpoints to land restoration, there are a variety of other developments, of landscape and recreation as well as industry and other more intensive uses. In an age when we are cultivating a love of wilderness, it must be remembered that some of the most attractive places in the world are man-made.

So the restoration of land requires imagination and sensitivity as well as science. And it requires knowledge that it

Figure 14.5. We can make derelict land into new and beautiful landscape at little expense: one of the first colliery spoil heaps to be afforested in Durham.

can be done, as well as the will to see that it is done. Let us hope that the steps we have begun to take towards imaginative and effective restoration continue. With the collaboration of different skills the possibilities are boundless.

'The tragedy is that although we have caught a few fine hares we do not in the least know what to do with them, for in the innermost depths of our souls we all realise we have lost our way and our bearing, and do not know in which direction to start for home. The finger posts to my—perhaps untutored—eyes point unmistakably in the direction of the land.'
SIR GEORGE STAPLEDON
The Way of the land. 1943.

Appendix
Conversion of Weights and Measures

Metric units are now being adopted universally and should be used wherever possible

To convert → multiply by to get ← divide by		to get to convert
inches	25·4	millimetres (mm)
feet	30·48	centimetres (cm) (10 millimetres)
yards	0·914	metres (m) (100 centimetres)
square feet	0·0929	square metres (m²)
square yards	0·836	square metres
acres	0·405	hectares (ha) (10000 m²)
ounces	28·3	grammes (g)
pounds	0·454	kilograms (kg) (1000 g)
hundredweights (112 lbs)	50·8	kilograms
tons (2240 lbs)	1·016	tonnes (t) (1000 kg)
short tons (2000 lbs)	0·907	tonnes
gallons (Imperial)	4·55	litres (l)
gallons (US)	3·79	litres
cubic feet	28·3	litres
ounces/square yard	23·7	grammes/square metre (g/m²)
pounds/acre	1·121	kilograms/hectare (kg/ha)
tons/acre	2·511	tonnes/hectare (t/ha)
gallons/acre	11·23	litres/hectare (l/ha)
grams/square metre	10	kilograms/hectare
P_2O_5	0·4364	P
K_2O	0·8301	K
CaO	0·7146	Ca
MgO	0·6031	Mg

Acknowledgments and Sources

Preface
Photographs of Pasture, Sonoma County by Ansel Adams

Chapter 1
Figures:
1·1 from Department of the Environment survey of derelict and despoiled land.
1·2 photograph from the National Coal Board.
1·4 data from University of Liverpool Environmental Advisory Unit.

Tables:
1·1, 1·3 from *Surface Mining and our Environment,* 1967. Washington: US Dept. of the Interior.
1·2 from Department of the Environment survey of derelict and despoiled land.

Chapter 2
Figures:
2·1 from Jeffrey D.W. *et al*. 1974. In *Minerals and the Environment* (ed. M.J. Jones). London: Institute of Mining & Metallurgy (modified).
2·3a,b photographs from Siedlungsverband Ruhrkohlenbezirk, Essen.
2·4 photograph by B.N.K. Davies.
2·5 photograph by John Markham.
2·6 from Ellis E.A. 1965. *The Broads*. London: Collins.
2·9 from Siedlungsverband Ruhrkohlenbezirk leaflet.

Tables:
2·1, 2·4 from Wallwork K.L. 1974. *Derelict Land*. Newton Abbot: David & Charles.
2·5 from information supplied by the Department of the Environment.
2·6 from Grim E.C. & Hill R.D. 1974. *Environmental Protection in Surface Mining of Coal*. Cincinnati: US Environmental Protection Agency.

Chapter 3
Figures:
3·1 from Epstein E. 1972. *Mineral Nutrition of Plants: Principles and Perspectives*. New York: Wiley.
3·2 from Bradshaw A.D. *et al*. 1960, 1964. *J. Ecol*. **48**, 631: **52**, 665.

3·4 photograph by A.J. Tollitt.

3·5 photograph by C.J. Veltkamp.

3·6 from Foth, H.D. 1978. *Fundamentals of Soil Science* (6th Ed). New York: Wiley.

3·8 from Bannister P. 1976. *Introduction to Physiological Plant Ecology*. Oxford: Blackwell Scientific Publications.

3·9 from Black C.A. 1968. *Soil Plant relationships* (2nd ed.). New York: Wiley.

3·10 from Grime J.P. & Lloyd P.S. 1973. *An Ecological Atlas of Grassland Plants*. London: Arnold.

3·11 from Mather J.R. 1974. *Climatology: Fundamentals and Applications*. New York: McGraw-Hill.

3·12 from Fitter A.H. & Bradshaw A.D. 1974. *J. Appl. Ecol.* **11**, 609.

Tables:

3·1 from Hewitt E.J. & Smith T.A. 1975. *Plant Mineral Nutrition*. London: English Universities Press.

3·2 from Black C.A. 1968. *Soil Plant Relationships* (2nd ed.). New York: Wiley.

3·3 from Dennington V.N. & Chadwick M.J. 1978. *J. Appl. Ecol.* **15**, 303.

3·4 from Salter P.J. & Williams J.B. 1965. *J. Soil Sci.* **16**, 310.

Chapter 4

Figures:

4·4 from Saltmarsh J. & Darby H.C. 1935. Economic History **3**, 34.

4·5 photograph from University of California Agricultural Experimental Station.

4·6 from Hayward H.E. 1954. In *Utilization of Saline Water*. Paris: UNESCO.

Tables:

4·1 from Allen S.E. *et al.* 1974. *Chemical Analysis of Ecological Materials*. Oxford: Blackwell Scientific Publications. Also personal communication.

Chapter 5

Figures:

5·1 photograph from the National Coal Board.

5·4, 5·9 from Bradshaw A.D. *et al.* 1975. In *The Ecology of Resource Degradation and Renewal* (ed. M.J. Chadwick & G.T. Goodman). Oxford: Blackwell Scientific Publications.

5·5 from Berg W.A. 1973. In *Ecology and Reclamation of Devastated Land* (ed. R.J. Hutnik & G. Davis). New York: Gordon & Breach.

5·6 from Dancer W.S. 1975. *J. Environ. Qual.* **4**, 150.

Tables:

5·3 data from Gina Bradley.

Acknowledgments

Chapter 6

Figures:

6·1 photographs by D.W. Lawrence.

6·2 from Crocker R.L. & Major J. 1955. *J. Ecol.* **43**, 427.

6·3 from Neumann U. 1973. In *Ecology and Reclamation of Devastated Land* (ed. R.J. Hutnik & G. Davis). New York: Gordon & Breach.

6·4 from Knabe, W. 1973. In *Ecology and Reclamation of Devastated Land* (ed. R.J. Hutnik & G. Davis). New York: Gordon & Breach.

6·5 photograph from Association of Portland Cement Manufacturers.

6·7 data from Hazel Bloomfield.

6·9 photograph from VEB Ltd.

6·10 from Sheldon J.C. & Bradshaw A.D. 1977. *J. Appl. Ecol.* **14**, 905.

6·11 from Kohnke H. 1950. *Adv. Agron.* **2**, 317.

6·12 photograph from the National Coal Board.

6·15 photograph by J.F. Handley.

6·18 data from A. Gilham.

Tables:

6·2 from Sheldon J.C. & Bradshaw A.D. 1977. *J. Appl. Ecol.* **14**, 905.

6·6 data from R.N. Humphries.

Chapter 7

Figures:

7·3 from Ludeke K.L. 1973. Mining Cong. J. **59**. 30.

7·4 photograph by A.J. Tollitt.

7·5 from Chadwick M.J. *et al.* 1978. *Nutrient Problems in Relation to Vegetation Establishment and Maintenance on Colliery Spoil*. London: Department of the Environment.

7·6 from Johnson M.S. *et al.* 1976. *Trans. Inst. Min. Metall.* **A85**, 32.

7·9 from Chadwick M.J. 1974. In *Grüne Halden im Ruhrgebiet*. Essen: SVR.

Tables:

7·2 from Chadwick M.J. 1974. In *Grüne Halden im Ruhrgebiet*. Essen: SVR.

7·3 from Richards L.A. *et al.* 1954. *Diagnosis and Improvement of Saline and Alkali Soils*. Washington: USDA.

Chapter 8

Figures:

8·3 from Caruccio F.T. 1973. In *The Ecology of Resource Degradation and Renewal* (ed. M.J. Chadwick & G.T. Goodman). Oxford: Blackwell Scientific Publications.

8·4, 8·14 from Chadwick M.J. *et al.* 1978. *Nutrient Problems in Relation to Vegetation Establishment and Maintenance on Colliery Spoil*. London: Department of the Environment.

8·5 from Harding C.P. 1970. D.Phil. thesis, Univ. of York.

8·9 data from P.J. Costigan.

8·10 from Williams P.J. 1973. In *The Ecology of Resource Degradation and Renewal* (ed. M.J. Chadwick & G.T. Goodman). Oxford: Blackwell Scientific Publications.

8·13 data from Hazel Bloomfield.

8·16 from James A.L. & Mrost M. 1965. *J. S. Afr. Inst. Min. Metall.* **65**, 488.

8·20 from Matter F.S. *et al.* 1974. *A Balanced Approach to Resource Extraction and Creative Land Development*. Tucson: University of Arizona.

8·22 data from Australian Mineral Development Laboratories.

8·23 data from T.M. Roberts.

8·24 from Nielson R.F. & Peterson H.B. 1973. *Utah Agric. Exp. Sta. Bull.* **485**.

8·26 from Bradshaw A.D. 1971. In *Ecological Genetics and Evolution* (ed. R. Creed). Oxford: Blackwell Scientific Publications.

8·28 from Jeffrey D.W. *et al.* 1974. In *Minerals and the Environment* (ed. M.J. Jones). London: Institute of Mining and Metallurgy.

8·29 photograph by K.Ludeke.

Tables:

8·1 data compiled by M.P. Palmer.

8·4 data from P.J. Costigan.

8·5, 8·6 from Chadwick M.J. *et al.* 1978. *Nutrient Problems in Relation to Vegetation Establishment and Maintenance on Colliery Spoil*. London: Department of the Environment.

8·7 data from Donna Baker.

8·8 from Cresswell C.F. 1973. In *Ecology and Reclamation of Devastated Land* (ed. R.J. Hutnik & G. Davis). New York: Gordon & Breach.

8·10 from Blessing N.V. *et al.* 1974. In *Minerals and the Environment* (ed. M. J. Jones). London: Institute of Mining and Metallurgy.

8·11 from Johnson M.S. 1977. Ph.D. thesis, University of Liverpool.

Chapter 9

Figures:

9·1 from Grim E.C. & Hill R.D. 1974. *Environment Protection in Surface Mining of Coal*. Cincinnati: U.S. Environmental Protection Agency.

9·3, 9·5 from the National Coal Board.

9·4, 9·12, 9·14 from Grim E.C. & Hill R.D. 1974. *Environmental Protection in Surface Mining of Coal*. Cincinnati: U.S. Environmental Protection Agency.

9·8 from Curtis W.R. 1971. *Trans. Amer. Soc. Agric. Engineers* **14**, 434.

9·9 photographs from the National Coal Board.

9·10 from Kohnke H. 1950. *Adv. Agron.* **2**, 317.

9·13 from Vogel W.G. 1973. Symposium on *Mined-land Reclamation*. Monroeville: Bituminous Coal Res. Inc.

9·15 photograph by P. Pere, Ministry of Forestry and Nature Conservation, Estonian SSR.

9·16, 9·19 photographs from Northamptonshire County Council.

9·18 from Leisman G.A. 1957. *Ecol. Monogr.* **27**, 221.

9·21 photograph by Erie Mining Co.

9·23, 9·25 photographs by G. W. Morgan.

9·26 from Morgan G.W. 1974. *Trop. Agric.* (Trinidad) **51**, 332.

9·29 photograph by J.K. St Joseph.

9·30, 9·33 from Bradshaw A.D. *et al*. 1975. In *The Ecology of Resource Degradation and Renewal* (ed. M.J. Chadwick & G.T. Goodman). Oxford: Blackwell Scientific Publications.

9·28, 9·34, 9·36 photographs from English China Clays Ltd.

9·35 from Bradshaw *et al*. 1978. In *The Breakdown and Restoration of Ecosystems* (ed. M.W. Holdgate & M.J. Woodman). New York: Plenum Press.

9·37, 9·38 photographs from Anglo-American Clays Corp.

Tables:

9·1 from Karr J.R. 1968. *Condor* **70**, 348.

9·2 from Beyer L.E. & Hutnik R.J. 1969. *Acid and Aluminium Toxicity as Related to Strip-mine Spoil Banks on Western Pennsylvania*. Pennsylvania State Univ. Special Res. Rep. SR-72.

9·3 from Curtis W.R. 1972. 4th Symp. on *Coal Mine Drainage Research*. Pittsburgh: Mellon Institute.

9·4 from Vogel W.G. 1976. 3rd Symp. on *Surface Mining and Reclamation*. Washington: National Coal Association.

9·5, 9·6 from Carter R.P. *et al*. 1974. *Surface Mined Land in the Midwest*. Washington: US Dept. of the Interior.

9·7 from Schmehl W.R. & McCaslin B.D. 1973. In *Ecology and Reclamation of Devastated Land* (ed. R.J. Hutnik & G. Davis). New York: Gordon & Breach.

9·8 data from T.G. Heafield, MAFF.

9·9 from Whyte R.O. & Sisam, J.W.E. 1949. *The Establishment of Vegetation on Industrial Waste Land*. Aberystwyth: Commonwealth Bureau of Pasture and Field Crops.

9·10 from Leisman G.A. 1957. *Ecol. Monogr.* **27**, 221.

9·11 from Smith, .M. *et al*. *W. Virginia Univ. Agric. Exp. Sta. Bull.* 604 T.

9·14 from Bradshaw A.D. *et al*. 1975. In *The Ecology of Resource Degradation and Renewal* (ed. M.J. Chadwick & G.T. Goodman). Oxford: Blackwell Scientific Publications.

9·15 photograph by P. Pere, Ministry of Forestry and Nature Conservation, Estonian SSR.

9·16 from Dancer W.S. *et al*. 1977. *Plant & Soil* **48**, 403.

9·17 from May J.T. 1975. In *The Ecology of Resource degrada-*

tion and Renewal (ed. M.J. Chadwick & G.T. Goodmam). Oxford: Blackwell Scientific Publications.

Chapter 10
Figures:
10·3,10·5,10·6 photographs from Norsk Vassdrags og Elektrisitetsvesen.
10·8 from Sheldon J.C. & Bradshaw A.D. 1975. *Landscape Design* **113**, 31.
10·10 photograph by N.A. Richards.
10·12 from Bradshaw A.D. *et al.* 1978. In *The Breakdown and Restoration of Ecosystems* (ed. M.W. Holdgate & M.J. Woodman). New York: Plenum Press.
10·13 from Danziger K, 1971. *Rehabilitation of the Nesher Quarry.* Israel: Israel Portland Cement Works.
10·15 photograph by Celia Bradshaw.
10·16, 10·17, 10·19, 10·20 photographs by Pamela Harrison.
10·18 photograph by Tilling Construction Services Ltd.
10·21 from Harrison J. 1974. *The Sevenoaks Gravel Pit Reserve.* Chester: WAGBI.
10·22 photograph by J.K. St. Joseph.

Tables:
10·1 from Clarke F.E. 1924. *The Data of Geochemistry* (5th ed.) Washington: US Geol. Surv.
10·2 from Tansley A.G. 1939. *The British Isles and their Vegetation.* Cambridge: Cambridge University Press.
10·3 data from R.N. Humphries.
10·4 from Bradshaw, A.D. *Proc. Roy. Soc. Lond. B* **197**, 77.
10·5 from Humphries, R.N. 1977. *Quarry Management & Products* **4**, 43.
10·6 from Harrison J. 1974. *The Sevenoaks Gravel Pit Reserve.* Chester: WAGBI.

Chapter 11
Figures:
11·1, 11·2 photographs by A.J. Tollitt.
11·3 from Darlington A. 1969. *Ecology of Refuse Tips.* London: Heinemann.
11·4 photograph from West Yorkshire County Council.
11·5 from Townsend, W.N. & Gilham, E.W.F. 1975. In *The Ecology of Resource Degradation and Renewal* (ed. M.J. Chadwick & G.T. Goodman). Oxford: Blackwell Scientific Publications.
11·6, 11·9 photographs from Central Electricity Generating Board.
11·7 from Hodgson D.R. & Buckley G.P. 1975. In *The Ecology of Resource Degradation and Renewal* (ed. M.J. Chadwick & G.T. Goodman). Oxford: Blackwell.
11·8 from Hodgson D.R. & Townsend W.N. 1973. In *Ecology and Reclamation of Devastated Land* (ed. R.J. Hutnik & G. Davis). New York: Gordon & Breach.
11·10 diagram from Central Electricity Generating Board.

Tables:

11·1 data from Kathryn Eley.

11·2, 11·3, 11·4, 11·5, 11·7, 11·8 from Hodgson D.R. & Townsend W.N. 1973. In *Ecology and Reclamation of Devastated Land* (ed. R.J. Hutnik & G. Davis). New York: Gordon & Breach.

11·6 from Townsend, W.N. & Gilham, E.W.F. 1975. In *The Ecology of Resource Degradation and Renewal* (ed. M.J. Chadwick & G.T. Goodman). Oxford: Blackwell.

11·9 from Barber E.G. 1975. *Win Back the Acres*. London: Central Electricity Generating Board.

11·10, 11·11 from Gemmell R.P. 1977. *Colonisation of Industrial Wasteland*. London: Arnold.

Chapter 12

Figures:

12·1, 12·2 from *Zuyder Zee—Lake Ijssel Guide. 1975. The Hague: I.D.G.*

12·3 photograph from KLM Aerocarto, Rotterdam.

12·4 diagram from Department of Applied Biology, Cambridge University.

12·5 photograph by Bart Hofmeester, Rotterdam.

12·7 photograph from Merseyside County Council.

12·10 data from P. Johnson.

Tables:

12·1 data from Department of Applied Biology, Cambridge University.

12·2, 12·3 from de Glopper R.J. & Smits H. 1974. *Outlook on Agriculture* **8**, 148.

12·5 from Brooks D.R. 1976. In *Landscaping and Land Use Planning as Related to Mining Operations*. Adelaide: Australasian Institute of Mining and Metallurgy.

Chapter 13

Figures:

13·7 photograph from Bougainville Copper Ltd.

13·8 photograph from Ministry of Transport.

13·9, 13·10 photographs by C.J. Gill.

13·11 photograph by A.J. Tollitt.

13·14 photographs from Civic Trust and Friends of the Earth, Redbridge.

13·15 photograph from Civic Trust.

13·16 photograph from South London Press.

Tables:

13·1 from Perring, F.H. 1969. In *Road Verges—Their Function and Management* (ed. J.M. Way). Monkswood: Institute of Terrestrial Ecology.

13·3 from Green J.T. *et al.* 1973. *Establishing Persistent Vegetation on Cuts and Fills along West Virginia Highways—Final Report*. Blacksburg: Virginia State University.

13·4 from Hottenstein W.L. 1969. In *Turfgrass Science* (ed.

A.A. Hanson & F.V. Juska). Madison: American Society for Agronomy.

13·5 from Ranwell D.S. *et al*. 1973. *Road Salting Effects on Soil and Plants*. London: Natural Environmental Research Council.

13·7 from Gill C.J. & Bradshaw A.D. 1971. *Landscape Design* **95**, 31.

13·8 data from Hazel Bloomfield.

Chapter 14

Figures:

14·1 from Trewartha G.T. 1969. *A Geography of Population: World Patterns*. London: Wiley.

14·2 photograph by F.W. Goldring.

14·3 photograph by J.F. Handley

Table:

14·1 from *World Bank Atlas* 1975. Washington.

Species Index

Atriplex nummularia   152
Atriplex patula   126, 223
Austrian pine   99, 259, 269
Autumn olive   99, 100, 169
Avena sativa   238
Aythya ferina   218
Aythya fuligula   218

Bahiagrass   198
Balm-leaved figwort   265
Banksia spp.   259
Banksia integrifolia   255
Banksia serrata   255
Barley   182, 238
Bay willow   275
Beach bean   255
Beach grass   97, 254, 255
Beaked hawksbeard   177
Becium homblei   148
Bee orchid   15, 211, 212
Beech   99, 238
Beet   238
Bell flower   272
Bell heather   272
Bent grass   29, 41, 51, 94,
     109, 125, 129, 148, 151,
     193, 206, 207, 214, 234,
     238, 266, 268, 269, 277
Berberis linearifolia   238
Berberis thunbergii   238
Bermuda grass   56, 148, 151,
     198, 268
Beta trigyna   265
Beta vulgaris   238
Betonica officinalis   272
Betony   272
Betula papyrifera   99
Betula pendula   99, 109, 125,
     136, 234, 238, 275
Betula pubescens   99, 205, 209
Bicolor lespedeza   96, 169
Bilberry   109, 206, 272
Birch   99, 205, 209
Bird's foot trefoil   96, 125,
     133, 140, 168, 169, 177,
     182, 193, 194, 214, 234,
     266, 269, 272
Birthwort   265
Black alder   99
Black cherry   269
Black locust   98, 99, 170,
     238, 239, 269
Black medick   125, 194, 234
Black poplar   275
Black walnut   170
Black willow   275
Blackbutt   254
Blackthorn   269, 272
Bladder campion   109, 148,
     272
Bloodwood   255
Blue eyed grass   241
Blue grama   268
Bluebell   272

Bohmers cat's-tail   265
Botrychium lunaria   212
Bouteloua gracilis   268
Brachypodium pinnatum   41,
     109
Bracken   109, 126
Bramble   125, 205, 272
Brassica napus   238
Brassica nigra   238
Brassica oleracea   238
Brassica rapa   238
Brigalow   166
Bristly locust   99
Brittle bladder-fern   206
Briza media   47, 109
Broad bean   238
Bromus inermis   169, 182, 268
Bromus mollis   109
Broom   125, 169, 238, 259,
     269, 272
Broom brush   49
Broomrape   241
Brown bent   29, 109, 206,
     266
Brown top   94
Brush box   255
Brussels sprouts   238
Bryum argenteum   228
Buchloe dactyloides   268
Buffalo grass   268
Buffel grass   167
Bupleurum falcatum   265
Burhinus oedicnemus   52
Bur-reed   217, 223
Bush grass   177
Buttercup   126, 272
Buttonball   275

Cabbage   238
Cakile maritima   109, 254
Calamagrostis epigeios   177
Calidris alpina   241
Callitriche stagnalis   217
Calluna vulgaris   51, 103,
     125, 206, 272
Caltha palustris   109
Calystegia sepium   126
Calystegia soldanella   254
Campanula latifolia   272
Campanula rotundifolia   272
Canada bluegrass   94
Canavalia maritima   255
Capsella bursa-pastoris   228
Carex arenaria   254
Carex digitata   212
Carex filiformis   265
Carex flacca   47, 212
Carex montana   265
Carex ornithopoda   212
Carex pendula   223
Carex riparia   223
Caribbean pine   186
Carlina vulgaris   241
Carline thistle   241

Species Index

Salix cinerea 99, 125, 194, 272, 275
Salix daphnoides 99
Salix fragilis 109, 224, 275
Salix herbacea 206
Salix lutea 275
Salix nigra 275
Salix nigricans 125
Salix pentandra 275
Salix phylicifolia 275
Salix purpurea 99, 169, 275
Salix repens 254
Salix triandra 275
Salix viminalis 99, 275
Sallow 99, 109, 194, 209, 218, 234, 272, 275
Salsola kali 254
Salt bush 151, 152, 215, 269
Saltwort 254
Salvia spp. 215
Salvia pratensis 265
Sambucus nigra 125
Sand fescue 254
Sand sedge 254
Sand spinifex 254, 255, 257
Sawtooth banksia 254
Saxifraga tridactylites 212
Scirpus maritimus 222, 223
Scirpus tabernaemontani 223
Scots pine 54, 99, 170, 209
Screw pine 184
Scrophularia scorodonia 265
Sea bindweed 254
Sea buckthorn 109, 238, 269
Sea club rush 222, 223
Sea couch 109, 254, 255
Sea holly 254
Sea lyme grass 254, 255
Sea oats 255
Sea poa 109, 248
Sea purslane 109, 254
Sea rocket 109, 254
Sea sandwort 109, 254
Sea spike rush 222, 223
Sea spurge 254
Sea-kale 109, 254
Secale cereale 29, 96, 182, 198, 238, 256
Self heal 212, 272
Senecio erucifolius 126
Senecio jacobaea 126, 177
Senecio squalidus 126
Senecio sylvaticus 125
Senecio viscosus 125
Senecio vulgaris 126, 228, 254
Sericea lespedeza 96, 168, 169, 198
Sessile oak 125, 205, 209, 269
Sheep's fescue 41, 47, 51, 94, 109, 125, 148, 193, 206, 207, 214, 266
Sheep's sorrel 109, 234
Shepherd's purse 228
Shortleaf pine 99, 170

Shrubby pear 265
Siberian dogwood 269
Silene dioica 272
Silene nutans 212
Silene otites 265
Silene vulgaris 109, 148, 272
Silver birch 99, 109, 125, 136, 234, 238, 275
Silver hairgrass 109
Silver leaf desmodium 96
Silver maple 170
Siratro 96, 167
Sisyrinchium bermudiana 241
Slender wheatgrass 268
Smooth brome 169, 182, 268
Smooth elm 269
Smooth-stalked meadow grass 94, 109, 125, 178, 193, 214, 234, 266, 268, 269
Snipe 218
Snowberry 126, 269
Soft brome 109
Solanum dulcamara 126
Solanum nigrum 126
Solanum tuberosum 238
Solidago gigantea 178
Solidago nemoralis 178
Solidago virgaurea 272
Sonchus arvensis 126, 178
Sonchus asper 70, 254
Sonchus oleraceus 126
Sorbus aria 272
Sorbus aucuparia 99, 272
Sorghum vulgare 90, 91, 96, 168, 256, 258
Sorrel 125, 206
Sowthistle 70, 254
Spanish catchfly 265
Sparganium spp. 223
Sparganium ramosum 217
Spartium junceum 238
Spear thistle 109, 125, 177, 228, 229, 263
Spergularia rubra 126
Sphagnum spp. 19, 208
Spike rush 223
Spindle tree 269, 272
Spinifex 179
Spinifex hirsutus 254, 255, 257
Sporobolus spp. 184
Sporobolus virginicus 152
Spotted cat's ear 265
Spring sandwort 109, 148
Spring tails 74
Stachys germanica 265
Star grass 139
Starwort 217
Stellaria holostea 272
Stellaria media 125
Sterile brome 109
Stitchwort 272
Stonewort 223

305

Species Index

Strawberry clover   272
Stylosanthes humilis   96
Subterranean clover   50
Sugar maple   170, 265
Swamp cypress   275
Swamp iron wood   275
Swamp privet   275
Swede   238
Sweet clover   96, 177, 178,
    182, 238, 239
Sweet vernal-grass   41, 148,
    206
Sweetgum   170, 275
Swietenia macrophylla   186
Switchgrass   169
Sycamore   99, 125, 170, 181,
    238
Symphoricarpus rivularis   126,
    269
Sysimbrium altissimum   234

Tacamahac   178, 275
Tall fescue   94, 125, 168,
    169, 198, 267, 268
Tall wheatgrass   173
Tamaria gallica-indica   238
Tamarisk   269
Tamarix spp.   269
Taraxacum officinale   70, 125
Tartarian honeysuckle   169
Taxodium distichum   275
Tea-leaved willow   275
Teasel   125, 272
Tephrosia longipes   148
Tetragonolobus maritimus   265
Teucrium scorodonia   126,
    205, 212, 272
Thalictrum minus   212
Thelycrania sanguinea   272
Thelypteris robertiana   212
Thlaspi alpestre   148
Thuja spp.   269
Thuja occidentalis   99
Thymus praecox   47, 212
Timothy   48, 94, 169, 178,
    180, 214, 238
Toad flax   126, 272
Torgrass   41, 109
Tormentil   51, 272
Townsville stylo   96
Traveller's joy   238, 272
Tree lupin   96, 194, 195,
    223, 259
Trefoil   265, 272
Trifolium dubium   125, 194
Trifolium fragiferum   272
Trifolium hybridum   96, 180,
    194, 238
Trifolium incarnatum   215
Trifolium pratense   96, 125,
    169, 178, 180, 193, 194,
    214, 234, 238, 239, 272
Trifolium repens   48, 51, 56,
    96, 125, 133, 136, 169,

177, 178, 180, 193, 194,
    198, 214, 234, 238, 239,
    266, 268, 269, 270, 277
Trifolium subterraneum   50
Tringa ochropus   218
Tringa totanus   218
Triodia spp.   179
Tripleurospermum
    maritimum   126, 265
Trisetum flavescens   41, 109,
    177, 212
Tristania conferta   254
Triticum aestivum   238
Trollius europaeus   205
Tsuga canadensis   238
Tuckeroo   254
Tufted duck   218
Tufted hair grass   94, 109,
    125, 206
Tulip poplar   170
Turnip   238
Tussilago farfara   109, 125,
    177, 234
Typha angustifolia   109, 177,
    217, 222
Typha latifolia   223

Ulex spp.   100
Ulex europaeus   70, 96, 109,
    125, 194, 234, 238, 272
Ulex gallii   272
Ulmus carpinifolia   269
Ulmus procera   125, 269
Uniola paniculata   255
Urtica dioica   125

Vaccinium myrtillus   109, 206,
    272
Vaccinium vitis-idaea   206
Valerian   272
Valeriana dioica   109
Valeriana officinalis   272
Veldt grass   139, 140
Verbascum pulverulentum   265
Veronica
    anagallis-aquatica   223
Veronica angustifolia   238
Veronica buxifolia   238
Vetch   125, 194, 214, 272
Viburnum lantana   272
Viburnum opulus   212, 272
Vicia faba   238
Vicia sativa   125, 194, 214
Vicia sepium   272
Viola calaminaria   148
Viola lutea   272
Violet   148
Violet willow   99, 169, 275
Virginia pine   99, 170, 199

Water cress   223
Water mint   217, 223

General Index

General Index